GRAMMAR L
WORKBOOK

GRAMMAR LINKS 3
A THEME-BASED COURSE FOR REFERENCE AND PRACTICE WORKBOOK

Charl Norloff

University of Colorado,
International English Center

Debra Daise

University of Colorado,
International English Center

M. Kathleen Mahnke, Series Editor

Houghton Mifflin Company   Boston   New York

Director, World Languages: Marketing and ESL Publishing   Susan Maguire
Senior Development Editor   Kathy Sands Boehmer
Editorial Assistant   Manuel Muñoz
Manufacturing Manager   Florence Cadran
Marketing Manager   José A. Mercado

Printed in the U.S.A.

ISBN: 0-395-82896-1

3456789-CRS-04 03

CONTENTS

Acknowledgments

We would like to thank the many people who helped us in writing this workbook. We are expecially indebted to Kathleen Mahnke, the *Grammar Links* series editor and our developmental editor, for her invaluable help, direction, and guidance in completing the manuscript.

We are indebted to Jan van Zante, our co-author of the *Grammar Links 3* textbook, for generously sharing her ideas and exercises for the workbook. We are thankful to Jan, Randee Falk, Mahmoud Arani, and the other authors in the *Grammar Links* series for their continued support and encouragement.

Our gratitude also goes to the people at Houghton Mifflin from whom we have received care and guidance throughout the writing of this book. We thank our editorial team, especially Kathy Sands Boehmer and Manuel Muñoz, for their thoughtful handling of our manuscript. We especially thank Susan Maguire, the director of ESL at Houghton Mifflin, who took a chance on two long-time teachers with little publishing experience. Thank you, Susan, for the opportunity to be part of the *Grammar Links* team and for your unwavering support and encouragement throughout the project.

Our thanks, too, to Erin Walshkirkman for reading through and completing the exercises in the workbook, Hana Sasaki for testing the materials, and all of our students at the International English Center, who gave us feedback and helped us write better.

Finally, we extend heartfelt love and thanks to those closest to us, Richard, Jonathan, and Joshua Norloff, and Lakhdar Benkobi for their patience, understanding, support, and hot soup. Without their willingness to allow us to devote our time and energy to the project, we would not have been able to write this book.

Charl Norloff
Debra Daise

GRAMMAR LINKS 3
WORKBOOK

Unit One

Present and Past: Simple and Progressive

chapter 1

Simple Present and Present Progressive

GRAMMAR PRACTICE 1: Simple Present and Present Progressive

1 Simple Present—Form and Function

A. Use the words in parentheses to complete the statements and questions in the simple present. Use contractions with *not*. Then complete Part **B**.

1. Science _____*divides*_____ (divide) time into precise units of clock time.

   _____*b*_____

2. _____ (people, schedule) all their activities, even the natural ones,

   according to the clock? _____

3. We _____ (not, think) about natural time very often in modern

   society. _____

4. _____ (the human body, follow) a natural, internal clock?

   _____

5. Our bodies _____ (run) on an internal clock. _____

6. However, most of us _____ (not, use) them to schedule our activities.

   _____

B. Why is the <u>simple present</u> used in the sentences in Part **A**? Write the letter of one of the following reasons in the blank at the end of the sentences in Part **A**.

a. Habitual or repeated action   b. Scientific fact

2 Present Progressive—Form and Function

A. Use the words in parentheses to complete the sentences in the present progressive. Use contractions with subject pronouns and with *not*. Then complete Part **B**.

1. In modern society nowadays, we'*re not paying / aren't paying* _____ (not, pay)

   enough attention to natural time. _____*b*_____

2. We _____ (always, complain) that we are late for scheduled activities.

   _____

3. I _____ (try) to schedule my activities in natural time these days.

   _____

4. I _____ (sleep) in natural time. _____

5. I _____ (eat) right now because I'm hungry. _____

6. _____ (you, listen) to your internal clock right now? _____

7. It _____ (not, tell) you to stop studying, is it? _____

B. Why is the present progressive used in the sentences in Part **A**? Write the letter of one of the following reasons in the blank at the end of the sentences in Part **A**.

   a. Action in progress at this moment

   b. Action in progress through a period of time including the present

   c. With *always*, often to express a complaint

3   Time Expressions with Simple Present and Present Progressive

Underline the verbs in these sentences. Circle the correct time expression for the meaning in brackets.

1. [Action in progress through a period of time including the present] I'm spending more time reading (now/on Mondays).

2. [Habitual or repeated action] Do you exercise (on the weekends/now)?

3. [Action in progress through a period of time including the present] They aren't watching a lot of TV (usually/these days).

4. [Habitual or repeated action] He goes to bed (at 10:00/tonight).

5. [Action in progress at this moment] Are you working (always/at this time)?

6. [Habitual or repeated action] She doesn't eat dinner (in the evening/this evening).

4   Simple Present and Present Progressive; Time Expressions

Use the verbs and the time expressions given to write sentences in the simple present and present progressive. Use contractions with subject pronouns and with *not*.

1. I / go to bed / usually / at 11:00   ___I usually *go to bed at 11:00.*___

2. He / get up / often / at sunrise / in the morning

   _____

3. We / eat a big breakfast / before work / nowadays

_____

4. John / work a flexible schedule / this year

_____

5. They / relax at home / on weekends

_____

6. You / study or work / more / at present?

_____

7. Briana / exercise / not / regularly / every day

_____

5 Guided Writing: Simple Present and Present Progressive

Do your activities follow natural or clock time? On a separate sheet of paper, use the verbs and the time expressions in Exercise 4 to write seven sentences about when you do these things. Give your sentences to your teacher for correction.

> Example: I usually *go to bed* when I feel tired. OR I usually *go to bed* at 10:00.
>
> Nowadays, I'm eating on a regular schedule. OR Nowadays, I'm eating when I feel hungry.

6 Simple Present and Present Progressive

Use the words in parentheses to complete the statements and questions in the simple present or the present progressive. In some cases, either form may be correct.

Astronomers and cosmologists are scientists. They _____study_____ (study) time
(1)

and the universe. How _____ (they, do) their work?
(2)

The earth, the sun, and other stars _____ (move) through space.
(3)

Some astronomers _____ (observe and record) their motions frequently.
(4)

These astronomers _____ (measure) the speed of the earth's orbit around
(5)

the sun and _____ (determine) the exact "mean solar time," or sun time.
(6)

Cosmology is related to astronomy. A cosmologist _____ (study) the
(7)

universe as a whole. Cosmologists often _____ (think) about distances,
(8)

times, and ideas that are very hard for most people to imagine. These days, cosmol-

ogists _____ (try) to understand the beginning of the universe and the
                (9)

nature of time. So somewhere right now a cosmologist _____ (ask) diffi-
                                                                          (10)

cult questions: Is it possible to understand the beginning of time? Why

_____ (we, remember) the past, but we _____ (not, remember)
         (11)   (12)

the future? Why _____ (time, run) forward? Where is the universe going?
                        (13)

GRAMMAR PRACTICE 2: Verbs with Stative Meaning

7 Verbs with Stative Meaning and Verbs with Active Meaning

A. Underline the verbs with stative meaning. Including the example, there are 13.

My husband <u>has</u> a busy schedule. He stays up late to watch TV programs that he
doesn't really hear because he's tired after a hard day. He rarely exercises and looks
tired all the time. He says he's being lazy, but he isn't lazy. He's really a morning person, so when he stays up late, he seems unwell in the morning. He knows his schedule is making him unhappy and he wants to do something about it.

Nowadays, I'm listening to my body's internal clock. I'm also paying attention to
natural time and my natural work cycle. I usually work best early in the day. These
days, I'm going to work early and leaving early, too. I go to bed when my body tells
me I'm tired, so I don't mind getting up early now. I like my new schedule. I'm feeling great.

Do you like your schedule? At present, are you following your natural cycle or
are you following clock time?

B. There are three verbs that usually have a stative meaning but have an active meaning
in Part **A**. Write them on the lines.

_____   _____   _____

8 Verbs with a Stative and an Active Meaning

Use the verbs in parentheses to complete the sentences. Use the simple present if the
verb has a stative meaning. Use the present progressive whenever the verb can have an
active meaning. Use contractions with subject pronouns.

1. a. I _____think_____ (think) Mars is the next frontier.

   b. I___'m thinking___ (think) about becoming an astronomer.

2. a. Astronomers _____ (look) for evidence of ice or water in the photographs of Mars.

   b. This photograph _____ (look) like a picture of ice.

3. a. Astronomers _____ (have) good telescopes now.

   b. We _____ (have) a good time studying about Mars.

4. a. Scientists _____ (weigh) the new meteor samples.

   b. Rocks _____ (weigh) less on Mars.

5. a. Astronomers _____ (feel) excited about the possibility that life existed on Mars.

   b. The surface of the meteor _____ (feel) rough.

6. a. Astronomers _____ (be) scientists and scientists need positive proof.

   b. At present, astronomers _____ (be) cautious about declaring the certainty of life on Mars.

chapter 2

Simple Past and Past Progressive

GRAMMAR PRACTICE 1: Simple Past and Past Progressive

▯ Simple Past—Form and Pronunciation

A. The following is a conversation between a college student and her advisor. Use the words in parentheses to complete the statements and questions in the simple past. Use contractions with *not*.

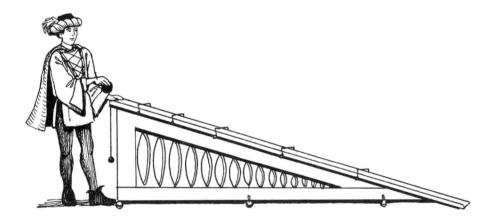

Student: I don't know whether I should study mathematics or music. I like both.

Advisor: You don't have to choose. After all, in his scientific experiments, Galileo

_____**used**_____ (use) both music and mathematics to find out about
        (1)

speed and time.

Student: How _____ (he, do) that?
                   (2)

Advisor: Galileo _____ (want) to know if a ball _____
                    (3)   (4)

(increase) its speed as it _____ (fall) through the air. He couldn't
                            (5)

determine changes in speed when he simply _____ (drop) a
                                            (6)

ball, so he had to find a different way to measure changes in speed.

Student: _____ (what, be) that?
(7)

Advisor: He _____ (set up) inclined planes, or flat pieces of wood with
(8)

one end higher than the other. He _____ (roll) some balls down
(9)

the inclined planes.

Student: Then _____ (Galileo, be) able to measure changes in speed?
(10)

Advisor: No. He _____ (need) a way to measure time first. He
(11)

_____ (not, have) a watch, but he _____ (know) that
(12)   (13)

music has a regular beat, or time between notes.

Student: So, _____ (he, play) the piano during his experiments?
(14)

Advisor: No. He _____ (put) strings across the inclined planes so that the
(15)

balls _____ (hit) the strings in regular intervals, like the beats in
(16)

music. The time that it _____ (take) a ball to go from string to
(17)

string was always the same, but the strings _____ (get) farther
(18)

and farther apart. In this way, Galileo _____ (demonstrate) that
(19)

the balls went faster and faster down the inclined plane.

Student: Wow! Thanks! I see that math and music can work together!

B. Circle the regular (*-ed* form) verbs in part **A**. Say each word and listen to the final
sound. Put each word in the correct list below according to its final sound. (See
Appendix 6 in the textbook for pronunciation rules for the *-ed* form of the verb.)

Example: *Galileo (1) (used) both music and mathematics.*

/t/	/d/	/id/
	used	

2 Simple Past and Past Progressive—Function

A. Read each statement. If the sentence is true for the simple past, put **SP** in the blank.
If the sentence is true for the past progressive, put **PP** in the blank.

_SP_ 1. talks about actions that began and ended in the past

_SP_ 2. is used with verbs with stative meaning to talk about states in the past

PP   3. talks about actions in progress at a particular moment or over an extended period in the past

PP   4. emphasizes that the action was in progress

PP   5. doesn't specify whether the action was completed

SP   6. emphasizes the completion of the action

PP   7. is used in narratives to provide background information

SP   8. is used for the action that follows background information in narratives

B. Use the verbs in italics in parentheses to complete the statements. Use the function in the same parentheses to determine the form of the verb: the simple past or the past progressive.

Tycho Brahe ___was___ (*be*, stative meaning) a Danish astronomer. One
(1)

night, while he _was attending_ (*attend*, background information) a party, he
(2)

was discussing (*discuss*, background information) mathematics. Brahe and
(3)

another student _were arguing_ (*argue*, background information) about a math
(4)

equation. The two men _started_ (*start*, action following background infor-
(5)

mation) to fight, but their friends _pulled_ (*pull*, action following back-
(6)

ground information) them apart. Neither Brahe nor the other man _forgot_
(7)

(*forget*, stative meaning) about the argument. A week later, they _fought_
(8)

(*fight*, completed action) again, this time with swords. While they _were fighting_
(9)

(*fight*, action in progress), the other student _cut off_ (*cut off*, completed
(10)

action) a big part of Brahe's nose. Brahe _wore_ (*wear*, completed action)
(11)

an artificial nose for the rest of his life.

3 Simple Past and Past Progressive

Use the words in parentheses to complete the statements and questions in the simple past or the past progressive. In some cases, either form may be correct.

Isaac Newton ___was___ (*be*) an English physicist. He was born in the
(1)

year of Galileo's death, 1642, and he _died_ (*die*) in 1727. As a young man,
(2)

Newton _was studying_ (*study*) at Cambridge University when a terrible disease,
(3)

the plague, _broke out_, (*break out*) and the university _closed_
(4)   (5)

(close). To avoid the plague, Newton _____stayed_____ (stay) in a village in the coun-
(6)

tryside for nearly two years. While he ___was waited/waiting___ (wait) in the countryside, he
(7)

was thinking
___thought___ (think) about mathematics and physics. Once, he ___was sitting___
(8)   (9)

(sit) in the garden when an apple _____fell_____ (fall) from a tree to the ground.
(10)

The falling apple ___helped___ (help) him understand that gravity is the force
(11)

that holds the planets in their orbits around the sun. Newton ___became___
(12)

worked
(become) a professor at Cambridge. While he ___was working___ (work) there, he
(13)

___made___ (make) many other important discoveries about the nature of
(14)

motion, light, and time. For Newton, time ___was___ (be) absolute—it was
(15)

constant and unchanging under all conditions.

4 Guided Writing: Simple Past and Past Progressive

On a separate sheet of paper, write a story about a science experiment, either a story
you know about or one that happened to you. Use the simple past at least seven times
and the past progressive at least three times. Write at least seven sentences. What was
happening when the experiment began? What happened during the experiment? Give
your story to your teacher for correction.

> Example: I really liked science when I was growing up. I was always taking
> things apart to see how they fit together. One day when I was taking apart
> an old radio, the phone rang . . .

GRAMMAR PRACTICE 2: Simple Past and Past Progressive in Time Clauses

5 Simple Past and Past Progressive in Time Clauses

Read the following sentences. Circle the time expressions that begin the time clause.
Underline the action or state that started first. If the actions or states happened at the
same time, put brackets [ ] around the sentence.

1. (Before) the United States had time zones and standardized time, clock time

   wasn't very important.

2. Many Americans were farmers and small business owners. [Most people were

   making their own schedules (while) only factory workers were listening for bells

   and whistles to tell them at what time to start and stop work.]

3. In the 1880s, when the United States was thinking about instituting standardized time, the railroads were very powerful.

4. Farmers and factory owners needed to get their products to the railway station before the train arrived. Knowing at what time the train arrived became very important.

5. After the farmers and factory owners started paying attention to clock time, other business owners and professionals began using it, too.

6. While clock time was taking over the business world, natural time remained important in the personal world.

7. For about forty years, workers chose their own activities when they had free time.

8. This changed after radios became popular and programs came on at a certain time.

9. Families often checked the radio schedules before they made plans for their free time.

10. After most families had radios, clock time became important in our personal lives.

6 Simple Past and Past Progressive in Time Clauses

Lauren and Paul wrote down their activities one day and compared their lists. Use the activities and time expression in parentheses to write a sentence about their days. Use a time clause in each sentence. Use the past or past progressive.

	Lauren's Day		Paul's Day
5: 00 A.M.	get up, eat breakfast	5:00 A.M.	sleep
7:00 A.M.	go to work	10:00 A.M.	get up
11:00 A.M.	eat lunch	3:00 P.M.	go to work
3:00 P.M.	leave work; do errands	7:30 P.M.	eat dinner
9:00 P.M.	go to bed	11:00 P.M.	finish work; meet friends
2:30 A.M.	sleep	2:30 A.M.	come home

1. (Lauren, get up; Paul, sleep; when) <u>When Lauren got up, Paul was sleeping.</u> OR

   <u>Paul was sleeping when Lauren got up.</u>

2. (Lauren, go to work; Paul, get up; after)_____

3. (Lauren, work; Paul, get up; while)_____

4. (Lauren, eat lunch; Paul, get up; before)_____

5. (Lauren, leave work; Paul, go to work; when)_____

6. (Lauren, leave work; Paul, eat dinner; before) _____

7. (Lauren, go to bed; Paul, work; while)_____

8. (Lauren, go to bed; Paul, meet friends; after)_____

9. (Lauren, sleep; Paul, come home; when)_____

GRAMMAR PRACTIVE 3: Used To

7 Used To—Form

A. Complete the statements and questions with the correct form of *used to*. Complete
the short answers. Use contractions with *not*.

Sally: The electricity was off for a while at school today, so I couldn't use the

computer to finish my paper. I had to use a pencil.

Grandpa: I ___<u>used to write</u>___ (write) all of my papers with a pencil or pen. Schools
(1)

_____ (not, have) computers.
(2)

Sally: The teacher usually puts on a CD while we clean up, but he couldn't

because he didn't have batteries for the CD player. _____ (your
(3)

teacher, play) music for you?

Grandpa: Yes, but she didn't have a CD player. She _____ (use) a record
(4)

player.

Sally: How _____ (you, check) your math problems? I check mine
(5)

with a calculator.

Grandpa: I _____ (check) them by doing them a second time.
                        (6)

Sally: Who _____ (help) you with your homework?
                        (7)

Grandpa: My grandpa _____ (help) me.
                              (8)

Sally: You see, Grandpa, some things don't change!

B. Go back to Part **A**. Replace *used to* with *would* wherever possible.

    would

I **used to write** (write) all of my papers with a pencil or pen.
    (1)

🔳 **Guided Writing: *Used To* and *Would***

On a separate sheet of paper, write five sentences about differences between you now and your grandparents when they were your age. Use *would* where possible. Use *used to* where *would* is not possible. Give your sentences to your teacher for correction.

UNIT WRAP-UP

ERROR CORRECTION

Find and correct the errors in verb forms and tenses. Some errors can be corrected in more than one way. Including the example, there are 9 errors.

                                   invented

Long before people ~~were inventing~~ clocks, they would look up at the sun to tell

time. Because the sun is reaching the highest point in the sky about once every

twenty-four hours, it is a convenient marker of time passing from one day to the

next. However, the earth doesn't moves around the sun on a consistent basis. It

varies from day to day by as much as sixteen minutes. This variation wasn't notice-

able until more and more people follows clock time instead of natural time.

    Nowadays we seldom realizing that clock time and sun time don't match. We

make appointments by our watches, not by the position of the sun in the sky.

Watches also help us agree on the time, with enough precision to satisfy most of our needs.

To satisfy their needs, scientists developed much more accurate and precise methods of measuring time. Now, they are depend on mathematical measurements of the motion of the sun and stars. They are also using an atomic clock, which relies on the change of cesium atoms from one state to another.

Although scientists are now measuring time with great accuracy and precision for any one place, we are knowing that time itself is not constant. Albert Einstein's theory of relativity predicted that motion and gravity are affecting time. An experiment in 1971 tested his theory. While one airplane was traveling west carrying an atomic clock, another is traveling east with another atomic clock. The atomic clock on the plane traveling east gained time while the one on the plane going west lost time.

Are our lives changing because we know more about the nature of time? Probably not. Have we lost something with our reliance on clock time? Who knows? Only time can tell!

Guided Writing: Present and Past, Simple and Progressive

On a separate sheet of paper, write a paragraph comparing your past and present habits and routines. What were you doing in the past? What are you doing now? What do you usually do every day? What did you use to do? Use simple present, present progressive, simple past, and past progressive. Use appropriate time expressions and time clauses. Give your paragraph to your teacher for correction.

> Example: I was a student last year, but now I'm working. I used to get up late every day, but now I'm getting up early. I go to work at 8:00 every day. When I was a student, I started class at 11:00. . . .

TOEFL TIME

Allow yourself 12 minutes to complete the 20 questions in this exercise.

Questions 1 through 10: Circle the letter of the one word or phrase that best completes each sentence.

1. While they _____ Paris last year, thousands of tourists saw Leonardo da Vinci's *Mona Lisa* at the Louvre.

    (A) visit
    (B) are visiting
    (C) were visiting
    (D) visiting

2. The telephone system in the United States didn't

    _____ be owned by many separate companies; at one time it was a monopoly.

    (A) use
    (B) using
    (C) used to
    (D) use to

3. Jurors often deliberate for many hours before they

    _____ a decision.

    (A) are making
    (B) were making
    (C) make
    (D) made

4. The number of cases of asthma _____ these days, perhaps partly because more people own cats.

    (A) is increasing
    (B) increases
    (C) was increasing
    (D) increased

5. How long before the American Civil War started

    _____ *Uncle Tom's Cabin*?

    (A) was Harriet Beecher Stowe completing
    (B) did Harriet Beecher Stowe complete
    (C) Harriet Beecher Stowe completed
    (D) Harriet Beecher Stowe was completing

6. Several people, who refused to leave,

    _____ on Mount St. Helens when it erupted in 1980.

    (A) still live
    (B) still living
    (C) are still living
    (D) were still living

7. Scientists now _____ that it is possible to clone organisms.

    (A) know
    (B) are knowing
    (C) were knowing
    (D) knew

8. George Balanchine _____ the New York City Ballet before 1948.

    (A) wasn't establishing
    (B) didn't establish
    (C) doesn't establish
    (D) used to establish

Go on to the next page

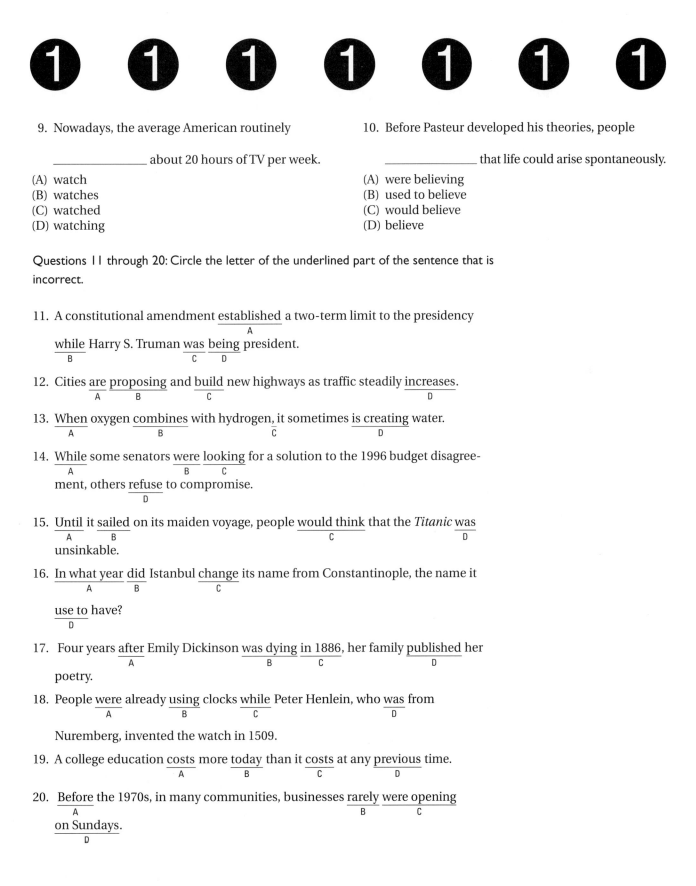

9. Nowadays, the average American routinely

_____ about 20 hours of TV per week.

(A) watch
(B) watches
(C) watched
(D) watching

10. Before Pasteur developed his theories, people

_____ that life could arise spontaneously.

(A) were believing
(B) used to believe
(C) would believe
(D) believe

Questions 11 through 20: Circle the letter of the underlined part of the sentence that is incorrect.

11. A constitutional amendment <u>established</u> a two-term limit to the presidency
       A
   <u>while</u> Harry S. Truman <u>was</u> <u>being</u> president.
   B   C   D

12. Cities <u>are</u> <u>proposing</u> and <u>build</u> new highways as traffic steadily <u>increases</u>.
   A   B   C   D

13. <u>When</u> oxygen <u>combines</u> with hydrogen, it sometimes <u>is creating</u> water.
   A   B   C   D

14. <u>While</u> some senators <u>were</u> <u>looking</u> for a solution to the 1996 budget disagree-
   A   B   C
   ment, others <u>refuse</u> to compromise.
   D

15. <u>Until</u> it <u>sailed</u> on its maiden voyage, people <u>would think</u> that the *Titanic* <u>was</u>
   A   B   C   D
   unsinkable.

16. <u>In what year</u> <u>did</u> Istanbul <u>change</u> its name from Constantinople, the name it
   A   B   C

   <u>use to have?</u>
   D

17. Four years <u>after</u> Emily Dickinson <u>was dying</u> <u>in 1886</u>, her family <u>published</u> her
   A   B   C   D
   poetry.

18. People <u>were</u> already <u>using</u> clocks <u>while</u> Peter Henlein, who <u>was</u> from
   A   B   C   D

   Nuremberg, invented the watch in 1509.

19. A college education <u>costs</u> more <u>today</u> than it <u>costs</u> at any <u>previous</u> time.
   A   B   C   D

20. <u>Before the 1970s</u>, in many communities, businesses <u>rarely</u> <u>were opening</u>
   A   B   C
   <u>on Sundays.</u>
   D

Unit Two

Present and Past: Perfect and Perfect Progressive

Present Perfect and Present Perfect Progressive

GRAMMAR PRACTICE 1: Present Perfect and Present Perfect Progressive

❶ Present Perfect—Form

At a conference about time management, a moderator and a participant are discussing ideas about the pace of life. Use the words in parentheses to complete their statements and questions in the present perfect. Use contractions with subject pronouns and *not*.

Moderator: You said technology ___**has taken**___ (take) up our time. It
(1)

___hasn't given___ (not, give) us more free time.
(2)

Participant: This is true. We ___'ve invented___ (invent) many things to save
(3)

time, but in the end they ___haven't done___ (not, do) this for us.
(4)

Moderator: What ___has happened___ (happen)? Why
(5)

___hasn't technology saved___ (technology, not, save) us time? Where
(6)

___has our time gone___ (our time, go)?
(7)

Participant: First, people ___have needed___ (need) to work harder and
(8)

longer to earn enough money to buy the new time-savers. Also, people

___have spent___ (spend) a lot of time learning how to use
(9)

them and taking care of them. Most importantly, the new inventions

___have made___ (make) it possible to do more, so people
(10)

___have wanted___ (want) to do more with them. They
(11)

___haven't changed___ (not, change) the fast pace of American life!
(12)

2 Present Perfect Progressive—Form

The participant and the moderator are continuing their discussion. Use the words in parentheses to complete their statements and questions in the present perfect progressive. Complete the short answer. Use contractions with subject pronouns and with *not*.

Moderator: So far, we ___'ve been talking___ (talk) about the fast pace of life in
(1)

the United States. Many Americans _have not been enjoying_ (not,
(2)

enjoy) this pace. Some of them _have been feeling_ (feel)
(3)

stressed. Why _have they been feeling_ (they, feel) this way?
(4)

Participant: We _'ve been trying_ (try) to do more in the time that we have.
(5)

Moderator: How _have we been doing_ (we, do) this?
(6)

Participant: We _'ve been speeding_ (speed up) each activity. Also, we
(7)

haven't been doing (do) two or three things at once. For exam-
(8)

ple, recently I _'ve been using_ (use) my computer and talking
(9)

on the phone while traveling on airplanes.

Moderator: So we _'ve been working_ (work) harder and faster. Why?
(10)

Participant: We _'ve been trying_ (try) to get more time to spend at home.
(11)

Moderator: But _have we been getting_ (we, get) more time as a result?
(12)

Participant: No, _we haven't_ .
(13)

3 Present Perfect and Present Perfect Progressive

Fill in each blank with the letter of the best meaning for each sentence.

1. __a__ Some Americans have been   a. actions not yet completed
         making changes to slow the
         pace of their lives.

2. _____ They have been happier   b. actions completed at an
         because they have had more   unspecified time in the
         time for simple pleasures.   past

3. _____ A friend of mine works in an office, c. progress toward a stated
         but he has used a computer   end result
         to "telecommute" to his company
         from home.

4. _____ I have taken time off from work twice in the last year to pursue other interests.

d. stating the number of times an action is repeated

5. _____ I have been building my own house for the last three years.

e. verb with stative meaning

4 Present Perfect versus Present Perfect Progressive

Look for the time expression in the following sentences. If there is one, underline it. Circle the correct tense(s) in the sentences. Both may be possible.

1. I have thought / have been thinking about changing the pace of my life lately.

2. I have written / have been writing a movie script for two years.

3. I have gone / have been going to six writers' conventions in the last two years.

4. I haven't watched / haven't been watching TV since I started writing the script.

5. My children and husband haven't seen / haven't been seeing much of me lately either.

6. I have traveled / have been traveling overseas and I'd like to do that again.

7. I have made a decision / have been making a decision to relax more when I finish this script.

8. Have you had / Have you been having time for all the things you want to do recently?

9. Is there anything that you haven't done / haven't been doing lately because you have no time?

5 Guided Writing

A. On a separate sheet of paper, write a paragraph about the pace of your life lately. Use the present perfect and present perfect progressive. What have you been doing? How long have you been doing it? What haven't you done because you don't have time? How have you been feeling about the pace of life? Give your paragraph to your teacher for correction.

Example: I have been writing a novel. I've been working on it for two years. I haven't watched TV in the evening since I began to write it.

B. Interview a family member or friend. On a separate sheet of paper, write a paragraph about the pace of his/her life. Give your paragraph to your teacher for correction.

GRAMMAR PRACTICE 2: Present Perfect versus Simple Past

6 Present Perfect and Simple Past—Function

Underline the present perfect and simple past in the sentences. Write the letter of the correct meaning on the line.

> For the present perfect decide if a past action:
>
>> a. happened at an unspecified time in the past
>>
>> b. continues to the present
>
> For the simple past decide if a past action:
>
>> c. cannot occur again
>>
>> d. happened at a specified time

1. I have seen a human walk on the moon. ____a____

2. Neil Armstrong became the first person to walk on the moon. _____

3. He has lived in Honolulu all his life. _____

4. What's the most exciting experience you have ever had? _____

5. They have been to New York. _____

6. They saw the Statue of Liberty two years ago. _____

7. She has painted pictures since she was a child. _____

8. I saw that movie last week. _____

7 Present Perfect versus Simple Past

Use the words in parentheses to complete the statements and questions. Use the present perfect where possible. Use the simple past elsewhere. Use contractions with subject pronouns and with *not*.

Shauna: I ___'ve just finished___ (just, finish) reading this book about sports
                        (1)

cars. Do you want to borrow it?

Karl: No, thanks. I _____ (read) it when it was published. I
                           (2)

_____ (be) interested in sports cars all my life. _____
        (3)   (4)

(you, ever, drive) one?

Shauna: No. I _____ (drive) my friend's old Ford Mustang a couple of
(5)

months ago, but I still _____ (not, drive) a real sports car.
(6)

Karl: I _____ (always, want) to own a Ferrari, but I _____
(7)   (8)

(never, have) enough money. I'm saving up to buy one now.

Shauna: Ferraris are really expensive. Do you have a good job?

Karl: I _____ (start) working at a fast-food restaurant a year ago.
(9)

Shauna: _____ (you, save) a lot of money since then?
(10)

Karl: So far, I _____ (save) enough to buy a spare tire for a Ferrari.
(11)

8 Guided Writing: Present Perfect versus Simple Past

On a separate sheet of paper, write a paragraph about your past accomplishments and
things you haven't accomplished yet. Use the present perfect and simple past. What
have you already accomplished in your life? When did you do it? Give details. What
haven't you done yet that you would like to do? Give your paragraph to your teacher for
correction.

> Example: I have graduated from the university. I graduated in 1997
>   with a degree in Business Administration. I have worked for
>   a company, too. But I haven't owned my own business yet.

9 Present Perfect, Present Perfect Progressive, and Simple Past

A reporter is talking to a former Boston resident who now lives on a ranch in New
Mexico. Use the words in parentheses to complete the statements and questions in the
present perfect, present perfect progressive, or simple past. In some cases you can use
either of two tenses. Use contractions with subject pronouns and with *not*.

Q: How long _have you lived/have you been living_ (you, live) in New Mexico?
(1)

A: We _____ (live) here for two years. We _____ (move) here
(2)   (3)

from Boston in 1996.

Q: Why _____ (you, leave) Boston?
(4)

A: Our lives _____ (be) too hectic and stressed there, and we
(5)

_____ (not, have) time for the important things.
(6)

Q: _____ (your lives, be) very different since you moved?
        (7)

A: Yes. Everything is different now. Since we came here, we _____ (live)
                                                                          (8)

very simply, without computers or television. Jack _____ (build) a
                                                              (9)

new barn, but he _____ (not, finish) it yet. For the last two years, I
                        (10)

_____ (teach) the children at home instead of sending them to
      (11)

school, so they _____ (have) freedom to develop their interests at
                       (12)

their own speed. For example, Cindy _____ (spend) a lot of time fish-
                                                 (13)

ing here, but so far she _____ (catch) only three fish. For the past two
                              (14)

days she _____ (write) a story about fishing.
              (15)

Q: It sounds like a big change from Boston. _____ (you, be) happy living
                                                        (16)

in New Mexico?

A: Yes. We _____ (be) happier here than we _____ (be) in
                  (17)   (18)

Boston.

Past Perfect and Past Perfect Progressive

GRAMMAR PRACTICE 1: Past Perfect and Past Perfect Progressive

---

■ Past Perfect

A. Sadatoshi is an exchange student in the United States. In sentences 1-5, tell what Sadatoshi had done before he came to the United States. In sentences 6-10, tell what Sadatoshi hadn't done before he came to the United States.

1. climb a mountain   *Before he came to the United States, he had climbed a mountain.*

2. drive a car

3. catch a fish

4. make many friends

5. ride a horse

6. leave home for so long   *Before he came to the USA, he hadn't left home for so long.*

7. sleep in a tent

8. go skiing

9. hear a coyote howl

10. write e-mail to his parents

11. read a novel in English

12. have so much fun

B. Circle the past participles in the sentences in Part **A.** Then look at the blanks below. Under each blank there are two numbers: the sentence number and another number. The other number is the position of the letter in the past participle that should go in the blank. For example, (*1*) indicates the first letter, (*2*) the second letter, etc. When all blanks are filled in, they should spell out the name of a city and state in the United States that Sadatoshi visited.

Example: *1. Before he came to the United States, he had* (climbed) *a mountain.*

M	I	A	M	I	,	F	L	O	R	I	D	A
1. (*4*)	2. (*3*)	3. (*2*)	4. (*1*)	5. (*2*)		6. (*3*)	7. (*2*)	8. (*2*)	9. (*4*)	10. (*3*)	11. (*4*)	12. (*2*)

2 Past Perfect versus Simple Past

Write sentences with the information from the timelines and the words given. Use the past perfect or the simple past. In cases where both tenses are possible, use the past perfect.

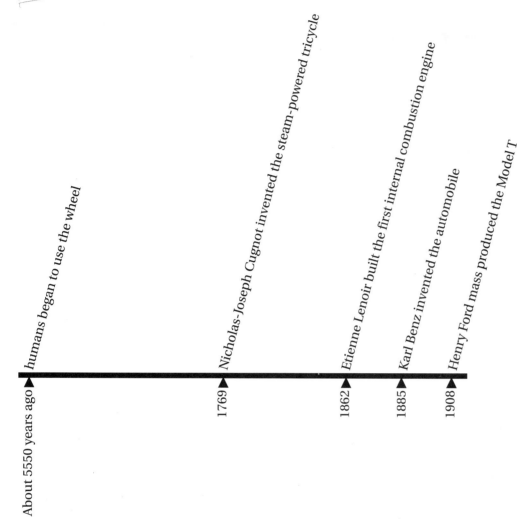

1. Etienne Lenoir / Nicholas-Joseph Cugnot / before

   1. *Before Etienne Lenoir built the first internal combustion engine, Nicholas-Joseph Cugnot had invented the steam-powered tricycle.* OR *Nicholas-Joseph Cugnot had invented the steam-powered tricycle before Etienne Lenoir built the first internal combustion engine.*

2. In 1885 / Karl Benz

   In 1885, Karl Benz invented the automobile.

3. Etienne Lenoir / already / Karl Benz / when

   E.L. had already built the 1ˢᵗ internal combustion engine when K.B. invented the automobile.

4. Until 1908 / Henry Ford / not *didn't mass produce*

  Until 1908, H.F. [hadn't mass produced] the Model T.

5. Humans / for thousands of years / before / Nicholas-Joseph Cugnot

  Humans had used the wheel for thousands of yrs before N.-J.C. invented the steam-powered tricycle.

the Wright brothers achieved powered flight — 1903

Paul Cornu designed the first helicopter — 1907

Charles Lindbergh flew the first trans-Atlantic solo flight — 1927

Frank Whittle performed a test flight on the first jet engine — 1941

the first supersonic jet passenger service began — 1976

6. By 1904 / the Wright brothers

  By 1904, the W. brothers had achieved powered flight.

7. Charles Lindbergh / Paul Cornu / after

  C.L. flew the 1st trans-Atlantic flight after P.C. had designed the 1st helicopter.

8. Until 1976 / the first supersonic jet passenger service / not

  Until 1976, the 1st supersonic jet passenger service hadn't begun.

9. Frank Whittle / the first supersonic jet passenger service / before

  F.W. had performed a test flight on the 1st jet engine before the 1st supersonic jet passenger service began.

10. The Wright brothers / already / Paul Cornu / when

  The W.B. had already achieved powered flight when P.C. designed the 1st helicopter.

3 Past Perfect versus Simple Past

Stories called fables are often used to teach a lesson about using time. Use the words in parentheses to complete the sentences in the fable. Use the simple past or the past perfect. In cases where both tenses are possible, use the past perfect. Use contractions with *not*.

no single action 1. Last fall, a grasshopper _____visited_____ (visit) some ants.

2. It ___asked___ (ask) them to give it some of the food they ___had stored___ (store).

Specific time by fall 3. During the summer, the grasshopper ___had sung___ (sing) and ___danced___ (dance), but the ants ___had worked___ (work).

4. The grasshopper ___didn't have___ (not, have) any food for the winter because it ___had played___ (play) all summer.

5. In the summer, food ___had been___ (be) plentiful, but in the fall the grasshopper ___wasn't able to___ (not, be able to) find any.

6. The ants ___thought about___ (think about) what the grasshopper ___had done___ (do) while they ___gathered___ (gather) food.

7. The ants ___made___ (make) a decision about what the grasshopper ___had requested___ (request).

same time frame 8. They ___picked up___ (pick up) the grasshopper and ___threw___ (throw) it out of their home.

9. The grasshopper ___realized___ (realize) that it ___hadn't used___ (not, use) its time wisely.

same time frame 10. It ___begged___ (beg) for a second chance, but the ants ___didn't change___ (not, change) their minds.

4 Past Perfect Progressive

Use the words in parentheses to write statements and questions. Use the past perfect progressive. Use contractions with *not*.

1. Last fall, a grasshopper didn't have any food. What ___had the grasshopper been___

   ___doing___ (the grasshopper, do) during the summer?

2. The grasshopper _____ (play). It _____ (not, gather) any food for the winter.

3. _____ (the ants, do) the same thing?

4. No, the ants _____ (work). They _____ (search) for food all summer.

5. Where _____ (the ants, look) for food?

6. They _____ (look) everywhere, especially at parties and picnics.

5 Past Perfect and Past Perfect Progressive

> *Hickory Dickory Dock. The mouse ran up the clock.*
> *The clock struck one; the mouse ran down.*
> *Hickory Dickory Dock.*
>
> —children's rhyme

Use the words in parentheses to complete the sentences. Use the past perfect or the past perfect progressive. In cases where both tenses are possible, use the past perfect progressive. Use contractions with *not*.

1. What ___had the mouse been doing___ (the mouse, do) before it ran up the clock?

2. It _had been looking_ (look) for food.

3. _Had the clock_ (the clock, strike) "one" before the mouse reached the top?

4. Yes. The mouse _had gotten_ (got) only half-way up when the clock struck one.

5. It _had been climbing_ (climb) up the clock, but then it turned and ran down.

6. Why did the mouse run down after the clock _had struck_ (strike) one?

7. It was scared. The clock _had struck_ (strike) many times before, but the

   mouse _had never heard_ (never, hear) the clock strike so loudly until then.

8. _Had it been feeling_ (it, feel) scared before it ran up the clock?

9. No. It _hadn't been thinking_ (not, think) about danger or loud noises.

⑥ Past Perfect, Past Perfect Progressive, and Simple Past

Another story about time talks about a tortoise (a turtle that lives on land) and a hare (an animal like a rabbit, but with longer ears and legs). Decide whether past perfect, past perfect progressive, or simple past can be used in the following sentences. In some cases, only one is possible. In other cases, both answers are possible. Circle all possible answers.

1. Long, long ago, a tortoise and a hare (lived / had lived) with many other animals.

2. When the animals got together, the hare (bragged / had bragged) about how fast he could run and (teased, had teased) the tortoise about being slow.

3. The tortoise (had told / had been telling) a joke to her friends and was unhappy at being interrupted by the hare.

4. The tortoise was angry, so she (challenged / had challenged) the hare to a race.

5. The tortoise (hadn't run / hadn't been running) a race before, but the hare (had run / had been running) many races.

6. The hare (accepted / had been accepting) the challenge before the tortoise could change her mind.

7. On the day of the race, all the animals (were / had been) excited.

8. The race started, and the tortoise and hare (took / had taken) off.

9. The night before the race, the hare (had danced / had been dancing) with his friends.

10. On the other hand, the tortoise (had gone / had been going) to bed early.

11. The hare ran fast until he (got / had gotten) tired and thirsty and fell asleep.

12. When the hare woke up, he (realized / had realized) that the tortoise was ahead.

13. Before the hare caught up, the tortoise (crossed / had crossed) the finish line.

14. The tortoise won because she (didn't stop / hadn't stopped) during the whole race.

Unit Wrap-up

Error Correction

Find and correct the errors in verb forms and functions. Some errors can be corrected in more than one way. Including the example, there are 10 errors.

       read
Recently I ~~had read~~ a book about people who use their time well. I had been

looking for role models and trying to be more like them when I ~~have~~ found this book

about CEOs.

Herb Kelleher, CEO of Southwest Airlines, is one such role model. During an

interview, someone asked him, "What does a typical day look like for you now?" He said that he didn't know. He said, "I have never ~~look~~ looked back. I have always tried to remain directed forward." He has decided what is important and has ~~setting~~ set his priorities based on those decisions.

Several years ago, he ~~has~~ delegated control of his schedule to his executive vice president, Colleen Barrett. Why did he do that? Herb Kelleher said that before Colleen began handling his appointments, scheduling his day took up too much of his time. When he spent time on scheduling, he ~~hasn't focused~~ didn't focus on other important matters.

Colleen Barrett had been ~~being~~ Herb Kelleher's secretary before she became his executive vice president. When she worked as his secretary, she learned a lot about the business and her boss, so it ~~had been~~ was easy for her to take over this duty. Since then, Herb has concentrated on running the company, while she has managed his daily activities.

So far, Herb Kelleher ~~was~~ has been a good role model for me while I have been trying to use my time well. I ~~had~~ have been managing my time better since I finished the book. There is just one problem. I don't have an executive vice president to schedule my day!

Guided Writing

On a separate sheet of paper, put the important events of your life so far on a timeline. Then write a paragraph about them. Use the past perfect, the past perfect progressive, the simple past, the present perfect, and the present perfect progressive at least once each. Use appropriate time expressions. Give your paragraph to your teacher for correction. Show your teacher your timeline as well.

Example: I was born 20 years ago. By the time I started kindergarten, I had already learned to read. I've been a good reader ever since. I had been enjoying life for seven years when my brother was born . . .

TOEFL TIME

Allow yourself 12 minutes to complete the 20 questions in this exercise.

Questions 1 through 10: Circle the letter of the one word or phrase that best completes each sentence.

1. Scientists _____ the effects of El Niño for many years, but they still don't agree on its impact on our weather.

   (A) have been studying
   (B) had been studying
   (C) are studying
   (D) were studying

2. Because the USA _____ trade with Cuba yet, cigars from that island nation are considered contraband by U.S. customs officials.

   (A) reestablished
   (B) has reestablished
   (C) hasn't reestablished
   (D) hadn't reestablished

3. The number of subscribers to Personal Cellular Service (PCS) has grown since the technology

   _____ available in the mid-1990s.

   (A) has become
   (B) has been becoming
   (C) had become
   (D) became

4. Voters _____ Franklin Delano Roosevelt four times before an amendment to the Constitution limited the number of terms a U.S. president could serve.

   (A) has been electing
   (B) had elected
   (C) has elected
   (D) had been serving

5. Data base companies _____ personal information about consumers for years before the government regulations became stricter.

   (A) had compiled
   (B) have been compiling
   (C) was compiling
   (D) are compiling

6. Toni Morrison _____ the 1988 Pulitzer Prize for fiction.

   (A) has won
   (B) was winning
   (C) had won
   (D) won

7. After the flood of 1997, health workers

   _____ residents to boil their drinking water until water purification systems could be repaired.

   (A) have advised
   (B) have been advising
   (C) advised
   (D) had advised

8. Since downsizing during the 1980s, many

   companies _____ trouble finding loyal new employees.

   (A) had had
   (B) have had
   (C) were having
   (D) had been having

9. Host cities usually _____ their major highways in preparation for the Olympic games.

    (A) had been repairing
    (B) have repaired
    (C) are repairing
    (D) were repairing

10. Special crews _____ avalanches for scientific studies until this practice was deemed too dangerous.

    (A) have filmed
    (B) have been filming
    (C) was filming
    (D) had been filming

Questions 11 through 20: Circle the letter of the underlined part of the sentence that is incorrect.

have been

11. Humans <u>are</u> <u>refining</u> ways of <u>communicating</u> with each other <u>for</u> thousands of
       A   B   C   D
    years.

12. Albert Einstein <u>had continued</u> <u>to work</u> on his theory of relativity even <u>after</u> he
               A   B   C
    <u>had published</u> it.
      D

13. The average score on standardized tests <u>has been</u> <u>dropping</u> <u>since</u> the last <u>ten</u>
                          A   B   *for* C   D
    years.

14. Scientists have developed new theories on the collapse of stars, but they <u>have</u>
                                                    A
    confirmed
    <u>not</u> <u>confirming</u> them <u>yet</u>.
     B C   D

15. Before he <u>became</u> famous for opposing the president's policies, Daniel Schorr
            A
    had
    <u>has already</u> <u>reported</u> the news <u>for</u> many years.
     B   C   D

16. The U.S. military <u>has</u> <u>been having</u> the FA18 Hornet fighter jet in service as a
               A *had* B
    replacement for the F14 Tomcat <u>for</u> <u>a number of years</u>.
                            C   D

17. The National Aeronautics and Space Administration <u>has</u> <u>ever</u> sent a manned
                             (already) or ∅ A B
    mission to the moon, but it hasn't <u>yet</u> <u>put</u> human astronauts on Mars.
                            C D

18. Life <u>became</u> easier for humans <u>while</u> they <u>had learned</u> to <u>use</u> tools.
        A   *when/after* B   C   D

19. Jessica Tandy <u>had</u> <u>been acting</u> <u>for</u> many years by the time she <u>has won</u> an Oscar
               A   B   C   *won* D
    for best actress.

20. Since fifteen people <u>lost</u> their lives on Mt. Everest in 1996, the climbing com-
                has A
    munity <u>had</u> <u>been</u> <u>discussing</u> whether amateurs should be allowed to climb that
         B   C   D
    mountain.

Unit Three

Future; Phrasal Verbs; Tag Questions

Future Time

GRAMMAR PRACTICE 1: Will and Be Going To

▯ *Will*—Form and Function

A. Vacations at amusement parks are becoming very popular. The roller coasters, in many different shapes and sizes, are the biggest attractions in those parks. Use the words in parentheses to complete the statements and questions with *will* about a popular amusement park in California. Use contractions with subject pronouns and *not*.

Josh: I'm so excited to be at Six Flags Magic Mountain. With all the roller coasters

here, this ___will be___ (be) a thrilling day.
            (1)

Rachel: How many roller coasters _____ (we, ride)?
                                        (2)

Josh: We _____ (try) to ride as many as possible, but the lines
           (3)

_____ (be) long so we probably _____ (not, be) able to
    (4)   (5)

ride them all.

Rachel: Which one _____ (we, go on) first?
                        (6)

Josh: Look, the sign says the wait time for the Viper _____ (be) one
                                                            (7)

hour in the morning and two hours in the afternoon. Let's wait in line for

the Viper first.

Rachel: The Viper. That sounds dangerous. I _____ (be) too scared.
                                                  (8)

Josh: Don't worry. I _____ (take care) of you, I promise. I
                              (9)

_____ (not, leave) you.
       (10)

Rachel: I _____ (ride) the others, but I _____ (not, ride) the
                (11)   (12)

Viper.

Josh: OK, but _____ (you, wave) at me when I go by?
                       (13)

B. Write the number of the answer from Part **A** that fits the meaning indicated next to
the line.

1. # 4 and # 7   ___4___ prediction

                        ___7___ formal announcement

2. #2 and #13   _____ prediction or expectation

                        _____ request

3. #3 and #9   _____ prediction or expectation

                        _____ offer or promise

4. #5 and #12   _____ prediction or expectation

                        _____ refusal

2 *Be Going To*—Form and Function

A. Use the words in parentheses to complete the statements and questions with *be
going to* about one of the popular roller coasters at Six Flags Magic Mountain. Use
contractions with subject pronouns and *not.*

Welcome to the Riddler's Revenge. You __'re going to take__ (take) the ride of
                                                  (1)

your life on the world's tallest and fastest stand-up roller coaster. First, the train

_____ (carry) you up a 156-foot tall hill. Be ready! Within seconds the
        (2)

train _____ (dive) 146 feet into a vertical loop. You _____
           (3)   (4)

(reach) a top speed of 65 mph. You _____ (experience) six inversions
                                            (5)

where you're riding upside down. You _____ (not, return) to the platform
                                              (6)

until you experience a gravity defying upward spiral. The ride _____
                                                                         (7)

(take) three minutes. The park has several more roller coasters. Which one

_____ (you, ride) next?
        (8)

B. Most of the sentences in Part **A** use *be going to* to express an expectation about the roller coaster ride. On the lines, write two sentences that express an expectation.

You're going to take the ride of your life on the world's tallest and fastest

stand-up roller coaster.

One sentence in Part **A** asks about intentions or plans. Write the sentence on the line.

3 *Will* and *Be Going To*—Function

Circle the function of each **boldfaced** verb.

1. *A:* We've made reservations for our vacation.

   B: When **are** you **going to leave**? [(plan) / prediction]

2. *A:* I've packed my winter jacket.

   B: Do you think the weather **will be** cold? [plan / prediction]

3. *A:* It's an outdoor adventure vacation.

   B: It**'s going to be** exciting. [plan / expectation]

4. *A:* My arms are getting tired. My suitcase is too heavy.

   B: Give it to me. I**'ll carry** it for you. [plan / offer]

5. *A:* This flight is getting bumpy.

   B: Yeah. Watch out! Your coffee **is going to spill**. [intention / prediction about immediate future]

6. *A:* Would you like a cheese sandwich or a turkey sandwich?

   B: I**'ll have** a turkey sandwich. [prediction / request]

7. *A:* I've never eaten enchiladas before. Are they good?

   B: You**'ll enjoy** them, I'm sure. [expectation / request]

8. *A:* Are you a vegetarian?

   B: Yes, I am. I **won't eat** meat. [prediction / refusal]

4 Expressing the Future in Sentences with Time Clauses

A. Use the words in parentheses to fill in each blank in the sentences about an exciting roller coaster at Six Flags Magic Mountain with the correct form of *be going to* or the simple present. Use contractions with subject pronouns.

1. When the riders ___*sit down*___ (sit down) on Batman the Ride, an inverted

   roller coaster, their feet ___*are going to dangle*___ (dangle) free.

2. The train _____ (dive) into a vertical loop as soon as it

   _____ (reach) the top of the first hill.

3. Before the riders _____ (travel) through the second 68-foot loop, they

   _____ (experience) a one-of-a-kind spin.

4. After they _____ (go) through the spin, the riders _____

   (proceed) through several twisting turns.

5. Until the ride _____ (be) over, the riders _____ (travel) at

   speeds up to 50 mph.

6. By the time the train _____ (arrive) at the end of the ride, some riders

   _____ (be) very dizzy.

B. Combine each pair of sentences about another thrilling roller coaster into one sentence using the time word given, the simple present, and *will*. In each pair, the action in the first sentence happens first. There are two ways to write each sentence.

1. when: You will ride the Viper.

                You will be upside down seven times.

   When you ride the Viper, you will be upside down seven times. OR You will be

   upside down seven times when you ride the Viper.

2. after: You will experience the first drop of 188 feet.

                You will go into the first vertical loop.

   _____

3. before: The train will enter a high-speed 180 degree turn.

                The train will go through two more vertical loops.

   _____

4. as soon as: The train will go through the loops.

                The train will fly up a hill.

   _____

5. when: You will go through the classic corkscrew inversion.

                You will finish the ride.

   _____

5   Guided Writing

On a separate sheet of paper, write a paragraph that describes the steps that someone is going to go through in experiencing an activity you know. Use *will* and *be going to*. Use time clauses with *when, before, after*, etc. Give your paragraph to your teacher for correction.

> Example: You're going to ride the Colossus, one of the largest wooden roller coasters in the world. You're going to climb to 115 feet before you experience the first drop. The train is going to travel at a top speed of 61 miles per hour. The ride will last for three minutes.

GRAMMAR PRACTICE 2: Expressing the Future with the Present Progressive, the Simple Present, and *Be About To*

---

6   Expressing the Future with Present Progressive, Simple Present, and *Be About To*

Match each form with the most appropriate function. Use each form and each function only once.

1. present progressive
2. simple present
3. *be about to*
4. *will* or *be going to*

a. predict unplanned events in the future
b. talk about the immediate or very near future
c. talk about future actions on a schedule or timetable that are not likely to change
d. talk about planned future actions

7   Expressing the Future with Present Progressive and Simple Present

A. Circle the function of each **boldfaced** verb.

Guide: Tomorrow we**'re going** to the Black Hills. (1) (prediction /(planned future) action) The bus **leaves** at 8:00 in the morning. (2) (prediction / action on a schedule)

Dudley: When **are** we **arriving** in Idaho? (3) (unplanned event / planned event)

Guide: We**'re** not **going** to Idaho. (4) (prediction / plan) The bus **gets** to Hot Springs, South Dakota, late in the day. (5) (unplanned event / planned event) It**'ll** probably **be** dark before we get there. (6) (prediction / plan) We**'re having** dinner at a buffalo ranch near there. (7) (prediction / planned event)

Dudley: **Are** we **riding** buffaloes after dinner? (8) (prediction / plan)

Guide: No, buffaloes are dangerous animals. Besides, I think you**'ll be** pretty tired

after dinner. (9) (prediction / plan)

B. Use the present progressive or the simple present and the words in parentheses to complete the statements and questions. Sometimes both are possible. If neither is possible, use *will.*

Dudley: When we're at the hotel, what time <u>does room service start</u> (room service,
(1)

start)?

Guide: I think that the kitchen _____ (open) at 5:00 A.M. Why?
(2)

Dudley: Tonight I _____ (pack) my earplugs in case my room is next to
(3)

the kitchen.

Guide: I see. Remember, everyone, that after breakfast, the tour _____
(4)

(go) to Mt. Rushmore and the Crazy Horse Memorial. It _____
(5)

(probably, be) cool in the morning, so please bring a jacket or a coat.

Dudley: When _____ (we, visit) the Jefferson Memorial? I _____
(6)   (7)

(bring) my camera because I want to get lots of pictures of it.

Guide: This tour _____ (not, go) to the Jefferson Memorial. That's in
(8)

Washington, D.C. Are you sure that you want to go on *this* tour?

Dudley: Yes, but it _____ (be) a lot different than I expected!
(9)

8   Expressing the Future with Present Progressive, Simple Present, and *Be About To*

Circle the form in parentheses that correctly completes the sentence.

1.

Marissa: Oh, you have the phone in your hand. Who (a) (are you about to)/ do you)

call?

Clare: I (b) ('m about to call / call) the travel agent to arrange our vacation cruise.

Marissa: Wow! Where (c) (are you going / do you go) this year?

Clare: I don't know yet. I (d) (know / 'll know) more after I call. The travel agent's

office (e) (closes / is about to close) in half an hour, so I need to call now.

2. (Later . . .)

Marissa: Your trip to the Bahamas sounds wonderful! I know I (a) (am / 'll be) jeal-

ous when you're there.

Clare: I (b) ('m telling / 'm about to tell) Tom when he gets home from work. I'm

so excited that we (c) ('re going / go) on this trip! As soon as Tom comes

home, we (d) ('re making / make) a list of all the things we have to pack.

Marissa: You're already making me jealous. I (e) ('m about to pick up / pick up) the

phone and make my own reservation. In fact, give me that phone. I (f) (go

/ 'm going) to the Bahamas, too!

9 Guided Writing

On a separate sheet of paper, write a paragraph about a trip that you would like to take. Use the present progressive and the simple present to describe your trip. Give the schedule for the time that you will leave and come back and for the activities that you will do. Give your paragraph to your teacher for correction.

> Example: *The bus leaves for Mt. Rushmore promptly at 9:00 A.M. We're spending two hours there. We're watching the video in the Visitors' Center and learning about how the monument was made . . .*

Future Progressive, Future Perfect, and Future Perfect Progressive

GRAMMAR PRACTICE 1: Future Progressive

1 Future Progressive with *Will* and *Be Going To*—Form

A. Scientists will be developing and using robotic submarines to explore and study the oceans. Use the words in parentheses to complete the statements and questions in the future progressive with *will*. Use contractions with subject pronouns and with *not*.

Before long, robotic submarines __will be exploring__ (explore) the oceans. These
(1)

small subs _____ (not, carry) passengers. What _____ (they,
(2) (3)

do)? These unmanned subs _____ (carry out) dangerous missions where
(4)

no one has been able to go before. They _____ (go) into dark caves. They
(5)

_____ (travel) in the ice-covered arctic regions. They _____
(6) (7)

(pass) over hypothermal vents where lava-heated water comes up from the ocean

floor. These AUVs (autonomous underwater vehicles) _____ (help)
(8)

scientists gather physical, biological, chemical, and geographical data.

B. Use the words in parentheses to complete the statements and questions in the future progressive with *be going to*. Use contractions with subject pronouns and with *not*.

One such vehicle, the Southampton Oceanography Center's Autosub One

__is going to be monitoring__ (monitor) natural hazards and environmental changes in
(1)

the ocean. It _____ (also, research) the roles that oceans play in climate
(2)

changes. A fleet of AUVs built by Florida Atlantic University's Sea Tech

_____ (take on) even more dangerous roles waiting for and recording
(3)

what is going on when storms hit. AUVs _____ (carry out) routine
(4)

sampling of the seabeds and ocean surface, too. So AUVs _____ (save) (5)
oceanographers from dangerous work. What _____ (these scientists, do) (6)
instead? They _____ (devote) more time to studying the data the AUVs (7)
provide.

2   Future Progressive versus Future

A. Put a check above each verb form that can be used in each sentence.

1. In the future, people (will travel ✓ / will be traveling ✓) across the ocean in hyper-sonic planes.

2. Transoceanic travel (will be ✓ *stative* / will be being) faster when hypersonic planes begin to fly.

3. The hypersonic plane (will fly ✓ / will be flying ✓) at five times the speed of sound.

4. With automated baggage handling, when you arrive, your luggage (will wait / will be waiting ✓) for you. *already in progress*

5. When the first hypersonic plane lands, the passengers (will cheer ✓ / will be cheering ✓).

6. (Are you going to ride ✓ / Will you be riding ✓) on a hypersonic plane one day?

7. The first one (will depart ✓ / is going to be departing ✓) in 2025.

8. (Will you be ✓ *stative* / Are you going to be being) on it?

B. In one sentence in Part **A** where both verb forms are possible, each form gives the sentence a different meaning. Write the number of the sentence on the line. _____

3   Future Progressive in Sentences with Time Clauses

Futurists make predictions about what will be happening in the future. Complete the sentences on their predictions about the future of personal transportation. Use the future progressive with *will* and the simple present. Use contractions with subject pronouns.

1. Most people __will be driving__ (drive) hybrid vehicles that combine electric and internal combustion engines when fuel cell cars (electric cars powered by fuel cells) __become__ (become) available around 2016.

2. By the time people __drive__ (drive) on automated highways two years

   later, everyone __will be using__ (use) fuel cell cars.

3. While cars __drive__ (drive) on automated highways, these highways

   __will be controlling__ (control) their speed, steering, and braking.

4. When automated highways __use__ (use) these intelligent transporta-

   tion systems, drivers __won't be causing__ (not, cause) so many accidents.

5. People in large metropolitan areas __will be riding__ (ride) in personal rapid

   transit (car-like capsules on guide rails) when large cities __install__
   (install) them in about 2024.

6. Before cities __have__ (have) personal rapid transit, people

   __will be living__ (live) in clustered, self-contained communities in large urban
   areas.

7. After cities __build__ (build) these clustered communities, people

   __won't be commuting__ (not, commuting) to work, which will reduce the amount of
   traffic on highways.

GRAMMAR PRACTICE 2: Future Perfect and Future Perfect Progressive

4 Future Perfect with *Will* and *Be Going To*—Form

A. Use the words in parentheses to complete the statements and questions in the
future perfect with *will*. Use contractions with subject pronouns and *not*.

Ron: Imagine living on Mars! Do you think I can explore there some day?

Carl: Maybe. Before anyone goes there, though, we __'ll have developed__
                                                              (1)
   (develop) a lot of new technology to deal with Mars' problems.

Ron: Oh, yeah? Like what? What problems __will we have solved__ (we, solve)?
                                                    (2)

Carl: By then, we __'ll have found__ (find) a way to keep warm at very cold tempera-
                          (3)
   tures. The night time low at the surface can be −130°F. Fahrenheit

Ron: Oooh, that's cold. I'm sure that I __'ll have put__ (put) a good heat source on
                                              (4)
   board my spaceship.

Carl: Yes, and scientists __will have *discovered*__ (discover) materials for your spacesuit to
(5)

keep you comfortable at Mars' high temperatures, too.

Ron: Hmm. Does Mars have an atmosphere? Will I be able to breathe the air?

Carl: No. The Martian atmosphere is 95% carbon dioxide and has almost no oxygen.

The atmosphere __won't have *changed*__ (not, change) by the time you get there.
(6)

Ron: __Will anything *have changed*__ (anything, change) on Mars?
(7)

Carl: Maybe not, but you__'ll have *gotten*__ (get) older, and everyone
(8)

__will have *learned*__ (learn) more about the planet.
(9)

B. Use the words in parentheses to complete the statements and questions in the
future perfect with *be going to.* Use contractions with subject pronouns and *not.*

Ron: How ___are we going to have learned___ (we, learn) more about Mars by the
(1)

time I get there?

Carl: In 1998, NASA set up a schedule of unmanned spacecraft to explore Mars. By

2010, five pairs of spacecraft __are going to *have gone*__ (go) to Mars, and one spacecraft
(2)

__is going to have *returned*__ (return) to Earth.
(3)

Ron: Yes, and . . .?

Carl: The first spacecrafts __are going to *have studied*__ (study) the atmosphere and one
(4)

__is going to have *mapped*__ (map) the surface, so you__'re going to *have learned*__ (learn) a lot of
(5)   (6)

information before you go.

Ron: __Are scientists *going to have collected*__ (scientists, collect) rocks and soil?
(7)

Carl: Yes, and they__'re going to have *looked*__ (look) for fossils and other signs of life.
(8)

Ron: __Are they going *to have found*__ (they, find) any life? Am I going to meet Martians?
(9)

Carl: Who knows what they'll find? That's the excitement of exploration.

Didn't assign 5-8

5 Future Perfect Progressive with *Will* and *Be Going To*

Ron's Terraforming Experiment

Activity	Day																				
	Week 1							Week 2							Week 3						
	1	2	3	4	5	6	7	8	9	10	11	⑫	13	14	15	16	17	18	19	20	21
plant seeds	X																				
start fan 1	X																				
write in journal	X	X	X	X	X	X	X	X	X	X	X	X	X	X	X	X	X	X	X	X	X
read about terraforming Mars		X	X	X	X	X	X														
read about wind erosion								X	X	X	X	X	X	X							
start fan 2													X								
read about reclaiming deserts															X	X	X	X	X	X	
end experiment																					X

A. Wind erosion is a problem on Mars, so Ron has set up an experiment on wind erosion and grass. Use the information in the chart above and the words in parentheses to complete the statements. Use the future perfect progressive and *will*.

1. Ron planted three plots with grass seeds on the first day of the experiment. By

   the end of the experiment, the grass ___will have been growing___ (grow) for

   ___21___ days.

2. Ron started a fan blowing on one plot of grass on the first day of the experiment.

   By the end of the experiment, the fan _____ (blow) for

   _____ days.

3. Today is the twelfth day of the experiment. Ron is starting a fan on the second

   plot of grass today. By the end of the experiment, the fan _____ (run)

   for _____ days.

4. Ron isn't going to start a fan on the third plot. At the end of the experiment, a fan

   _____ (not, blow) on the third plot at all.

5. Ron started a journal on the first day to record his observations. By the end of

   the experiment, Ron _____ (write) in his journal every day for

   _____ days.

6. This week, Ron has been reading about wind erosion. By the end of the week, he

   _____ (read) about wind erosion for _____ days.

7. Next week, Ron is going to read about deserts. By this time next week, he

   _____ (read) about deserts for _____ days.

8. By the end of the experiment, what _____ (Ron, look at) every day?

9. He _____ (observe) whether the grass can grow with wind from the

   fans blowing on it.

B. Go back to Part **A** and change the form of each of the verbs in the blanks to the future perfect progressive and *be going to*.

   The grass is going to have been growing for 21 days. _____

⑥ Future Perfect and Future Perfect Progressive with *Will* and *Be Going To*

YEAR	PREDICTION
2018	Scientists manufacture chemicals and metals in space that cannot be manufactured on Earth.
2019	Private companies send up most of the spaceships that are launched.
2028	A permanent moon base is established.
2037	Astronauts go to Mars.
2042	Scientists send a spaceship to explore another star system.
2062	Spaceships travel at almost the speed of light.

Use the information in the chart above to decide whether future perfect or future perfect progressive can be used in the following sentences. Circle the letter of the forms that can be used. In some cases, only one is possible. In other cases, both are possible.

1. By 2020, scientists _____ new metals and chemicals in space for two
   years.
   a. will have produced   b. will have been producing

2. By 2020, some private companies _____ for their own launches for
   many years.
   a. are also going to have paid   b. are also going to have been paying

3. Nine years before astronauts reach Mars, we _____ a permanent moon base.

   a. will have established   b. will have been establishing

4. Before 2042, spaceships _____ pictures back from another star system.

   a. aren't going to have sent   b. aren't going to have been sending

5. Spaceships _____ at the speed of light until at least 20 years after astronauts land on Mars.

   a. won't have traveled   b. won't have been traveling

6. _____ life on other planets before the end of the twenty-first century?

   a. Will we have found   b. Will we have been finding

7. What other things _____ before 2100?

   a. are we going to have discovered   b. are we going to have been discovering

7 Time Clauses, Future Perfect, and Future Perfect Progressive

Henry is an engineer at the National Aeronautics and Space Administration (NASA). Use information from the time line and the time expression given to combine each pair of sentences into one sentence.

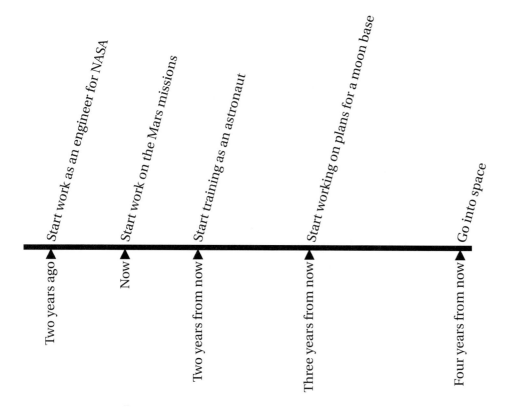

A. Use the simple present and the future perfect with *will*. There are two ways to write each sentence.

1. by the time   He will start training as an astronaut.

He will work at NASA for four years.

By the time he starts training as an astronaut, he will have worked at NASA

for four years.   OR   He will have worked at NASA for four years by the time he

starts training as an astronaut.

2. before   He will work on the Mars missions for three years.

He will begin plans for a moon base.

3. when   He will train as an astronaut for two years.

He will go into space.

4. by the time   He won't work at NASA for ten years.

He will go into space.

B. Now use the simple present and the future perfect progressive with *will*. There are two ways to write each sentence.

1. when: He will be training as an astronaut for a year.

He will start working on the moon base.

He will have been training as an astronaut for a year when he starts working on

the moon base.   OR   When he starts working on the moon base, he will have

been training as an astronaut for a year.

2. before: He will start working on the moon base.

He will be working on the Mars missions for three years.

3. when: He will start working on the moon base.

                  He will be working for NASA for five years.

_____

_____

4. by the time: He will go into space.

                  He will be working for NASA for six years.

_____

_____

8 Guided Writing

Predict the important events of your life and put them on a time line on your own paper.
Include activities beginning in the past, present, and future. Then, on a separate sheet of
paper, write a paragraph about what you will be doing and what you will have
accomplished in ten years. Use the future progressive, the future perfect, and the future
perfect progressive. Use appropriate time expressions. Give your paragraph to your
teacher for correction. Show your teacher your time line as well.

> Example: In ten years, I will be working as an international business profes-
>   sional. I'll have been working for three years by then.
>   I will have gotten married, but I won't have had any children yet . . .

Phrasal Verbs; Tag Questions

Phrasal Verbs Without Objects

A. Complete the crossword puzzle with the phrasal verbs for the meanings given. Look at the verbs in the box if you need help.

Across

2. begin to happen

5. end or result

6. return

7. begin

Down

1. start on a journey

2. appear

3. fail to function

4. continue

break down	come back	go on	set in
✓ set off	show up	start out	turn out

B. Use the appropriate form of the phrasal verbs from the crossword puzzle in Part **A** to complete the paragraph.

Norwegian explorer Borge Ousland _____*set off*_____ alone across Antarctica
                                                    (1)

on November 15, 1996. The journey _____ well. In 1995, he had tried
                                              (2)

to cross the Antarctic continent solo, but only reached the South Pole. He said,

"I _____ to try again. I am determined to succeed and I _____
        (3)   (4)

to the end this time." Luck was with him. None of his equipment _____
                                                                        (5)

and no bad weather _____ to stop him. The second crossing
                          (6)

_____ well and he _____ as planned at New Zealand Scott
        (7)   (8)

Base on January 17, 1997, the first man to cross the Antarctic continent solo and

unassisted.

2 Phrasal Verbs; Placement of Pronoun Object

Underline the phrasal verbs and circle the noun objects in the questions about Borge Ousland's journey. Complete the answers to the questions. Use pronoun objects.

1. Q: How did Borge Ousland bring off <u>bring off</u> (the feat) of crossing Antarctica
   alone?

   A: He ___*brought it off*___ it off through careful planning and endurance.

2. Q: Did he use dogs to pull along his sled?

   A: No, he didn't have any help with his sled. He _____ himself on his
      skis.

3. Q: Did he carry out his plan in the 100 days that he estimated?

    A: No, he didn't. He actually _____ in 64 days.

4. Q: How did he keep up the pace he needed to accomplish this?

    A: He _____ by making better time than he thought using his
    parasail.

5. Q: When did he first try out the parasail?

    A: The winds were too strong until the third day, so he _____
    (not) until then.

6. Q: What held up Borge Ousland?

    A: The lack of wind _____ and he only traveled a few
    kilometers some days.

7. Q: Was he able to make up the time?

    A: Yes, he was always able to _____ when the wind picked up.

8. Q: What did Borge Ousland say after he arrived at Scott Base and took
    off his skis?

    A: He _____ and said, "It's done."

3 Phrasal Verbs—Meaning

Circle the appropriate particle for each phrasal verb in **bold** to complete the sentences.
(If necessary, look in Appendix 9 in the student book for help.)

1. Polar explorers won't let their fears **keep** them (back, up) from reaching their
    goals.

2. They will **take** (on, over) the challenge of being the first to succeed.

3. Unless the weather is very bad, they won't **call** (off, up) the expedition.

4. They must **check** (a) (in, out) their equipment carefully before they **set** (b)
    (back, off) on their journey.

5. The media **plays** (down, up) their successes with many interviews and articles.

6. It's easy to **run** (a) (off, up) thousands of dollars in expenses to **bring** (b) (off,
    out) an expedition successfully.

7. These explorers will never **turn** (down, off) a chance for a new adventure.

GRAMMAR PRACTICE 2: Verb-Preposition Combinations; Phrasal Verbs with Prepositions

4   Verb-Preposition Combinations

Complete the conversation between an interviewer and Borge Ousland. Use the appropriate form of the verb-preposition combinations given in the box above each part of the conversation. (If necessary, look in Appendix 10 in the student book for help.)

depend on	happen to	✓ hear of	learn from	plan for	protect from

Interviewer: Congratulations on being the first man to cross the continent of

Antarctica alone and unsupported. Everyone ___has heard of___ your
                                                      (1)

amazing feat and wants to know what contributed to your success.

Borge: I knew I would succeed. I can _____ myself. I always
                                              (2)

_____ an expedition carefully. I _____ my experi-
        (3)   (4)

ence reaching the South Pole last year, too. I _____ myself
                                                      (5)

_____ bad weather, but I also know I'm lucky that nothing

bad _____ me.
        (6)

care about	come from	suffer from	recover from	think about	worry about

Interviewer: What about injuries and loneliness? Did you _____ those?
                                                                  (7)

Borge: Yes, I did. When you're alone you always _____ accidents
                                                          (8)

and injuries. I _____ several injuries during my journey, but
                      (9)

I _____ them all. It was also hard to _____
      (10)   (11)

Norway without my family, but I know they _____ me and
                                                    (12)

support me.

pay for   read about   talk about   write about

Interviewer: What will you do now?

Borge: I wrote in a journal each day of my journey. I plan to _____
(13)

my expedition in a book, and I _____ my expedition to
(14)

interested groups. I _____ my next expedition with the
(15)

money I make on my book and lectures.

Interviewer: Thanks for talking about your incredible adventure.

We _____ it when you publish your book.
(16)

5 Phrasal Verbs with Prepositions

A. Match the phrasal verb with preposition with its meaning. Write the letter of the correct meaning on the line. (If necessary, look in Appendix 11 in the student book for help.)

1. ___c___ come up with   a. return from

2. _____ get along with   b. meet unexpectedly

3. _____ get back from   ✓c. discover (an idea)

4. _____ get down to   d. be careful of

5. _____ meet up with   e. visit unexpectedly

6. _____put up with   f. enjoy the company of

7. _____watch out for   g. begin

          h. tolerate

B. Complete the sentences with the correct phrasal verb-preposition combination from Part **A.** Use each verb-preposition combination only one time.

Borge Ousland had to:

1. ___watch out for___ crevices

2. _____ the expedition safely

3. _____ extreme cold and loneliness

4. _____ work

5. _____ a plan for the expedition

Borge Ousland didn't have to:

6. _____ other people

7. _____ anyone until he got near Scott Base

6 Guided Writing

A. Choose three verbs from the list. These verbs are phrasal verbs with one or more meanings. On a separate sheet of paper, write a sentence using each verb you choose in one of its meanings. (If necessary, look in Appendix 9 in the student book for help.)

bring in	call off	come over	keep up	think over	work out

B. Choose three verbs from the list. These verbs are verb-preposition combinations. On a separate sheet of paper, write a sentence using each verb you choose in one of its meanings. (If necessary, look in Appendix 10 in the student book for help.)

come from	forget about	pass over	play with	search for	worry about

C. Choose three verbs from the list. These verbs are phrasal verbs with prepositions. On a separate sheet of paper, write a sentence using each verb you choose in one of its meanings. (If necessary, look in Appendix 11 in the student book for help.)

come up with	drop in on	get through with	meet up with
run out of	stand up to	start out for	watch out for

D. Choose three verbs from the list. These verbs are both phrasal verbs with one or more meanings and verbs + preposition. On a separate sheet of paper, write sentences using each verb you choose in two different meanings. (If necessary, look in Appendix 9 and Appendix 10 in the student book for help.)

look over	look up	run off	run up	turn down	turn up

Give your sentences to your teacher for correction.

BRIEFING TO PRACTICE: Tag Questions

7 **Tag Questions—Form**

Complete the tag questions and short answers.

1. Q: Learning about explorers past and present is fun, __isn't it?__

    A: Yes, __it is.__

2. Q: All of the explorers faced danger and hardship, _____?

    A: Yes, _____.

3. Q: Nothing stopped them from pursuing their goals, _____?

    A: No, _____.

4. Q: Borge Ousland was very brave to cross Antarctica alone, _____?

    A: Yes, _____.

5. Q: Others had gone before him, but had never gone alone, _____?

    A: No, _____.

6. Q: These stories of adventure inspire others to do the same, _____?

    A: Yes, _____.

7. Q: Explorers have always wanted to travel into the unknown, _____?

    A: Yes, _____.

8. Q: Someone is always trying to be the first to go somewhere, _____?

    A: Yes, _____.

9. Q: We'll continue to explore new places in the future, _____?

    A: Yes, _____.

10. Q: There aren't many places left on earth to explore, _____?

    A: No, _____.

11. Q: The ocean still offers unknown territory, _____?

    A: Yes, _____.

12. Q: I am interested in exploration, _____!

    A: Yes, _____ (you).

Unit Wrap-up

Error Correction

Find and correct the errors in verb forms and tenses. Some errors can be corrected in more than one way. Including the example, there are nine errors.

1. will land / will be landing

In the future, robots and other devices that ~~will be land~~ on Mars and other

celestial bodies will probably have gone to Antarctica before they ever leave Earth.

Scientists will be using this cold continent more and more as they design devices for

Mars exploration. They want to take the machines there and try out them because of

the similarities in climate between Mars and Antarctica. Both of these places have

frozen soil, and Antarctic lakes resemble the Martian lakes of long ago. Before any-

one will set foot on Mars, scientists are going to have been exploring Lake Hoare in

Antarctica for many years. They will have been looking at the algae that live at the

bottom of the ice-covered lake. They want to know it about because it is a very sim-

ple form of life. In the future, they search for similar algae under the surface of Mars

in what they think are old lake beds. The water dried up long ago, but the remains of

the algae, if there are any, might still be there. By 2010, a spacecraft is going to have

been returning to Earth with soil samples. When the spacecraft comes off, scientists

will find algae fossils in the soil, won't they? Maybe, but regardless of what they find,

scientists aren't going to give up their search for life too easily. They will keep in

looking in other places until they close in on their goal, don't they?

Guided Writing

On a separate sheet of paper, write two travel advertisements or announcements. Your advertisements can be for: 1) a travel agency, 2) a trip or tour, 3) a lecture about exploration, and/or 4) any other travel-related idea you have. Use at least three future forms and two phrasal verbs or verb-preposition combinations in each one. Use a tag question at least once. If you want, you can include drawings. Give your paper to your teacher for correction. (If necessary, look at the Introductory Tasks in the student book on pages 78–79 for examples.)

TOEFL TIME

Allow yourself 12 minutes to complete the 20 questions in this exercise. Questions 1 through 10: Circle the letter of the one word or phrase that best completes each sentence.

1. Hip replacement surgery will become more com-

   mon when the population _____.
   - (A) ages
   - (B) will age
   - (C) is going to age
   - (D) age

2. Before a single term of office is over, a US President _____ a State of the Union Address four times.
   - (A) is delivering
   - (B) is about to deliver
   - (C) will have been delivering
   - (D) will have delivered

3. If a student can't find a particular source of information, a reference librarian will

   _____ for them.
   - (A) look it up
   - (B) look up it
   - (C) look up
   - (D) look it

4. By 2010, the Internet _____ to meet the needs of a growing number of users.
   - (A) will have expanded
   - (B) expands
   - (C) is expanding
   - (D) is about to expand

5. Jobs open up when an economy expands,

   _____?
   - (A) aren't they
   - (B) are they
   - (C) don't they
   - (D) won't they

6. The *Farmer's Almanac* tells on what days the new

   moon _____ in the coming year.
   - (A) is about to fall
   - (B) falls
   - (C) will have been falling
   - (D) will have fallen

7. Today's fads _____ completely in a few years or even a few months.
   - (A) are disappearing
   - (B) will have been disappearing
   - (C) are going to have been disappearing
   - (D) will have disappeared

8. Because of their economic value, grains are never

   going to lose importance, _____?
   - (A) don't they
   - (B) do they
   - (C) are they
   - (D) aren't they

Go on to the next page →

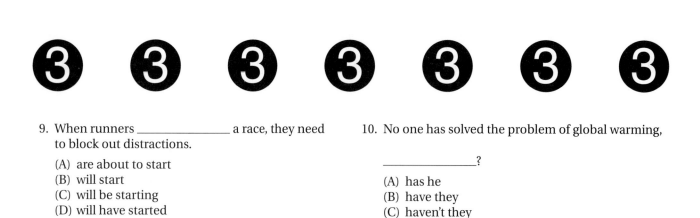

9. When runners _____ a race, they need to block out distractions.

    (A) are about to start
    (B) will start
    (C) will be starting
    (D) will have started

10. No one has solved the problem of global warming,

_____?

    (A) has he
    (B) have they
    (C) haven't they
    (D) hasn't he

Questions 11-20: Circle the letter of the underlined part of the sentence that is incorrect.

11. In the future, engineers will have figure out how to avoid collisions so that acci-
                    A   B   C
dents will not tie up traffic.
          D

12. Halley's Comet is coming back in 2062 after it will complete another orbit.
           A   B   C   D

13. Many homes will be having more computers when engineers build more "smart
               A   B   C
houses," isn't that right?
        D

14. It is possible that scientists are going to to reclassify the planet Pluto as an aster-
   A   B
oid after they will have studied it further.
         C   D

15. Perhaps in the future, detergents will treat any stain and get out it without
                 A   B   C
damaging the fabric.
   D

16. In future elections, computers will count up results while the voters will be
                  A   B   C
casting their ballots.
  D

17. There is hope that nations will get along each other, isn't there?
              A   B   C   D

Go on to the next page

60

18. World-class athletes <u>will</u> <u>be succeeding in</u> <u>breaking</u> many records before the
                           A   B   C

    next Olympic Games <u>end</u>.
                   D

19. Some people <u>believe</u> that taking vitamin C when a cold <u>be about to</u> start <u>will</u>
              A   B   C

    help them <u>get over it</u>.
                 D

20. Because the present generation <u>doesn't preserve</u> natural resources, it <u>will have</u>
                                         A   B

    <u>used up them</u> and there <u>will be</u> nothing left for future generations.
        C   D

Unit Four

Noun Phrases

Nouns and Determiners

GRAMMAR PRACTICE 1: Types of Nouns and Determiners

1 Proper and Common Nouns

Read the following passage. Capitalize the proper nouns. Underline the common nouns.

<u>Conquest</u>, <u>travel</u>, and <u>trade</u> have helped spread different <u>kinds</u> of <u>food</u> and <u>methods</u> of <u>cooking</u> throughout the <u>world</u>. For example, ~~r~~^Romans redesigned the gardens of the countries they conquered, and Christian soldiers returned from religious wars in the middle east and north africa with new ingredients and recipes. The travels of marco polo of venice, italy, helped establish trade with china and india, which gave europeans tea, spices, and the practice of heating the cooking pot with coal. When columbus and other explorers returned to europe from america, they brought new food and recipes with them. Then, italians traded these things with turks, who in turn traded with other Eastern europeans, thereby helping to spread new food throughout most of europe.

2 Using Articles with Proper Nouns

Write *the* in front of the proper nouns that use *the*. If a proper noun does not use *the*, write *NA* for "no article". (Look in Appendix 12 in the student book for help.)

1. _____*the*_____ Pacific Ocean

2. _____*NA*_____ Indonesia

3. _____ *Queen Elizabeth II* (a ship)

4. _____ Southwest

5. _____ Lake Michigan

6. _____ Julia Child

7. _____ Colorado River

8. _____ Ural Mountains

9. _____ California

10. _____ White House

11. _____ West Coast

12. _____ Philippine Islands

13. _____ Hawaii

14. _____ Indian Ocean

15. _____ South Pole

16. _____ Thanksgiving

17. _____ July   20. _____ Tuesday

18. _____ Africa   21. _____ Mediterranean Sea

19. _____ World Trade Center   22. _____ Boston

3 Proper Nouns Acting as Common Nouns

Circle the appropriate determiner or, if a determiner is not appropriate, circle ND for "no determiner."

Scott: Hey, Jenny, do you ever have (1) [a, the] Saturday free?

Jenny: Well, I usually do yoga on (2) [a, ND] Saturday. Why do you ask?

Scott: I was wondering if you'd like to come to my cooking class. The instructors,

(3) [the, ND] Crèvecoeurs, said that we could bring a guest sometime.

Jenny: (4) [The, ND] Crèvecoeurs? I met (5) [the, a] Paul Crèvecoeur once. Are they

from (6) [a, ND] Lafayette, Louisiana?

Scott: There's (7) [a, ND] Lafayette in Louisiana? I didn't know that. I only know

about (8) [two, the] Lafayettes, one in Indiana and one in Colorado. No,

they're from (9) [a, ND] New Orleans, and his name is (10) [a, ND] Robert.

Jenny: Now that I think of it, I've heard of (11) [a, ND] Robert Crèvecoeur that has a

restaurant downtown. I'd love to know if your instructor is (12) [a, the]

Robert Crèvecoeur that has the restaurant.

Scott: Well, come to the class with me (13) [a, ND] next Saturday and find out.

4 Count and Noncount Nouns

Mark the count nouns in bold with a **C** and the non-count nouns in bold with an **N.**

                                                    C   N

The Internet has also been instrumental in spreading **ideas** about **cooking.**

Many on-line **bookstores** have a **section** for **cookbooks** that includes **reviews** about

the **books**. Television and radio **programs** often have corresponding **websites** that

give **recipes** and further **information** and **advice** about different **kinds** of **food**.

Some **companies** use the Internet to give **consumers help** with their **products**. For

example, one **company** that sells frozen **turkeys** has a very popular **website** about

the Thanksgiving **holiday.**

5   Count Nouns versus Noncount Nouns; Plural Count Nouns

A. Use the correct form of the noun in parentheses.

Some new ___employees___ (employee) were listening to their two
                (1)

_____ (boss) talk to them about the _____ (work) at a produce
        (2)   (3)

market. "Let me give you some _____ (advice)," said the first one. "There
                                        (4)

are no _____ (party) here! _____ (fun) is for our
            (5)   (6)

_____ (husband), _____ (wife), and _____ (child),
        (7)   (8)   (9)

not for us! Our _____ (vegetable) are our _____ (life).
                    (10)   (11)

_____ (fly) are our _____ (enemy)! _____ (mouse)
        (12)   (13)   (14)

and their tiny, little _____ (tooth) are not welcome! We won't talk about
                          (15)

harmful _____ (bacterium) because we won't have any! The
            (16)

_____ (health) of our _____ (customer) is more important
        (17)   (18)

than the _____ (money) that we make.
            (19)

"Look over there," said the second of the two _____ (man). "The
                                                      (20)

_____ (tomato) are in strong, wooden _____ (crate). You can
        (21)   (22)

pick them up easily. The _____ (garlic), on the other hand, is in flimsy,
                            (23)

cardboard _____ (box). You must be careful when you pick them up.
                (24)

I'm warning you: if you workers are careless with the garlic, _____ (head)
                                                                    (25)

will roll!"

B. The last line in Part **A** is a double entendre; that is, it has two meanings. One meaning comes from the idiom *heads will roll*, which means that people will lose their jobs.
What is the other meaning of the last line? (Hint: consider the fact that *garlic* is a
non-count noun. How do we "count" garlic?)

6   Subject-Verb Agreement

Circle the correct form of the verb.

1. Food science (has/have) long included more areas than just recipes.

2. Stimuli for studies (has/have) come from many sources.

3. For example, lead sometimes (enters/enter) food through decorated plates.

4. Hypotheses about safe food (has/have) led to better public health.

5. Physics (plays/play) a role in developing food for the space program.

6. The basis of such research (rests/rest) on adapting many substances for space travel.

7. Certain means of cooking (isn't/aren't) available in space, either.

8. A group of food scientists also (looks/look) at where food comes from.

9. Exciting news about food (is/are) reported every day.

7 Nouns Used as Count and Noncount Nouns

Circle the correct form of the noun phrase.

1. I don't really know much about (business)/ a business).

2. But I'm thinking about becoming a partner in (business / a business).

3. (Pressure / A pressure) that I'll have to face is dealing with employee problems.

4. Well, of course (pressure / a pressure) comes in many forms.

5. Should I do this? I might not have (chance / a chance) like this again.

6. My mother always said that both (chance / a chance) and skill were important in business.

7. Maybe I'll just light (fire / a fire) and make something to eat.

GRAMMAR PRACTICE 2: Definite and Indefinite Articles

8 The Definite Article—Function

Fill in each blank with the letter of the correct meaning for the noun and article in bold.
Use each letter only one time.

1. __d__ **The earth** appears blue from space.

   a. the noun has already been mentioned

2. _____ Did you feed **the cat**?

   b. the noun is a part of or related to something that has already been mentioned

3. _____ I bought a cookbook. **The recipes** in it are really good.

   c. the noun is made definite by a modifier

   d. the noun is unique

4. _____ Please pass **the salt and pepper**.

   e. the noun is part of everyday life for both speaker and listener

5. _____ I saw a chef on TV. **The chef** was talking about his new cookbook.

   f. the noun is part of larger social context of the speaker and listener

6. _____ **The cookbook** on that shelf is new.

   g. the noun is part of the immediate situation

7. _____ **The Vice President** came for the ceremony.

9   The Indefinite and [0] Article

Fill in each blank with the letter of the sentence that contains the type of noun and article in bold. Use each letter only one time.

1. ___*b*___ singular count noun

2. _____ subject complement

3. _____ plural count noun

4. _____ indefinite quantity

5. _____ category

a. That man is **a food critic**.

b. He has written **a cookbook**.

c. He likes **some coffee** after dinner.

d. I prefer **tea: black, green, or herbal**.

e. He visits **restaurants** and writes about the food.

10   Definite and Indefinite Articles

Complete the following conversation with *a, an, the,* or [0].

Sara: I want _____*a*_____ (1) new cookbook.

Dana: But, you already have _____ (2) bookshelf full of _____ (3) cookbooks.

Sara: I know, but _____ (4) cookbooks I have aren't like a cookbook I saw in the bookstore yesterday.

Dana: Why? What's so special about it?

Sara: It's _____ (5) astrological cookbook. It lists foods we should eat based on our astrological sign and _____ (6) position of _____ (7) sun, moon and stars.

Later . . .

Dana: So, did you buy _____ (8) astrological cookbook that you wanted?

Sara: Yes, I did. I've already tried out _____ (9) recipe, too. I had _____ (10) fruit, _____ (11) salad, and _____ (12) bread for _____ (13) lunch.

Dana: That sounds like _____ (14) normal lunch. I thought _____ (15) recipes in it would be more interesting than that.

Sara: I didn't tell you about _____ fruit. It was a carambola.
                                       (16)

Dana: What's that?

Sara: It's also called "star fruit" because when you slice it, it looks like

_____ star. _____ cookbook claims it will help me find
      (17)   (18)

_____ happiness.
      (19)

Dana: Let me have _____ cookbook. I want to find _____
                           (20)   (21)

recipe for my sign that will make me happy, too. Here's one. Enchiladas with

_____ tomatillos. According to _____ recipe, it's going
      (22)   (23)

to add spice to my life!

▐▐▐ Definite and Indefinite Articles

Circle the correct article in the recipes. Where both choices are correct, circle both.

Apple Salad

3 apples, cored and cut into small pieces
1/2 cup raisins
1/2 cup chopped celery
juice of (1) [an, the] orange
8 ounces of yogurt
(2) [[O], some] cinnamon

In (3) [a, the] medium bowl, combine (4) [an, the] apples,
raisins and celery. Blend (5) [the, [O]] orange juice into (6)
[a, the] yogurt. Pour this mixture over (7) [[O], the] salad
and toss well. Sprinkle (8) [O], some] cinnamon on top.

Scrambled Eggs

12 eggs
1/4 cup milk
(9) [the, [0]] salt and fresh ground pepper
butter

Beat (10) [the, some] eggs and milk together. Melt (11)
[a, the] butter in (12) [a, the] skillet. Pour (13) [a, the]
mixture into (14) [a, the] skillet and stir it until it thickens.
Add (15) [some, the] salt and pepper. Continue cooking
until (16) [[0], the] eggs are soft.

---

12 Generic Statements

A. Complete the statements about exotic fruit with *a* or *an, the,* or [0]. Show all possible
articles. Two of the statements about the exotic fruit are generic. One is not.

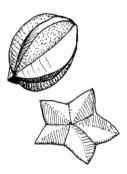

1. a. _____[0]_____ guava are native to tropical America but grow in Africa,
   Australia, India and the U.S., too.

   b. ___The/A/[0]___ guava can be white, yellow, red or green.

   ⓒ You can replace an apple with _____a_____ guava in that recipe.

2. a. _____ Asian pear is round and resembles an apple.

   b. _____ Asian pears are grown in Japan, China, Taiwan, and Korea.

   c. _____ Asian pear that I ate was fresh and delicious.

3. a. _____ carambolas are known as star fruit.

   b. The chef used _____ carambola to make jelly.

   c. _____ carambola will keep at room temperature for several days.

4. a. _____ tomatillos in the salsa gave it a good flavor.

   b. _____ tomatillos, also called Mexican husk tomatoes, are actually
      berries.

   c. The husk of _____ tomatillo is inedible (you can't eat it).

B. Circle the letter of the statement in each question in Part **A** that is not a generic
statement.

13 Guided Writing

On a separate sheet of paper, write three or four sentences describing an unusual fruit
or vegetable that you are familiar with. Use [0], *a* or *an*, and *the* with generic statements.
Give your sentences to your teacher for correction.

> Example: *Papayas are pear-shaped fruit. The papaya grows in Central
> America. A papaya can weigh from a few ounces up to 20 pounds. I like to
> have a papaya for breakfast.*

GRAMMAR PRACTICE 3: Quantifiers

14 Numbers and Measure Phrases

Use the appropriate numbers and measure phrases from the boxes to complete the list
of ingredients in the recipes. Use each number and measure phrase only one time.

1. tossed salad

a bag of	a bottle of	a bunch of	✓a head of	a slice of

a. __a head of__ lettuce   d. _____ tomato

b. _____ carrots   e. _____ salad dressing

c. _____ croutons

2. Cornish game hens for two

a can of	a couple of	a half pound of	a pair of	both	either

a. _____ Cornish game hens   d. _____ cream of chicken soup

b. _____ pieces of celery   e. _____ oregano or thyme

c. _____ stuffing mix   f. _____ salt and pepper to taste

15 *Much and Many*

Ask questions with *how many* and *how much* to learn about food ideas for a longer life.

1. _____How much_____ tea is good for me? Drink some every day.

2. _____ fruits and vegetables should I eat in a day? At least five servings.

3. _____ olive oil should I use? Use it sparingly in place of other fats.

4. _____ fish should I eat? Eat two or three servings a week.

5. _____ garlic do I have to have? As much as you can. Take it in a pill form if you don't like the flavor.

6. _____ servings of soybeans are good for me? Eat several servings a week for their anti-aging effect.

16 Quantifiers

Circle the correct choice. Where both choices are correct, circle both.

(1) (Many of / Much of) today's popular foods have been enjoyed for (2) (thousands / thousands of) years. The fig is (3) (no / none) exception. It has (4) (quite a little / quite a few) stories to its credit. It was probably (5) (one / one of) the first fruits that humans dried and stored. The first recorded history of figs is from about 4000 (6) (year / years) ago, when (7) (several / a large amount of) countries in Southwest Asia, as well as Egypt, Greece, and Italy, cultivated figs. People in these areas showered (8) (a great many / a great deal of) honor on the fig. Indeed, at one time, (9) (none / any) of the figs that were grown in Greece were allowed to leave the country. (10) (All / All of) were kept for the Greeks. When the Persian King Xerxes lost a battle to the Greeks, he had (11) (several / some) figs served at (12) (each / every) meal to remind him of his defeat.

(13) (Plenty of / Lots of) exporters recognized the value of figs, although (14) (not all / not much) of them were successful in reestablishing the plant in other areas of the world. In 812 A.D., Charlemagne of France tried to plant figs in the

Netherlands, but (15) (none / not any) flourished in the colder climate. In 1759,

(16) (some / any) Spanish priests planted the first fig trees in California, and today

(17) (many / most) figs in the United States are grown there.

17 Guided Writing

On a separate sheet of paper write down one of your favorite recipes. Include a list of
ingredients and complete instructions for preparing the food. Use articles, measure
words, and quantifiers. Give your recipe to your teacher for correction.

Modifiers, Pronouns, and Possessives

GRAMMAR PRACTICE 1: Modifiers

▮ Modifiers

A. Find the modifiers that come before nouns in the sentences. Underline them and circle the nouns they modify.

Every good (cook) knows that even a great (recipe) isn't going to result in a delicious dish without quality ingredients. Professional chefs use only fine, fresh produce. They usually prefer to buy healthy organic fruit and vegetables at small farmer-owned stands at local markets instead of in large grocery stores. For example, they select dark green leafy lettuce and smooth, round tomatoes at the peak of freshness for their summer salads. They pick ripe red strawberries, sweet Persian melons, and exotic tropical fruit for luscious, light desserts.

B. Find adjectives in Part **A** for:

Opinion _____ good _____ _____

Appearance _____ _____

Shape _____

Color _____ _____

Origin _____

Find a noun used as a modifier. _____

Find a compound modifier. _____

2 -Ing and -Ed Adjectives

Add -ing or -ed to the word stem in bold to complete the sentences with the correct participial adjective.

1. Some cookbooks promise **sooth**_ing_ food.

2. **Interest** _____ diners will try a **tempt** _____ new dish.

3. After eating too much chocolate, the **stimulat** _____ child couldn't sleep.

4. There are **heal** _____ recipes in that cookbook.

5. An **excit** _____ new restaurant opened downtown last week.

6. The **refresh** _____ woman had enjoyed the cold, **refresh** _____ iced tea.

7. There's a lot of **confus** _____ information about food and nutrition.

3 Noun Modifiers; Compound Modifiers

A. Change the words in parentheses to noun modifier + noun and complete the titles of the cookbooks. Use capital letters for the important words in the titles.

1. Recipes from a Country _Vegetable Garden_   (vegetables grown in a garden)

2. The _____ Cookbook   (a machine that makes bread)

3. _____ Cooking   (a pot made of clay)

4. The Great _____ Cookbook   (sauce made of chili)

B. Change the words in parentheses to a compound modifier + noun and complete the titles of the cookbooks. Use capital letters for the important words in the title.

1. Great _____Low-Fat Recipes_____   (recipes that are low in fat)

2. 100 Wonderful _____   (meals that have four courses)

3. Fabulous _____   (recipes that win awards)

4. Quick and Easy _____   (meals that take twenty minutes)

5. The _____ Cookbook   (a meal that has 300 calories)

4 Order of Modifiers

Write the modifiers in parentheses in an appropriate order.

1. This cookbook promises <u>really quick, easy</u> (easy/quick/really) meals.

2. This one offers _____ (authentic/old/Southern) food.

3. Here is a cookbook with recipes from _____ (food/great/American) companies.

4. This cookbook has recipes from _____ (art/famous) museums.

5. This one has recipes for _____ (modern/nonstick) cookware.

6. I like this _____ (French/herb) cookbook.

7. Here's a cookbook with _____ (interesting/regional/very) dishes.

8. There are _____ (coffee/delicious/international) drinks in this one.

5 Guided Writing

On a separate sheet of paper, write five cookbook titles of your own. Use more than one modifier and put the modifiers in an appropriate order. Give your titles to your teacher for correction. Refer to exercise three for examples.

GRAMMAR PRACTICE 2: Pronouns

6 Reflexive and Reciprocal Pronouns

Circle the correct form of the pronoun or phrase.

Randy: I need help. I have to do a restaurant review. Will you come to the restaurant

   with (me)/ myself)? I don't want to go (myself / by myself).
                (1)   (2)

Lee: Yes, unless the restaurant is Bad Bart's Barbecue. The President

   (himself / by himself) couldn't get me to go there. If that's where you're
            (3)

   going, you'll have to go (yourself / by yourself).
                             (4)

Randy: Why? I thought you'd like the restaurant. After all, you barbecue for

   (you / yourself) almost every weekend.
        (5)

Lee: That's the point. We could take turns cooking for (us / each other) every
(6)

Saturday night, and our food would still be more interesting than Bart's food.

Randy: We could sit (ourselves / by ourselves) and just talk to (us / each other). If
(7)   (8)

Bart came to our table, we wouldn't have to talk to (him / himself).
(9)

Lee: The three of us certainly wouldn't have much to say to (us / one another).
(10)

Randy: I don't get it. Is it the food (itself / by itself) that you don't like, or is it Bart?
(11)

Lee: Oh, I love Bart. It's his cooking. Don't you know that he's my brother? Our

mother could never get (us / ourselves) to agree with (us / each other).
(12)   (13)

7 Indefinite Pronouns

Use combinations of the words in the box to complete the sentences. In some cases,
more than one answer is possible. In sentences with verbs in parentheses, circle the
correct verb.

some		one
any	+	body
no		thing
every		

Henry: Tell me _____something_____. What are your plans for tonight? Are you doing
(1)

_____ special?
(2)

James: I'm not doing _____ so far. What do you have in mind?
(3)

Henry: There's a new restaurant downtown. _____ at the office (was /
(4)

were) talking about it, but she hadn't been there yet.

James: Is it the new Indian restaurant? _____ that I know (has / have)
(5)

been there, either, but it's the main topic of conversation at the office.

_____ (wants / want) to go there.
(6)

Henry: I hadn't heard _____ about an Indian restaurant. I know absolutely
(7)

_____ about it. I was talking about a new Algerian restaurant. I
(8)

haven't heard _____ say _____ negative about it.
(9)   (10)

James: It sounds interesting. It's _____ I'd like to try. Let's go!
(11)

8 Forms of *Other*

Complete the sentences by using *another, others, the other,* or *the others.*

Sara: The food in this restaurant is wonderful! I love places like this! Do you know

   some _____others_____ that we can try?
             (1)

Bernie: Tonight? I'm full, and I like this restaurant. Do you really want to go to

   _____ one tonight?
      (2)

Sara: Very funny. I was just suggesting that since our first date is going well, we

   might have _____ next Saturday. What do you think?
                  (3)

Bernie: I'm happy with that. For next Saturday, I have three ideas. One is that we go

   to a little French place that I know. _____ is that we pack a lunch
                                            (4)

   and go on a hike. _____ is that you cook something at your
                         (5)

   place.

Sara: I like those ideas. Do you have any _____?
                                                (6)

Bernie: Yes, but I'm not telling you about them. I'm keeping _____ a
                                                                    (7)

   secret.

Sara: Hmm. It sounds as if this won't be the only Saturday night that we spend

   together. Am I right? Are there going to be _____?
                                                  (8)

Bernie: I hope so. I hope there will be many more.

GRAMMAR PRACTICE 3: Possessives

9 Possessives

A. Underline the possessives and the words that they modify in the following sentences.

1. About 9000 years ago, <u>people of Mexico</u> started cultivating chilies.

2. In the 1500s, European traders' ships carried the chilies to other places.

3. The length of a century was the time needed for chilies to spread throughout the world.

4. A Hungarian cook has her recipes for chili peppers, and a Chinese cook has his, too.

5. Mexico's chili peppers are especially famous for their flavor and heat.

6. The chili pepper's seeds and ribs make it hot.

7. If your skin is as sensitive as mine is, wear gloves when handling hot chilies.

B. Fill in the chart with examples from Part **A**.

Form	Function
1. possessive determiner: *their*	1. ownership
2. singular possessive noun	2. amount
3. plural possessive noun	3. part of a whole
4. possessive pronoun	4. origin
5. possessive phrase	

🔟 Possessive Determiners, Possessive Pronouns, and Possessive Nouns

Complete the sentences with the correct possessive form of the pronoun or noun in parentheses.

Can you imagine living without rice? _Archaeologists'_ (Archaeologists) discoveries about rice include grains that are about 7000 years old. These grains were found in an ancient village in _____(2)_____ (China) Yangtze River valley.

European cooks expanded _____(3)_____ (they) skills when rice came to Europe, and Native Americans in South America sharpened _____(4)_____ (they), too, when the Europeans introduced it. Africans have long cultivated this crop, and in the United States, _____(5)_____ (South Carolina) rice fields date back to the 1600s.

More than half of _____ (the world) population eats rice every day.
                        (6)

Many _____ (people) nutrition depends on _____ (it) avail-
            (7)   (8)

ability. Some _____ (Asians) diets may contain over a pound of rice every
                   (9)

day. One of _____ (I) friends eats rice at every meal. _____
                (10)   (11)

(She) eating habits are much different from _____ (I) _____
                                                      (12)   (13)

(family) eating habits. _____ (We) diet includes more wheat and corn,
                              (14)

whereas _____ (she) doesn't include wheat at all.
               (15)

▐▐ Possessive Nouns versus Possessive Phrases

Complete the phrases by forming possessive nouns and possessive phrases with the
words in parentheses. In each, use the preferred possessive form.

__Mama's kitchen__ (Mama, kitchen) was always the _____ (house's
        (1)   (2)

activities, center). On chilly mornings, the _____ (stove, warmth) drew us
                                                    (3)

there. The kitchen was the first place the neighbors came to tell the _____
                                                                              (4)

(neighborhood and wider community, gossip). On holidays, the whole family would

gather at _____ (my parents, house). The _____ (cooking holi-
               (5)   (6)

day food, smells) permeated the house, and again we found ourselves in the kitchen

as _____ (my uncles, funny stories) kept us entertained.
        (7)

Unit Wrap-up

Error Correction

Find and correct the errors. Some errors can be corrected in more than one way.
Including the example, there are 15 errors.

   The cultivation of cacao is very precarious: the trees won't produce fruit if they

                         Earth's
are too far from the the ~~Earth~~ equator. They also won't grow in high altitudes if the

temperature falls below 60° F (about 16° C). The growing trees require year-round

moisture and is sensitive to a number diseases. Squirrels, monkeys, and rats tend to

eat the soft pulp that surrounds the trees' hard, bitter seeds, and a seeds will

promptly die without the proper humidity and temperature.

The seeds, though, are valued for producing a much-loving product: chocolate. Researchers disagree with one other about the exact origins of chocolate, but they tend to agree that the first domestication of tree was in the low-lying forests of what is now Mexico, at least 3000 years ago. The mayans, who lived there, probably spread their chocolate-drinking habits to others in Central America, eventually reaching the Aztecs in the highlands of Mexico. The Native Americans had several ways, not just a single mean, of preparing his processed chocolate, including flavoring it with chilies peppers.

The Aztecs valued the caffeine-rich seeds so highly that they used them as currency. Because of this, only royalty and the upper class consumed the rich, bitter chocolate drinks. Montezuma by himself, one of the Aztec last rulers, probably gave chocolate to Hernán Cortés, a Spanish explorer. The Spanish introduced some chocolate into the Europe, where the bitter drink was first mixed with sugar. Nowadays, people from all over the world enjoy this treat from the Americas.

Guided Writing

On a separate sheet of paper, write a review of a restaurant you are familiar with. Imagine you are a restaurant critic and describe the setting, the food, and the service in the restaurant you choose. Use nouns, determiners and modifiers in your paragraph. Give your paragraph to your teacher for correction.

> Example: I would give the Chinese Jade Restaurant a high rating. There is a warm, friendly atmosphere and the helpful servers are very willing to explain the more unusual oriental dishes. The appetizers I had were crisp tasty Crab Cheese Won Tons and delightful egg rolls made with fresh sweet cabbage and shrimp . . .

TOEFL Time

Allow yourself 12 minutes to complete the 20 questions in this exercise.

Questions 1 through 10: Circle the letter of the one word or phrase that best completes each sentence.

1. For the indigenous people of Australia, the land and everything on it are deeply woven into all

   aspects of _____.

   (A) the life
   (B) a life
   (C) life
   (D) lives

2. Orchids come in two basic types: one type grows at

   the base of the tree, and _____ grows on the tree itself.

   (A) others
   (B) other
   (C) another
   (D) the other

3. Americans get _____ of their news from television rather than from newspapers.

   (A) much
   (B) many
   (C) several
   (D) few

4. Many composers have extensive formal training,

   but Rimsky-Korsakov taught _____ the fine points of music.

   (A) himself
   (B) he
   (C) his
   (D) him

5. Although Buddhism was founded in India, there

   are _____Buddhists living there now.

   (A) a few
   (B) few
   (C) a little
   (D) little

6. The woolly mammoth, which has been extinct

   since the Ice Age, had _____ tusks.

   (A) long-sixteen-foot
   (B) long-sixteen-feet
   (C) sixteen-foot-long
   (D) sixteen-feet-long

7. Although some of the vitamin C that a person

   ingests is retained, _____ is lost and must be replenished.

   (A) several
   (B) any
   (C) a great many
   (D) a great deal

8. _____ seed will sometimes germinate

   after 200 years.

   (A) An unpreserved flowering lotus
   (B) A flowering lotus unpreserved
   (C) A lotus unpreserved flowering
   (D) An unpreserved lotus flowering

Go on to the next page ➡

9. A government employee with a high-level security clearance isn't permitted to discuss his or her work

with _____.

(A) one another
(B) anyone
(C) any other
(D) each other

10. _____who killed Abraham Lincoln, John Wilkes Booth, was a very popular actor of his time.

(A) The man
(B) A man
(C) Some man
(D) Man

Questions 11-20: Circle the letter of the underlined part of the sentence that is incorrect.

11. Some of archeologists believe that people from the Americas have been cultivat-
        A   B
    ing hot peppers for 6,500 years.
        C   D

12. Research has shown that efficient care in a hospital usually results in
      A   B   C
    shorter stay.
      D

13. Wood from the the white oak is not only burned in fireplaces but also used to
      A   B
    make the furniture and whiskey barrels.
        C   D

14. Some of of the interested hanging bridges that the Incas built lasted for over
      A   B   C   D
    500 years.

15. Cadiz, in the south of Spain, is the oldest continuously inhabited city in
      A   B   C
    Western world.
      D

16. Some of Van Gogh's most famous paintings are of fields of sunflower.
      A   B   C   D

17. Richard G. Drew, a Minnesota-born engineer, was person who invented
            A   B   C
    adhesive tape in 1925.
      D

18. In hers 1929 book, *A Room of One's Own*, Virginia Woolf described the benefits
      A B   C
    of having a fixed, steady income.
            D

Go on to the next page

82

19. <u>Cats and dogs</u> tend to favor one front paw or <u>the other</u>; that is, they prefer to use
       A   B

    either <u>the</u> their left or right <u>paw</u>.
           C   D

20. <u>Shakespeare's</u> characters Romeo and Juliet loved each <u>another</u> even though
      A   B

    <u>their</u> <u>families</u> were enemies.
     C   D

Unit Five

Adjective Clauses and Adjective Phrases

Adjective Clauses

GRAMMAR PRACTICE 1: Adjective Clauses; Subject and Object Pronouns

1 Forming Adjective Clauses; Subject Relative Pronouns

Use the adjectives to form adjective clauses with *be* to complete the sentences. Use each adjective only one time. Use any appropriate subject relative pronoun (*who, which, that*).

adventurous ✓creative dangerous stressful talkative

1. A person _who OR that is creative_ often becomes an artist or writer.

2. A person _____ might be among the first to colonize Mars.

3. People _____ might become teachers or salespeople.

4. A job _____ is good for a thrill-seeking person.

5. Careers _____ aren't good for nervous people.

2 Forming Adjective Clauses; Object Relative Pronouns

Use the adjectives to form adjective clauses with *we consider* to complete the sentences. Use each adjective only one time. Use a different object relative pronoun (*who, whom, which, that, [0]*) in each clause.

conscientious ✓dynamic enterprising exciting important

1. A person _who OR whom OR that OR [0] we consider dynamic_ would make a good CEO.

2. A person _____ should do well in business.

3. People _____ will be good workers.

4. A profession _____ is professional sports.

5. Jobs _____ will keep our attention and interest.

3 Relative Pronouns

Fill in the blanks with all the choices (*who, whom, which, that,* [0]) that are possible.

The Keirsey Temperament Sorter is a personality test __that/which__
                                                        (1)

categorizes people into four basic temperaments: artisan, guardian, idealist,

and rational. People _____ take the test answer a series of questions
                            (2)

_____ are designed to determine their temperament. Traits
        (3)

_____ are associated with each temperament are also associated with
        (4)

careers. For example, artisans are people _____ we find in fields
                                                  (5)

_____ allow them to use their creativity, like art and entertainment. A
        (6)

famous artisan was Elvis Presley. Guardians are people _____ are good
                                                              (7)

at logistics, so they make good supervisors. A President of the United States

_____ was a guardian was George Washington. Idealists are people
        (8)

_____ want deep and meaningful relationships. Plato, a famous Greek
        (9)

philosopher, was an idealist. Rationals are abstract thinkers _____ are
                                                                    (10)

good at planning. Bill Gates, the founder of Microsoft, is a rational.

The Keirsey Temperament Sorter is a test _____ you can take on the
                                                (11)

Internet to help direct you to a career _____ is right for you.
                                              (12)

4 Forming Adjective Clauses; *Someone, Everybody, Something*

Complete the sentences with *someone, everybody, or something* + all appropriate relative
pronouns (*who, whom, which, that,* [0]).

1. Personality traits are __something which/that/ [0]__ everyone has.

2. A psychologist is _____ we trust to help us learn about our
   personalities.

3. A personality test is _____ helps people understand their unique
   traits and characteristics.

4. A personality test can help almost _____ takes it.

5. _____ knows his or her positive traits can make better career
   decisions.

6. A career is _____ you should think about carefully.

5 Combining Sentences to Form Sentences with Adjective Clauses

Use the second sentence to form an adjective clause modifying the appropriate noun in
the first sentence. Use any relative pronoun (*who, whom, which, that,* [0]) that is possible.

1. Psychologists develop tests. The psychologists are interested in personality.

   Psychologists who OR that are interested in personality develop tests.

2. They are personality tests. They indicate a person's traits.

   _____

3. People will probably succeed. People have the right personality traits for a certain job.

   _____

4. These are traits. We consider these traits important for a particular job.

   _____

5. Someone probably won't be happy at a job. He or she doesn't have these traits.

   _____

6 Guided Writing

On a separate sheet of paper, describe each of the following people and things in two or
three sentences. Use adjective clauses with subject and object relative pronouns. Give
your paper to your teacher for correction.

> Example: *My mother is someone who is always kind and gentle. She has a
> smile which makes everyone feel good.*

My best friend   The job I would most like to have

The person I admire most   My favorite activity

GRAMMAR PRACTICE 2: Relative Pronouns as Objects of Prepositions; Possessive Relative Pronouns

7 Adjective Clauses with Prepositions

Underline the adjective clause in each sentence. Then change each adjective clause to
show all possible patterns.

1. A job <u>that you are interested in</u> should fit your personality.

   which you are interested in / you are interested in / in which you are interested

2. For a short time you can probably do a job that your personality isn't well suited
   for.

   _____

3. In the long run, however, you will be better off if you do a job that you are happy at.

_____

_____

4. A person that you can talk with honestly may help you decide on a good career.

_____

_____

8   Combining Sentences; Clauses With *Whose*

Combine these pairs of sentences using the second sentence as an adjective clause with *whose*.

1. A test asks questions about a person's thought and feelings.

   Its purpose is to match personality with careers.

   A test whose purpose is to match personality with careers asks questions

   about a person's thought and feelings.

2. An immediate response on these tests is preferred to a later response.

   A later response's accuracy may be decreased by too much thought.

   _____

   _____

3. People may answer as they wish they were, not as they really are.

   Their responses are slow.

   _____

   _____

4. Answers based on wishes will not help a person.

   His/Her personality is actually quite different.

   _____

   _____

5. A person has a strong preference in one aspect of work.

   His/Her answers tend toward a specific trait.

   _____

   _____

6. For example, a person probably prefers to work with other people.

   His/Her responses indicate an outgoing personality.

   _____

   _____

9 Relative Pronouns as Objects of Prepositions; Possessive Relative Pronouns

Fill in the blanks with all appropriate relative pronouns. Use *whom, who, which, that, whose,* and *[0].*

1. I've been thinking about taking a personality test, but I'm afraid it will be a test

   ___that / which / [0]___ I won't do well on.

2. My ex-girlfriend told me I had the personality of a rock. When we broke up, I

   wanted to return the personality, but I didn't know the rock _____ I

   had borrowed it from.

3. My ex-girlfriend also told me that you can tell a guy _____ personal-

   ity is like mine, but you can't tell him much.

4. I know what kind of personality I have. I am someone for _____

   "living in the moment" is important. I think that that moment was sometime

   in 1993.

5. My mother tried to get me to keep my eyes open and my mouth shut. This is an

   awkward way in _____ to work when you're a radio announcer.

6. I am a person _____ mind is always made up. Well, it's made up until

   someone changes it.

7. There are some things _____ I just won't speak about. I'd tell you

   what they were, but then I'd have to speak about them.

8. I've always thought of myself as someone _____ others don't talk

   about much. Why should they? I talk about myself enough for all of us.

10 Relative Pronouns

Fill in the blanks, using *whom, who, which, that, whose,* and [0]. Show all the possible completions.

Personality tests often use terms ___which/that___ have one meaning in
(1)

"everyday" language and a different, specific meaning for the test. The ideas

_____ the terms represent are more important than the terms
(2)

themselves. For example, one personality test contrasts "factual" with "sensitive",

two terms _____ we usually don't think of as opposites. This contrast is
(3)

between people _____ like to deal with facts and logic and people to
(4)

_____ feelings and intuition are more important. Someone
(5)

_____ answers indicate a strong tendency to be "factual" may prefer work
(6)

situations for _____ there are clear objectives. A job _____
(7)   (8)

allows for more personal expression appeals to someone _____ tends to
(9)

be more "sensitive". Remember that these are terms _____ the test
(10)

designers have used in specific ways.

More about Adjective Clauses; Adjective Phrases

1 Adjective Clauses with *Where*

A. Use the information in the box to write sentences about John and George with *the place* + adjective clauses. Use *where* or *which* + an appropriate preposition.

John	George
study / in a quiet corner of the library	study / in the student union
eat / at a small table alone	eat / at a large round table with friends
relax / at home with a good book	go / to a lively night spot
feel comfortable / in a small group of close friends	feel comfortable / in a large noisy crowd

1. The place where John studies is a quiet corner of the library. OR The place in

   which John studies is a quiet corner of the library. OR The place which John

   studies in is a quiet corner of the library.

   The place where George studies is the student union. OR The place in which

   George studies is the student union. OR The place which George studies in is

   the student union.

2. _____

_____

_____

3. _____

_____

_____

4. _____

_____

_____

B. An introvert is shy and an extrovert is outgoing. Look at the sentences in Part **A**

about John and George. Who is the introvert? _____ the extrovert?

_____

2 Adjective Clauses with *When*

A. Use the appropriate adjective clause with *when* to complete the sentences.

an artist feels creative	students feel many emotions
✓a couple feels happy	you felt bored
an employee feels nervous	we feel confused or frustrated

1. A day _____*when*_____ ____*a couple feels happy*____ is their wedding day.

2. A period in life _____ _____ is before we decide on a career.

3. A time _____ _____ is the first few days of a new job.

4. A month in life _____ _____ is the last month of high school.

5. A time in life _____ _____ is the most productive period for that
   person.

6. Was there a time in your life _____ _____ with what you were
   doing and wanted a change?

B. Replace *when* in each sentence in Part **A** with an appropriate preposition + *which*.

   A day on which a couple feels happy is the day they get married.
   _____

3 Guided Writing

On a separate sheet of paper, write two or three sentences about each of the following times and places. Give your sentences to your teacher for correction.

A time when my life changed   A place where I had a great adventure

A moment when I felt creative   A place where I feel comfortable

---

GRAMMAR PRACTICE 2: Restrictive versus Nonrestrictive Adjective Clauses

4 Nonrestrictive Adjective Clauses

Use the second sentence in each pair to write a nonrestrictive adjective clause modifying the appropriate noun or nouns in the first sentence. Be sure to include commas.

1. Intelligence and creativity are often considered a part of a person's personality.

   Intelligence and creativity are two areas that psychologists study.

   Intelligence and creativity, which are two areas that psychologists study,

   are often considered a part of a person's personality.

2. Howard Gardner has studied human development for over 30 years.

   He is a professor at Harvard University.

   _____

3. Gardner developed theories on intelligence.

   He did research on artistic talents in children.

   _____

4. He proposed that intelligence is made up of many different aspects.

   Intelligence can be measured in many different ways.

   _____

5. These aspects work together to form a person's intellect.

   Gardner called these aspects "multiple intelligences."

   _____

6. Gardner studied the relationship between types of intelligence and creativity.

   Intelligence and creativity both come in many different forms.

   _____

5 Restrictive versus Nonrestrictive Clauses

Underline the adjective clauses. Put commas in if necessary.

1. Gardner first studied Sigmund Freud and Pablo Picasso, <u>who demonstrated different kinds of intelligence.</u>

2. Freud whom Gardner called "linguistic" and "logical" was interested in psychology.

3. Picasso whose "intelligences" were "spatial" and "bodily" was known for his painting.

4. Both men were considered creative because of the innovations which they made in their fields.

5. The places where they spent most of their lives were in western Europe.

6. Freud died in 1931, the year when Picasso turned 50 years old.

7. The traits of the people he studied helped Gardner develop ideas about creativity.

6 Restrictive versus Nonrestrictive Clauses; All or Some? One or More?

Circle the letter of each correct choice.

1. Jobs, which may or may not be creative, can be more than just a source of income.

   a. This is talking about all jobs.　　　　　　b. This is talking about some jobs.

2. People, who are creative, can demonstrate their creativity in many ways.

   a. This is talking about all people.　　　　　b. This is talking about some people.

3. Artists who express their ideas in music can be very popular.

   a. This is talking about all artists.　　　　　b. This is talking about some artists.

4. My sister who has her own business is very creative in running her company.

   a. I have one sister.　　　　　　　　　　　b. I have more than one sister.

5. My cousin's job, which he does on the weekends, lets him design golf courses.

   a. My cousin has one job.　　　　　　　　　b. My cousin has more than one job.

7 Nonrestrictive and Restrictive Clauses—Pronouns and Punctuation

Complete the passage with *who, whom, which, that, whose, when, where,* or *[0]*, and add commas where they are needed. If more than one relative pronoun or adverb is possible, give all correct forms.

The traditional view of creativity is that a creative person is someone

___**who/that**___ finds a new solution to a problem. This definition _____
    (1)   (2)

underlies many "creativity tests" has been expanded by psychologists

_____ work enlarges older views of creativity. A place _____
    (3)   (4)

there is some disagreement is in the idea of general creativity. The definition

_____ Howard Gardner came up with says that people are creative in a
         (5)

specific domain. A gifted musician may show innovation in music but not in

another area in _____ she has less talent. An expansion of the traditional
                     (6)

theory says that there are many periods of time _____ people are cre-
                                                      (7)

ative. Fashioning new products and asking new questions _____ are not
                                                              (8)

part of traditional creativity tests are part of Gardner's definition of creativity.

Gardner's definition also differs in that creativity is a judgment _____
                                                                       (9)

must be made by a group of people.

GRAMMAR PRACTICE 3: Adjective Phrases

8   Forming Adjective Phrases

A. Change the underlined adjective clauses to adjective phrases.

Howard Gardner studied creativity in people ~~that had been~~ recognized for

contributions to their fields. Along with Freud and Picasso, Gardner studied other

famous creators who lived at approximately the same time. Albert Einstein,

who was the most famous physicist of the 20th century, and Igor Stravinsky,

who was an innovative composer, were two more of Gardner's subjects. T.S. Eliot

and Martha Graham, who were both born in the United States, were a poet and a

dancer, respectively. Gardner's seventh subject reflected "interpersonal intelli-

gence," which relates to human interactions, and is credited with developing nonvi-

olent, passive resistance in political struggles. That person was Mahatma Gandhi.

B. Change the underlined adjective phrases to adjective clauses.

                      who were
The creators ↑ in Gardner's study came from many fields of work, yet they had cer-

                                                   which helped
tain personality features in common. These features, ↑ ~~helping~~ them to become

outstanding in their fields, were self-confidence, alertness, unconventionality, hard work, and an obsessive commitment to their work. However, other people <u>sharing</u>

<u>these traits</u> aren't so successful. What's the difference? Is it something <u>running in a</u>

<u>family</u>? Or is it the method <u>used to raise a "creator"</u>? The facts <u>answering these</u>

<u>questions</u> aren't clear.

9 Guided Writing

which allows me to have freedom	that uses my natural talents
who supports others	who is confident in his/her abilities
that is well-known for being innovative	that is alert and unconventional

Choose five adjective clauses, either from those in the box or your own clauses. On a separate sheet of paper, write the adjective clauses and the corresponding adjective phrases. Then use each of the five phrases in a sentence that talks about personality or creativity. Give your paper to your teacher for correction.

> Example: *which allows me to have freedom* (clause); *allowing me to have freedom* (phrase); *I am a person who needs a schedule allowing me to have freedom to come and go as I want.*

Unit Wrap-up

Error Correction

Find and correct the errors in adjective clauses and phrases. Some errors can be corrected in more than one way. Including the example, there are ten errors.

For hundreds of years, people have been noticing that human beings tend to

have different personality types. Plato, ~~that~~ *who* was a Greek philosopher, wrote about

four kinds of character who humans have. Because Plato was interested in the socie-

tal role that these types of character played, he focused on the actions and charac-

teristics that each type displayed them. He wrote about artisans, guardians, ideal-

ists, and rationals.

Aristotle, Plato's student, defined four types of people, also, but he defined them

on the basis of happiness. Someone which happiness came from sensual pleasure was different from someone whom wanted to acquire assets. Others found happiness in acting in a moral fashion, while Aristotle's fourth type of person enjoyed logic.

During the time when Plato was alive in, Hippocrates a Greek physician proposed that people have distinct temperaments from the day that they are born. He identified, in about 370 B.C., four personality types based on bodily fluids: eagerly optimistic, doleful, passionate, and calm. Galen, was a Roman physician in the second century A.D., furthered Hippocrates' ideas. These two physicians looked for reasons for our thoughts and actions from within our bodies, not from our surroundings. That our physiology helped to determine our personality, which was new to Western thought.

The four personality temperaments whose Hippocrates and Galen described complemented Plato's four descriptions of social actions. Hundreds of years later, others interested in personality types also found four types. Perhaps our personalities haven't changed much in the last 2000 years.

Guided Writing

work alone	work in groups	work with things
work with ideas	use numbers	use words
use tools or machines	make your own schedule	have a fixed schedule

On a separate sheet of paper, describe the kind of job that you would like, based on your personality. Use the phrases in the box or your own phrases. Use at least one adjective clause with whose, one adjective clause with *where*, one adjective clause with *when*, one nonrestrictive adjective clause, and one adjective phrase. Give your paper to your teacher for correction.

Example: My ideal job, which I hope will be my real job, is one where I can make my own schedule and my own rules. I don't want to work in a company that has a lot of people . . .

TOEFL TIME

Allow yourself twelve minutes to complete the 20 questions in this exercise.

Questions 1 through 10: Circle the letter of the one word or phrase that best completes the sentence.

1. Scientists all over the world are trying to save

   species _____ are endangered.

   (A) what
   (B) in which
   (C) that
   (D) who

2. Placido Domingo, _____ Spain, is a well-known opera singer.

   (A) which is from
   (B) from
   (C) is from
   (D) that is from

3. Garage sales are a way many Americans recycle

   possessions _____.

   (A) that they don't want to keep
   (B) they don't want to keep them
   (C) which they don't want to keep them
   (D) what they don't want to keep

4. James Michener was an American author

   _____ books were bestsellers for years.

   (A) of whose
   (B) whose
   (C) who's
   (D) his

5. Although he has been dead for many years, Elvis

   Presley is a personality _____ many people continue to be interested.
   (A) in that
   (B) in whom
   (C) whom
   (D) in him

6. Anthropologists research the habits of people who

   _____ in the past.

   (A) was living
   (B) has lived
   (C) lived
   (D) living

7. The Pentagon is a five-sided building

   _____.

   (A) where the U.S. Army headquarters are located in
   (B) where the U.S. Army headquarters are located
   (C) where are the U.S. Army headquarters located
   (D) which the U.S. Army headquarters are located

8. Geography is a subject about _____ many Americans know very little.

   (A) that
   (B) it
   (C) whom
   (D) which

Go on to the next page

98

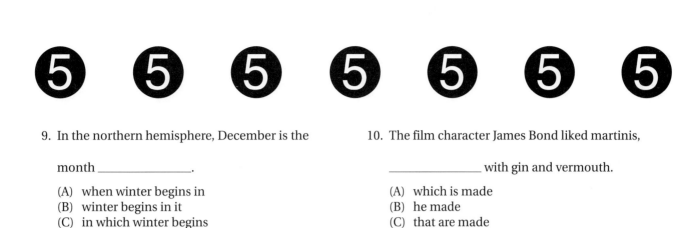

9. In the northern hemisphere, December is the

month _____.

(A) when winter begins in
(B) winter begins in it
(C) in which winter begins
(D) then winter begins

10. The film character James Bond liked martinis,

_____ with gin and vermouth.

(A) which is made
(B) he made
(C) that are made
(D) which are made

Questions 11 through 20: Circle the letter of the underlined part of the sentence that is incorrect.

11. The subatomic particle <u>which called</u> the quark, <u>which is</u> believed to be the fun-
                         A   B
damental <u>unit of matter</u>, <u>was first proposed</u> by the physicist Murray Gell-Mann.
                C   D

12. George Washington Carver, <u>who</u> was trying to improve agriculture in the South,
                                  A
showed <u>the peanut</u> could replace soil minerals <u>that</u> growing cotton had
          B   C
depleted <u>them</u>.
        D

13. Mineralized water <u>dripping</u> in caves <u>forms</u> both stalagmites, <u>which build up</u>
                    A   B   C
from the floor, and stalactites, <u>which hangs down</u> from the ceiling.
                                  D

14. American news organizations, <u>include</u> radio and television, <u>were criticized</u> for
                                A   B
<u>their reporting on</u> the presidential race in <u>1996, when</u> Bob Dole ran against Bill
         C   D
Clinton.

15. New York, <u>the capital of which</u> is Albany, is one of several American states
                   A
where <u>have</u> a capital <u>that</u> is not the biggest, or most important, <u>city in</u> the state.
        B   C   D

16. There are some American authors <u>whose</u> <u>their</u> books have been translated into
                                  A   B
<u>many</u> languages, <u>including</u> Spanish and Japanese.
     C   D

17. The Pennsylvania Dutch <u>are</u> the descendants of a group of German immigrants
                        A
<u>who</u> settled in eastern Pennsylvania, where <u>they</u> began farming <u>in</u>.
 B   C   D

Go on to the next page ➡

18. Somebody <u>that</u> is amazing to many people <u>is</u> Bill Gates, <u>who's</u> fortune was made
    _A   _B   _C
    in a relatively short <u>time in</u> the computer industry.
                          _D

19. After 1929, <u>when</u> the stock market crashed, the program <u>known</u> as the New Deal
                _A   _B
    was <u>begun</u> to improve economic conditions during the Great Depression, <u>that</u>
    _C   _D
    had put millions of Americans out of work

20. In 1876, at a <u>place</u> near the Little Big Horn <u>River is</u>, Indian warriors, <u>whose</u>
                   _A   _B   _C
    leader was Crazy Horse, killed General Custer and most of the

    <u>soldiers he commanded</u>.
                _D

Unit Six

Gerunds and Infinitives

Gerunds and Infinitives

chapter

12

GRAMMAR PRACTICE 1: Overview of Gerunds and Infinitives; Gerunds

1 Overview of Gerunds and Infinitives

Read the passage. Then underline the gerunds and circle the infinitives.

One result of <u>launching</u> Music Television (MTV) in 1981 was that both the television and the music industries took off in new directions. Before this time, it was unusual (to see) music videos, but televising them 24 hours a day became a winning formula for attracting young viewers. News and documentaries about music and performers were included on the broadcasts to supplement the videos. Young "VJ's", or Video Jockeys, hosted the programs and recommended listening to artists that they liked to hear. By promoting rock concerts and by holding interviews with artists, MTV not only attracted viewers but also exposed those viewers to a wide variety of performers.

2 Gerunds as Subjects, Objects of Verbs, and Objects of Prepositions

A. Correct the passage by changing verbs to gerunds where appropriate.

    Appearing
~~Appear~~ on television helped the career of musician Ricky Martin. At the 1999 Grammy Awards, ~~sing~~ *singing* "The Cup of Life" earned Martin a standing ovation. He certainly must have been happy about ~~receive~~ *receiving* this recognition of his music, and he also must have enjoyed ~~accept~~ *accepting* the award for Best Latin Pop Performance. After his appearance on the Grammys, Martin's fame kept ~~increase~~ *increasing*. His song, "Livin' La Vida Loca", soared to the top of the pop charts, and people looked forward to ~~buy~~ *buying* his album. From ~~grow~~ up *growing* in San Juan, Puerto Rico, to ~~live~~ *living* the crazy life, Martin has always loved ~~sing~~ *singing*.

B. Find examples in the passage in Part **A** of gerunds performing these functions.

subject of a sentence   _Appearing_   _singing_

object of a verb   _accepting_   _increasing_   _singing_

object of a preposition   _living_   _buying_   _growing_

be + adjective + preposition   _receiving_

3 Gerunds; *By* + Gerund; *Go* + Gerund

A. Correct the passage by changing verbs to gerunds where appropriate.

    becoming
    By ~~become~~ famous, Ricky Martin increased both his problems and his
              dancing   blending
pleasures. If he goes ~~dance~~ or on a date, he has a problem ~~blend~~ into the crowd.
              approaching   Maintaining
Fans can't help ~~approach~~ him for an autograph. ~~Maintain~~ his private life is hard. On
                            performing
the other hand, he is having a good time ~~perform~~. When he goes out on stage, he
         exposing   shopping
finds himself ~~expose~~ his thoughts and feelings to his fans. Perhaps he can't go ~~shop~~
          drawing (attracting)   reminding
by himself without ~~draw~~ attention, but by ~~remind~~ himself of the line between his

personal life and his private life, he may be able to live quite well with his fame.

B. Find examples in the passage in Part **A** of gerunds performing these functions.

by + gerund   _becoming_   _reminding_

go + gerund   _dancing_   _shopping_

subject   _maintaining_

object of a preposition   _drawing_

gerunds used with other expressions   _blending_   _approaching_   _performing_   _exposing_
                                   "have a problem"   "can't help"   "a good time"   "find ___self"
                                                      ↓
                                                   in the TXBK

4 Guided Writing

You can use a real-life role like a parent, a student, a nanny, a mechanic

Imagine that you are a pop musician. On a separate sheet of paper, use gerunds and other appropriate words to finish the sentences that tell about your life as a musician. Give your sentences to your teacher for correction.

1. Since I've become famous, *a teacher* I really appreciate... *having free time.*

2. Nowadays, it's not worth... *sitting around doing nothing.*

3. Before I was ~~famous~~ *a teacher* I used to go... *walking every day*

4. On the other hand, I enjoy... *helping people in my free time.*

5. I think I'll keep my sanity by... *meeting up with my friends and doing something fun.*

6. I'm always busy... *preparing for my classes.*

7. I avoid... *talking to my friends during the day.*

8. I had to quit... *taking personal enrichment classes at CSM.*

9. I miss... *having my free evenings.*

> Example: Since I've become famous, I really appreciate having some time alone.

GRAMMAR PRACTICE 2: Infinitives

5 *It* + Infinitive, Infinitive as Subject

A. Restate each sentence using *it* + infinitive

1. To choose a program on TV isn't easy these days.

   It isn't easy to choose a program on TV these days.

2. To learn about all the programs takes time.

3. To decide what to watch is difficult.

4. Not to waste time on programs that don't interest you is a good idea.

B. Restate each sentence using the infinitive as the subject.

1. It's fun to channel surf.

   To channel surf is fun.

2. It's necessary to have a remote control.

3. It's interesting to see how quickly you can become interested in each program.

4. It's a good idea not to channel surf when someone else is trying to watch a program.

⑥ Verb + Infinitive Patterns

A popular type of television program is a situation comedy. *I Love Lucy*, starring Lucille Ball, was one of the first situation comedies on American television, and some of the episodes are still running on TV today. Complete the sentences about this classic episode with an infinitive or an appropriate pronoun and infinitive.

In most episodes of *I Love Lucy*, Lucy managed _____to get_____ (get) herself
                                              (1)

into trouble. Her husband, Ricky, often needed _____ (rescue) her. In a
                                                   (2)

famous episode entitled "Job Switching," Lucy and her good friend Ethel Mertz

decided _____ (take) jobs in a candy factory while their husbands
           (3)

attempted _____ (take care of) the house.
             (4)

Lucy and Ethel had no experience in factory work, but they talked to the man

who was the manager of the candy factory and persuaded him _____ (let)
                                                                (5)

them try the job. Lucy and Ethel claimed _____ (know) how to do the
                                             (6)

work. Their supervisor, a woman, told _____ (put) the chocolate candies
                                         (7)

into paper wrappers as they came down a conveyor belt. The supervisor warned

_____ (not, work) too slowly or they would fall behind. She
   (8)

expected _____ (do) the job satisfactorily. Lucy and Ethel attempted
            (9)

_____ (do) the job well, but very quickly they were struggling
   (10)

_____ (keep up). They failed _____ (wrap) all the chocolates,
   (11)   (12)

so they began stuffing chocolates into their hats and mouths. Falling further behind,

Lucy and Ethel refused _____ (give up) and ate even more chocolates and
                          (13)

stuffed the rest in their pockets. The supervisor discovered what they were doing.

They begged _____ (keep) their jobs, but the candy company chose
               (14)

_____ (fire) them anyway.
   (15)

7   Adjectives Followed by Infinitives

Daytime talk shows are another popular type of program in the United States, but they are also controversial and not everyone thinks they are good television. Here are some reactions to what happens on these shows. Use an appropriate form of *be* + the adjective and verb in parentheses to complete the sentences.

1. I __was astonished to see__ (astonished / see) people fighting on yesterday's show.

2. We _were ashamed to admit_ (ashamed / admit) that we watched the guests tell embarrassing things about their personal lives on the show.

3. People _were stunned to learn_ (stunned / learn) that some guests on a talk show were actors who were paid to fight with each other.

4. Viewers _were delighted to hear_ (delighted / hear) that a popular talk show host was not going to air people's fights on her show anymore.

5. In the future, _will you be surprised to hear_ (you / surprised / hear) what people say on these talk shows?

8   Infinitive of Purpose

A murder mystery is another favorite type of TV program. In one popular show, the murder has often happened before the first scene. Complete the sentences with the phrases in the box. Use infinitives of purpose with *to* or *in order to*.

arrest the murderer	✓fool us
figure out if they are lying	find out who committed the crime
✓find clues	conceal his or her guilt

1. As the show begins, the detective examines the crime scene

   __(in order) to find clues__.

2. _(In order) to figure out if they are lying_, the detective asks people questions to which he or she knows the answers.

3. The murderer lies _(in order) to conceal his or her guilt_.

4. _(In order) to fool us_, the writer always includes another suspect who seems to have committed the crime.

5. The detective hunts for the proof he or she needs _(in order) to arrest the murderer_.

6. We watch the show _(in order) to find out who committed the crime._

9   **Infinitives with *Too* and *Enough***

A. Jon and Matt are cousins. Write sentences about each boy with an appropriate
adjective + *too* or *enough* + infinitive to complete the sentences about them.

Jon, 12
too + adj + inf

Matt, 24
adj + enough + inf

1. drive a car

   Jon is too young to drive a car.   Matt is old enough to drive a car.

2. watch an R-rated movie at a theater alone

   Jon is too young to watch an R-rated movie at a theater alone.
   Matt is old enough to watch " " " " " " —

3. buy a child's ticket to a movie

   Jon is young enough to buy a child's ticket to a movie.
   Matt is too old to buy " " " " —

B. Write sentences about Jon and Matt with the words given + *enough* + infinitive to
complete the sentences.

enough + noun + inf

1. Jon / time / play video games

   Jon has enough time to play video games.

2. Matt / money / go to a concert

   Matt has enough money to go to a concert.

3. Matt / sense / not / spend all day playing video games

   Matt has enough sense not to spend all day playing video games.

4. Jon / not / money / buy a lot of music CDs.

   Jon doesn't have enough money to buy a lot of music CDs.

10   Guided Writing: Infinitives as Adjectives

Listening to music can be beneficial. Think of some of the benefits of music. On a separate sheet of paper, write four sentences with infinitive phrases used as adjectives. Use each noun in the box one time. Give your paper to your teacher for correction.

ability	desire	possibility	way

Example: Listening to music is a good way to relax.

11   Guided Writing

On a separate sheet of paper, complete the following sentences. Use infinitives. Give your paper to your teacher for correction.

1. It's fun

2. I can't wait

3. I'm too young

4. We listen to music

5. Students have enough time

6. I'm glad

7. My friend trusts

8. It isn't a good idea

Example: It's fun to watch cartoons on TV.

chapter
13
More about Gerunds and Infinitives

1 Verbs Taking Only Gerunds or Only Infinitives

Use the words in parentheses to complete each sentence with an infinitive or gerund.

The prize that most movie actors hope ___to win___ (win) is an Academy
(1)

Award. Since 1929, people in the motion picture industry have aspired

___to earn___ (earn) the gold-plated statue, or Oscar, given with this award.
(2)

Winners appreciate ___attaining___ (attain) this recognition. No one can deny
(3)

___feeling___ (feel) honored when they receive a nomination. Imagine
(4)

___hearing___ (hear) your name announced as the best actor of the year. In the
(5)

excitement, you may forget what you have planned ___to say___ (say). You will
(6)

need ___to thank___ (thank) many people before you finish ___speaking___ (speak).
(7)   (8)

2 Verbs Taking Gerunds and Infinitives

Use the words in parentheses to fill in each blank with a gerund or an infinitive. *Rule* $\begin{cases} V+G \\ V+N+I \end{cases}$

I don't always advise ___looking___ (look) for deep meanings in pop movies,
(1)

but the continuing popularity of the *Star Wars* saga has required ___searching___
(2)

(search) for the origin of its appeal. Please permit me ___to explore___ (explore) this
(3)

with you.

The *Star Wars* films encourage us ___to see___ (see) the characters in terms
(4)

of good and evil. As the heroes fight external forces and internal passions, they urge

us ___to examine___ (examine) the darkness in our lives. The films allow us
(5)

___to be___ (be) heroes, too, and they encourage ___believing___ (believe) in
(6)   (7)

the power of good.

3   Verbs That Take Both Gerunds and Infinitives

Circle the gerund or infinitive that better completes each sentence.

1. I'd like to see *Star Wars* again; we should remember _____ at the video store.

   stopping   (to stop)

2. Some fans remember _____ to the first showing of the movie *Star Wars* in 1977.

   (going)   to go

3. If they forgot _____ early for tickets, they didn't get in the theater.

   going   (to go)

4. Darth Vader was so imposing that I've never forgotten _____ him for the first time.

   (seeing)   to see

5. When Luke Skywalker was learning to use a light saber, he tried

   _____ it in his left hand and then in his right hand to see which felt better.

   (holding)   to hold

6. R2D2 got hurt. C3PO tried _____ him, but he didn't have the parts he needed.

   repairing   (to repair)

7. Han Solo, a rough, rugged pilot, got _____ the refined Princess Leia.

   meeting   (to meet)

8. Princess Leia got Solo _____ the rebellion.

   joining   (to join)

9. The heroes got _____ when they realized that the Death Star was almost ready.

   (moving)   to move

10. Did Darth Vader ever regret _____ to the Dark Side?

    (turning)   to turn

11. I have bad news. I regret _____ you that Obi Wan Kenobi was killed.

    telling   (to tell)

12. Classic heroes such as Luke Skywalker never stop _____ the forces of evil.

    (opposing)   to oppose

13. From time to time, the heroes stopped _____ their good fortune and celebrate.

    enjoying   (to enjoy)

4 Guided Writing

On a separate sheet of paper, write a paragraph about a character in a movie or story that you like. Use at least three of these verbs followed by a gerund or infinitive: *forget, remember, stop, try,* and *regret.* Also, use at least two verbs that are followed only by gerunds and at least two that are followed only by infinitives. Give your paragraph to your teacher for correction.

> Example: My favorite character in the movie *To Kill a Mockingbird* was Atticus Finch. In the movie, Finch always tried to do the right thing even when others were afraid, and he hoped to teach his children to be like him . . .

GRAMMAR PRACTICE 2: Performers of Gerunds and Infinitives; Progressive Infinitives; Perfect Gerunds and Infinitives

5 Performers of Gerunds and Infinitives

Use the words in parentheses to complete the sentences with a gerund or infinitive. When a noun phrase or pronoun is given, include an appropriate form of the performer of the action.

With the movie *Toy Story,* Disney and Pixar Studios succeeded in

__creating__ (create) the first all computer-animated full-length movie. The
(1)

animators planned __for the toys to look__ (the toys / look) realistic. They
(2)

intended _____ (the audience / recognize) many of the toys from their
(3)

childhood. Movie viewers enjoyed _____ (watch) the toys behave like
(4)

humans. They tolerated _____ (the humans / look) less than life-like
(5)

because the story was really about the toys.

The story was a tale of rivalry between the two main characters. Disney per-

suaded _____ (we / believe) in the struggle between Cowboy Woody and
          (6)

Buzz Lightyear. Viewers understood _____ (Woody / feel) jealous of Buzz
                                      (7)

Lightyear, the new toy. It was believable that _____ (Buzz / become) the
                                                (8)

favorite toy annoyed Woody.

Disney Studios chose _____ (popular actor Tom Hanks / do) the
                       (9)

voice of Woody. They hoped _____ (he / make) the character appealing.
                             (10)

They were eager _____ (Tim Allen / do) Buzz Lightyear's voice for the
                  (11)

same reason. The studio trusted _____ (these two actors / bring) the toys
                                  (12)

to life.

6 Progressive Infinitives; Perfect Gerunds and Infinitives

A. Special effects are an important element of movies. Use the words in parentheses
to complete the sentences with progressive infinitives.

1. In a minute-long movie called *The Conjurer*, magician Georges Melies appeared

   ___to be disappearing___ (disappear).

2. Then, he seemed _____ (turn) himself into his female assistant.

3. Today, whole cities appear _____ (vanish) with great realism in
   movies like *Independence Day*.

4. In *Honey, I Blew Up the Baby*, the baby seems _____ (grow) right
   before our eyes.

5. The creators of special effects hope _____ (create) even better illu-
   sions in future films.

B. Use the words in parentheses to complete the sentences with perfect gerunds and
infinitives.

1. However special effects are created, every movie-goer enjoys ___having seen___
   (see) them.

2. How do filmmakers create scenes where people and things appear

   ___to have disappeared___ (disappear)?

3. Why did the magician seem _____ (turn) into his female assistant?

4. What made the baby appear _____ (grow) larger?

5. Who could have anticipated _____ (experience) what it would be like to travel inside the human body?

6. Imax Theaters showed the movie *Everest*. Movie-goers appreciated

   _____ (stand) on top of the world without leaving their seats.

7 Sensory Verbs and Causative Verbs

Use the words in parentheses to complete the sentences. In some cases, more than one form is correct. Give all correct forms.

1. a. In 1899 audiences watched George Melies _disappear / disappearing_
      (disappear) in *The Conjurer* and were amazed.

   b. He made himself _____ (disappear) by stopping the camera, changing the scene, and restarting the camera.

2. a. In *Honey I Blew Up the Baby*, we saw the baby _____ (grow) larger right before our eyes.

   b. Filmmakers make people and things _____ (appear) larger or smaller by changing the perspective.

3. a. In the 1977 movie, *Star Wars*, movie-goers looked at spaceships

      _____ (battle) in outer space.

   b. In this film, George Lucas, the director, had his special effects crew

      _____ (create) complex battle scenes using a computer.

   c. Computerized motion control let him _____ (create) specialized effects.

4. a. Viewers also heard the lasers _____ (fire) as Han Solo fought the Empire.

   b. With digital compositing, directors can get the computer _____ (add) different elements into their scenes, including realistic sounds.

8 Guided Writing

On a separate sheet of paper, give your own examples of special effects from movies you have seen. Use progressive infinitives, perfect infinitives and gerunds, sensory verbs, and causative verbs. Use the verbs in exercises 6 and 7 or any others you choose. Give your paper to your teacher for correction.

> Example: In *Raising Arizona*, a speeding car appeared to be stopping within inches of a baby on a highway. I saw the baby move, so I knew it wasn't a doll, but I couldn't believe any mother would let her child sit there with a car coming so fast . . .

Unit Wrap-up

Error Correction

Find and correct the errors in the passage. Including the example, there are eleven errors.

playing

Eric Clapton earned his fame through ~~play~~ his guitar, but he may have kept his solo career alive because of his singing. As a teenager, Clapton took up playing the guitar, and he later started performing in public. Practicing the guitar improved his music but left little time for schoolwork, so he stopped to go to school for pursuing a career in music. After he joined The Yardbirds, he became known for be one of the best blues guitarists playing at that time. As his reputation grew, Clapton seemed to be moving from one band to another, often because the musicians' egos were too big to keep the band together. Within ten years of him having dropped out of school, Clapton was considered to be a leading rock guitarist. He was enough famous to be invited to play with many other musicians. However, he didn't appreciate to have become so well-known, and at one time he seemed to be trying to hide in an unknown band. Clapton's popularity faded for a while, but he continued to record albums. The soundtrack of the 1992 film *Rush* included for Clapton singing "Tears in Heaven," a tribute to his son, who had recently died. Clapton's performance of "Tears in Heaven" and other songs on a special television program made it possible for him reaching a new audience. This success let him to release another album, and he kept on to sing in other movies.

9 Guided Writing

On a separate sheet of paper, write eight statements that are true about your
preferences and activities. In each statement use a different verb or expression from the
list + a gerund or infinitive. Give your paper to your teacher for correction.

Example: *I enjoy listening to pop music.*

1. enjoy
2. dislike
3. refuse
4. be afraid

5. be interested in
6. be used to
7. have a good time
8. like + go + a recreational activity

TOEFL TIME

Allow yourself twelve minutes to complete the 20 questions in this exercise.

Questions 1 through 10: Circle the letter of the one word or phrase that best completes each sentence.

1. _____ to Ireland in the late 1990s was surprising, especially given their exodus in the 1980s.
   (A) It was thousands of Irish emigrants returning
   (B) For thousands of Irish emigrants to return
   (C) Thousands of Irish emigrants returned
   (D) Thousands of Irish emigrants return

2. Proponents of gun control legislation were disappointed _____ that it hadn't passed.
   (A) them to learned
   (B) learning
   (C) to learn
   (D) having learned

3. The surgeon general recommends that everyone who smokes try _____.
   (A) to stop smoking
   (B) stopping to smoke
   (C) to have stopped smoking
   (D) having stopped to smoke

4. Fans of Emily Dickenson appreciated _____ her work, which she had chosen to keep secret while she was alive.
   (A) to publish
   (B) publish
   (C) her family to publish
   (D) her family's publishing

5. Some ethicists dispute the Hemlock Society's position that for the terminally ill, life is not worth _____.
   (A) living
   (B) to live
   (C) live
   (D) to be living

6. Injuries and deaths on the highway can be prevented _____ that children are properly buckled into an appropriate seat.
   (A) making sure
   (B) to make sure
   (C) by making sure
   (D) for making sure

7. Recognizing that _____ to a new home can be time consuming, some companies are assisting their employees in relocating.
   (A) by moving
   (B) for moving
   (C) to move
   (D) to have moved

8. Individual Retirement Accounts, IRAs, let _____ money for retirement.
   (A) employees accumulating
   (B) employees to accumulate
   (C) for employees to accumulate
   (D) employees accumulate

Go on to the next page

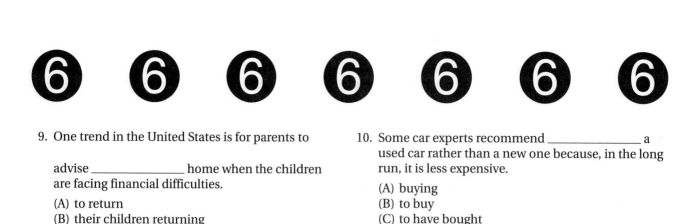

9. One trend in the United States is for parents to

advise _____ home when the children are facing financial difficulties.

(A) to return
(B) their children returning
(C) their children to return
(D) returning their children

10. Some car experts recommend _____ a used car rather than a new one because, in the long run, it is less expensive.

(A) buying
(B) to buy
(C) to have bought
(D) having bought

Questions 11-20: Circle the letter of the underlined part of the sentence that is incorrect.

11. Arctic mosquitoes, which can make a caribou herd <u>to stampede</u>, tend <u>to grow</u>
                                                          A   B

to be a quarter of an inch long and are known for <u>swarming</u> around unlucky
<u> </u>   D
C

mammals.

12. Doctors sometimes remove the tonsils of children who fail <u>to sleep</u> well
                                                                 A

<u>to unblock</u> their airways, thereby helping them <u>to stay</u> asleep instead of
B   C

<u>to wake up</u> throughout the night.
D

13. <u>By stroking</u> her baby's chin and throat, a mother may assist the child <u>in learning</u>
    A   B

<u>to nurse</u>, an action which is crucial for newborns <u>mastering</u> .
C   D

14. In a 1996 survey, which 950 people were willing <u>to participate</u> in, <u>doing</u>
                                                      A   B

household chores <u>were</u> among the top three things that couples reported
C

<u>fighting</u> about.
D

15. It's difficult <u>to watch</u> television without <u>see</u> reports of harmful bacteria, but food
                   A   B

safety experts have recommendations <u>to keep</u> us from <u>ingesting</u> unsafe food.
C   D

Go on to the next page

118

16. <u>For preparing</u> a stranded gray whale <u>to reenter</u> the ocean, rehabilitation
    _A _B
    specialists are prohibited from <u>spending</u> time with the animal once they
    _C
    <u>have finished working</u>.
    _D

17. Financial experts don't advise <u>investing</u> all of one's money in a single company
    _A
    as, <u>by doing</u> that, one risks <u>losing</u> everything at once; instead, they suggest
    _B _C
    <u>to diversify</u> one's assets.
    _D

18. "Pingers" prevent dolphins from <u>becoming</u> entangled in fishing nets by
    _A
    <u>scaring or alerting</u> them, and they allow fishermen <u>working</u> without <u>hurting</u>
    _B _C _D
    marine mammals.

19. Researchers are telling doctors <u>to urge</u> <u>to eat</u> dark, green, leafy vegetables <u>to get</u>
    _A _B _C
    more vitamin K, which seems <u>to strengthen</u> bones.
    _D

20. Once patients get used <u>to using</u> digital hearing aids, these aids may give them
    _A
    the opportunity <u>to hear</u> more sounds that have been <u>too high</u> or
    _B _C
    <u>not enough loud</u>.
    _D

Unit Seven

Modals

Modals

chapter 14

GRAMMAR PRACTICE 1: Overview of Modals; Ability Modals

☐ Overview

Read the passage. Circle the one-word modals.
Underline the phrasal modals. Put a check above the other forms that act like modals.

<u>Tony's Tips for Meeting People</u>

Can you walk into a room full of people and start talking imediately? You ought to try it sometime. All of us are supposed to be able to meet new people, but some of us find that a little hard. Try my tips and start making new friends today.

✓ You must show confidence! If you think you are worth knowing, other people will agree! You could try saying to yourself, "I am an interesting person!" Believe it.

✓ You should look people in the eye! People aren't going to speak to you if you look at their shoes!

✓ Of course, you ought to smile! You may be able to get someone else to speak with just a nice smile. Try it and see!

✓ You have got to say something! "Hi!" is a good start! You are allowed to keep your remarks simple. You don't have to be funny; just be sincere!

✓ You must not talk only about yourself! In fact, you had better let the other person talk more than you do. You might learn interesting things if you just listen.

So, what do you think? Are you going to be able to do these simple things? Of course you are! Start today! You should see results soon!

2   Present, Future, and Past Ability

Complete the sentences with appropriate forms of *be able to*. Where *can* or *could* is possible, write it as well. Use negatives where indicated. Use contractions with *not*.

What attracts people to others? Research ___is able to / can___ tell us some-
                                                        (1)

thing about attractiveness. A research team asked people to judge which faces were

most attractive. They _____ (not) experiment with real, live faces, but
                         (2)

they _____ alter photographs to make them more feminine or masculine.
         (3)

Using computers, a researcher _____ make the chin smaller (a feminine
                                   (4)

trait) or the eyebrows bigger (a masculine trait). Even though the photos were very

similar, the people in the study _____ select the same faces consistently.
                                     (5)

A Scottish researcher _____ get the same results as researchers in Japan
                          (6)

and South Africa did. Thus, the researchers _____ draw conclusions
                                                 (7)

across three different ethnic groups: feminine features, e.g., fuller lips and smaller

noses, were preferred for both men and women.

An interesting side note to this story is that many people are using the Internet

to meet each other. On the computer, one person _____ (not) see
                                                     (8)

another without special equipment. Couples _____ focus on things
                                               (9)

besides physical attributes. An attractive person _____ feel that he or she
                                                      (10)

isn't being judged on looks alone. In the future, some of the current Internet couples

_____ meet in the real world, but some of them _____ (not)
     (11)   (12)

get together. Will physical attractiveness still be important for the couples that

_____ meet in person? People who have already met this way think that
     (13)

we _____ (not) completely forget our ideas about beauty, but we also
       (14)

don't have to make them our first priority.

GRAMMAR PRACTICE 2: Belief Modals

3 Belief Modals—Degrees of Certainty About the Present

Gerald is giving a report on attraction. Look at his notes below and complete the
sentences with *must, have to, have got to, should, ought to, may, might,* and *could.* In each
blank, write one of the forms that you think express the intended meaning.

possible	most likely possibility	almost certainly true
• subconsciously looking for kind man • men with feminine features: gentler • looking very feminine not good	• women concerned with protection • choosing well leads to finding a good mate • no regrets about decision	• reason for attraction • feminine features not the only factor: other influences, too

Why do people seem to be attracted to feminine faces? No one knows for sure,

but, because the evidence is so strong, there ___must OR has to OR has got to___ be a
(1)

reason. One idea that _____ explain this phenomenon is that, subcon-
(2)

sciously, a woman _____ be looking for a man that will be kind to her. A
(3)

man with softer, more feminine-looking features _____ seem gentler
(4)

than a man with harder, more masculine-looking features. On the other hand, look-

ing too feminine _____ not be good, either, as a woman _____
(5)   (6)

be concerned with finding someone who looks like he can protect her. Evidence

shows men with all kinds of features are selected as mates, so feminine facial fea-

tures alone _____ not be the only factor in women's decisions. There
(7)

_____ be other influences. In the long run, if a woman chooses well, she
(8)

_____ end up with a man who will be good for her, and she
(9)

_____ not regret her decision.
(10)

4 Belief Modals—Degrees of Certainty About the Future

Circle the correct form; if both forms are correct, circle both.

Some trend watchers expect that increasing numbers of people (will) (are going to)
(1)

be using the Internet to find potential mates. The use of on-line dating services

(should, ought to) grow as users become more comfortable with the technology. Even
(2)

though it is now possible to see someone on another computer through the use of a

camera, this option (may, has got to) not become more popular because many people
(3)

seem to enjoy being able to ignore physical characteristics. What other changes

(will we, do we have to) see in dating practices? We (might, could) find services that
(4)   (5)

cater to international couples who have met over the Internet, or we (may, might) find
(6)

more localized services that bring together only people in the same geographical area.

We (should, ought to) not expect to see people give up on more traditional ways of
(7)

meeting each other, but we (may, could) see an increase in electronic "matchmakers".
(8)

A computer (might, must) set you up with others that you (may, must) not meet
(9)   (10)

otherwise. Whatever the future holds, it (will, has to) be interesting!
(11)

5 Guided Writing

A. On a separate sheet of paper, for each statement about marriages and families in the
United States, tell whether you think it is almost certainly true, possibly true, or
almost certainly untrue. Make affirmative and negative statements using the following modals: *must, could, might, may, can.* Tell your reason for thinking a statement is
true or false. Give your paper to your teacher for correction.

1. More weddings occur in New York than in any other state.

    Example: That might be true because there are a lot of people in New York.
    OR That couldn't be true because California must have more weddings.

2. Couples are engaged for an average of two years before getting married.

3. January is the most popular month for weddings.

4. Nine out of ten Americans are married at some point in their lives.

5. Americans are marrying at a younger age than ever before.

6. The bride is older than the groom in one out of four marriages.

7. The average number of children in an American family is four.

B. Look at the end of the unit to find out which statements are true.

GRAMMAR PRACTICE 3: Social Modals

6 Permission, Requests, and Offers

Use an appropriate modal and the information given to complete the sentences. More than one modal may work. Use each modal once.

1. ✓can   could   shall   will

Keiko: What are you reading?

Emily: It's a book about marriage and wedding customs around the world.

Keiko: It looks interesting. _____Can_____ I borrow it when you're finished?
                                    (a)

Emily: I'm sorry, but I checked it out of the library and it's due tomorrow. I

_____ ask them to hold it for you.
       (b)

Keiko: That's fine. _____ we go to the library together? Then, I can check
                              (c)

it out as soon as you return it.

Emily: Sure. _____ you be ready at 9:00?
                      (d)

2. can   may   would

Librarian: _____ I help you?
                    (a)

Keiko: My friend is returning this book and I want it. _____ I check it
                                                                  (b)

out now?

Librarian: Yes, that's not a problem. I see you have some other books.

_____ you like to check them out as well?
       (c)

7 Guided Writing: Permission, Requests, and Offers

On a separate sheet of paper, write a dialogue for each of the following situations. Make polite requests and offers or ask permission. Use appropriate responses for the information given. Give your paper to your teacher for correction.

1. Steve wants to know the number of Matematch Dating Service. The operator knows the number.

> Example: Operator: Directory assistance, may I help you?
>   Steve: Yes, could you give me the number of Matematch
>   Dating Service?
>   Operator: One moment please. The number is 800 get-mate
>   (438-6283).

2. You're at your brother's home. You ask your ten-year-old nephew to show you how to play a new computer game. He is happy to show you the game.

3. You're at a store. You ask the salesperson to gift wrap the wedding present you've just bought. The salesperson agrees, but asks you to come back later.

4. You don't have any money. You ask a friend to lend you some. He refuses because he doesn't have any money either.

5. You ask a classmate to go hiking with you this weekend. The classmate agrees.

6. Create a dialogue for a situation of your own.

8   Suggestions, Expectations, Advice, and Necessity

With her international students, a teacher is discussing how young people find marriage partners. Use any appropriate modal to complete the sentences with the meaning given in parentheses.

Teacher: I've been reading this book about marriage customs and weddings

around the world. The author states that young people in almost every

culture in the world are expected to find a marriage partner. They

<u>   are supposed to OR are to   </u> (expectation) get married. According
               (1)

to this book, in many cultures families still _____ (necessity)
                                    (2)

take an active role in arranging for the marriage of their children. How

do young people find a marriage partner in your country?

Abdullah: In Saudi Arabia, to find a bride the man _____ (expectation)
                                      (3)

get help from the female members of his family. Most families still

agree that young people _____ (prohibition) meet before
                              (4)

marriage arrangements have begun. However, contrary to what some

people believe, the woman _____ (lack of necessity) accept
                                 (5)

the man's proposal. She can refuse.

Hye Won: In Korea, a family _____ (suggestion) consult a matchmaker
                          (6)

to find a suitable partner for their son or daughter. But, young people

_____ (lack of necessity) do that. Many find a mate on their
         (7)

own, nowadays.

Toshi: In Japan, most people still believe a couple _____
(8)

(advice/opinion) have equal social standing. Computer-based mar-

riage information agencies are available now, and young people

_____ (advice/opinion) use one if they haven't found a suit-
(9)

able partner on their own.

Wornpahol: In Thailand, although we are free to date now, a Thai son or daughter

_____ (necessity) pay a debt of gratitude to his or her par-
(10)

ents which often delays the marriage.

Jaime: In Mexico, couples used to be chaperoned on dates, but they may now

meet on unchaperoned dates. The couple _____
(11)

(advice/opinion) have the approval of the woman's parents first,

though.

Teacher: Although there are differences in the customs of your cultures, there

are also similarities. This has been so interesting, but we

_____ (warning) stop now. I see that our time is up. Thank
(12)

you all for sharing your ideas.

🢒 Guided Writing

On a separate sheet of paper, write a paragraph about marriage customs and finding a mate. Use modals for expectation, advice, suggestion, and necessity. Tell what is necessary, what isn't necessary, and what is prohibited. Give your paper to your teacher for correction.

> Example: In the United States, you should find a husband or wife on your own. You could use a dating service, or you might go to places where young single people socialize. You must get the person to agree to marry you. You don't have to get the approval of your family, but it's better if you do . . .

chapter 15

More about Modals

1 Perfect Modals—Form

Julie has made a choice to remain single and is satisfied with her lifestyle, but her mother doesn't agree. Use the words in parentheses to complete the sentences with perfect modals. Use contractions with *not* where possible.

Mom: You ___should have been married___ (should / marry) by now.
                                (1)

Julie: I'm happy with my life. My career is going well and I have a very active social

life. I _____ (may / not / be) so happy as a wife.
                (2)

Mom: That's silly. I'm sure you _____ (could / be) just as happy as a mar-
                                        (3)

ried woman. You have dated some very nice men. What about Jeff? You

_____ (might / marry) Jeff. You _____ (should / not /
        (4)   (5)

tell) him that you planned to remain single. Maybe he's still interested.

Julie: He _____ (must / get) married by now. Besides, I _____
            (6)   (7)

(could / not / be) happy with him because he wanted a stay-at-home wife

and children.

Mom: (Sigh.) I _____ (could / have) grandchildren by now.
                    (8)

Julie: What made you think of Jeff anyway?

Mom: I saw his mother at the supermarket just last week and I . . .

Julie: Oh, Mother! I just had a message from Jeff's mother on my voice mail. You

_____ (must / say) something about me to her!
        (9)

Mom: Well, I did tell her you are still single.

Julie: You _____ (ought / tell) her that I like my life as it is.
            (10)

Mom: I _____ (should / not / raise) you to be so independent. You
        (11)

_____ (might / not / choose) a career instead of marriage.
        (12)

Julie: You raised me fine. I'm a well-adjusted single person with an exciting career!

2 Belief Modals in the Past

No one has seen Caroline, her fiancé Eric, or her former boyfriend Gene since yesterday afternoon. Caroline is supposed to marry Eric soon. Read the statements and complete the sentences with *must have, have to have, have got to have, should have, ought to have, may have, might have,* and *could have.* In each blank, write the modals that work best in the context. Use *not* where necessary. Use contractions with *not* where possible.

1. Caroline

   a. Caroline is missing and her bed wasn't slept in.

      Caroline ____might have / may have / could have____ (not very certain) stayed with her best friend Sally last night.

   b. When Caroline's mother called Sally, Sally hadn't seen Caroline in two days.

      Caroline _____ (strongly certain, not) stayed with Sally.

   c. Caroline is planning to marry Eric next month.

      Caroline _____ (most likely) looked happy, but she has seemed sad lately.

   d. Caroline was engaged to Gene a year ago.

      Caroline _____ (strongly certain) been serious about him then.

2. Gene

   a. Gene is missing and his friends haven't seen him since yesterday afternoon.

      Gene _____ (not very certain) gone on a business trip.

   b. Gene never travels on business. His friends aren't sure about where he went.

      Gene _____ (strongly certain, not) gone on a business trip.

   c. Gene and Caroline had a fight and she broke off their engagement a year ago.

      Gene _____ (strongly certain) felt sad because he stayed home a lot and never dated anyone else.

   d. Gene has seemed happier lately.

      Gene _____ (not very certain) found a new girlfriend.

3. Eric

   a. Eric wasn't at home when Caroline's mother called.

      Eric _____ (not very certain) gone away with Caroline.

   b. Eric's boss told Caroline's mother that he sent him on a business trip.

      Eric _____ (strongly certain, not) gone anywhere with Caroline.

3 Guided Writing

On a separate sheet of paper, write what you believe happened to Caroline, Gene, and Eric. Write sentences about what might have happened to them, what couldn't have happened to them, and what must have happened to them. Give your paper to your teacher for correction.

> Example: Eric might not have gone on the business trip for his boss. He
> and Caroline could have gone away together. OR Gene and Caroline might
> have fallen in love again . . .

GRAMMAR PRACTICE 2: Social Modals in the Past

4 Social Modals in the Past

Read the letter to Addy Viser, an advice columnist, as well as Addy's response. Complete each sentence with an appropriate social modal in the past. Use *not* where necessary. Use contractions where possible.

Dear Addy Viser,

My husband loves to cook, but he really had too much equipment for our small

kitchen. We ____had to____ (necessity) do something. So yesterday I got rid of
                (1)

some things that he _____ (advice/opinion) thrown out long ago. When
                        (2)

my husband came home after work, he said I _____ (a bad idea, but it
                                                (3)

happened) touched his things without consulting him. He also said that I

_____ (warning) thrown out his favorite stew pot. When he found out
    (4)

that I had, he was really angry and said that I _____ (prohibition) use any
                                                    (5)

of his equipment again.

Addy, I know that I _____ (suggestion) asked him to get rid of things
                        (6)

himself, but I have tried that and nothing ever happens. He _____
                                                                (7)

(expectation) cleaned out the kitchen last month. What do you think?

                                                    Adele

Dear Adele,

Your head was obviously in the right place, but you _____ (sugges-

(8)

tion) been a little more diplomatic. You _____ (lack of necessity) get rid of

(9)

your husband's things when he was at work. You _____ (good idea, but it

(10)

didn't happen) waited until he got home. Next time, talk more and act slowly.

Addy Viser

5 Belief and Social Modals in the Past

Luis and Taka are walking downtown. Complete their conversation. Circle the correct
choice. If both are correct, circle both.

Luis: Do you know where there's a phone near here? I (should, ought to) have

(1)

called my girlfriend about five minutes ago.

Taka: Yeah, after all, it (must, had to) have been all of 30 minutes since you last

(2)

talked to her.

Luis: Give me a break, will you? She (might, could) have changed her mind about

(3)

going out tomorrow.

Taka: No way. She (couldn't, must not) have changed her mind that fast. Besides,

(4)

she (didn't have to have, mustn't have had) much to do if she agreed to go out

(5)

with you.

Luis: Very funny. Her grandfather was visiting, and he (must, had to) leave soon, so

(6)

she (couldn't talk, must not have talked) very long when I called before.

(7)

Taka: So what makes you think she (might, could) have decided not to go out?

(8)

Luis: Oh, I don't know. I probably (shouldn't, must not) have said anything.

(9)

Taka: Yeah, you know she (didn't have to accept, couldn't have accepted) your invi-

(10)

tation. She (must, had to) have been excited about it.

(11)

Luis: Well, maybe. So where's that phone? I (must have called, was supposed to call)

(12)

her ten minutes ago. Is there a phone on the next corner?

Taka: Even better! Isn't that your girlfriend on the next corner?

6 Guided Writing

On a separate sheet of paper, write sentences using *could have*, *might have*, *should have*, and *ought to have*. What do the people say to each other or themselves in these situations? Give your paper to your teacher for correction.

1. Rex didn't call Marta until a week after he promised to. Marta was unhappy with him. She complained to him: *You could have called me a week ago.*

2. I wanted to go to a movie with Emily on Saturday night, but she had made other plans. I waited until Saturday to call her. I'm sorry about this. I said to myself:

3. Jane kept all of the love letters that her boyfriend had sent her. She discovered that her roommate had found and read them. Jane was angry. She told her roommate:

4. Hilda's boyfriend gave her an electric can opener for Valentine's Day. She wanted a romantic gift. Hilda was unhappy. She told her boyfriend:

5. Bart, a talented college football player, was asked to play for a professional team, but his girlfriend didn't want him to do it, so Bart became a football coach instead. All Bart's friends thought that he had lost an opportunity. They said to each other:

6. I went out with a group of people last night. I talked about myself the whole evening. I was sorry about this. I said to myself:

GRAMMAR PRACTICE 3: Progressive Modals and Perfect Progressive Modals

7 Progressive and Perfect Progressive Modals

Complete the sentences in the following conversations with the words in parentheses. If possible, put the modals into the progressive or perfect progressive form. (Remember that some verbs can't be used in the progressive.) Use contractions with *not* where possible.

Liz: What's wrong? Your eyes are red and your face is wet. You

   <u>must have been crying</u> (must, cry) before I got here.
         (1)

Diane: Oh, it's nothing. I was just watching a movie on TV. I _____
                                                (2)

   (should, do) other things, but the movie was too interesting.

Liz: Tell me about it. I _____ (might, sit) here with you if I had come
                  (3)

   earlier.

Diane: Well, one young woman had diabetes, and she _____ (should,
                                       (4)

   not, think) about having a baby, but she really wanted one.

Liz: She and her husband _____ (must, talk) a lot about their options,
        (5)

right?

Diane: Maybe. They _____ (might, fight), too, because the woman told
         (6)

her mother that they had been having problems.

Liz: They _____ (could, not, feel) very happy about their situation.
        (7)

Diane: No, probably not. They _____ (ought to, look) for other options,
         (8)

but they went ahead and had their own baby.

Liz: Oh, I've seen this movie! Julia Roberts _____ (must, play) the role
        (9)

of the woman with diabetes, right?

Diane: You're right. It was Julia Roberts. Do you know what's she doing now?

Liz: I don't know for sure. She _____ (may, take) some time off, but
        (10)

she _____ (might, make) another movie.
     (11)

Diane: She _____ (should, choose) her roles carefully these days. She
         (12)

_____ (must, not, accept) every part that she is offered. After all
(13)

she's not just another pretty woman.

Unit Wrap-up

Error Correction

Find and correct the errors in modals and modal-like expressions. Some errors can be
corrected in more than one way. Including the example, there are 9 errors.

                                           find
Anthropologists have seldom been able to ~~finding~~ a society in which men and

women don't marry, even though when and how they marry might vary. In some

                           be
cultures, couples are supposed to marry as soon as they reach adulthood. In others,

couples may be delay marriage until they want children. But, most cultures believe

that couples should to marry.

Types of marriage also vary. The most prevalent practice is monogamy, a

marriage between one husband and one wife. There are also polygamous societies.

In these, a man may have more than one wife, but he must not. A wife, however,

doesn't have to

mayn't have more than one husband. Polyandry, in which a wife can have more than

one husband, is extremely rare, occurring in only one percent of the world

population.

Young people in many cultures can have made their own decisions about mar-

riage, but freedom to choose one's spouse is a fairly recent development in the his-

tory of marriage. In the past, marriages had to be arranged in most cultures.

★ should

Although arranged marriages may have been more common in the past, they still

occur today where people believe that marriage ought to maintain family ties or

to choose

social bonds. Nowadays, even in these cultures, young people may be choosing

their own mates. When they do, their families often believe they mustn't have.

Will you marry? Will you can choose your own mate? Many societies are chang-

ing, and attitudes about marriage should be changing along with them. It is unlikely,

however, that marriage, in some form, is going to be disappear any time soon.

Guided Writing

On a separate sheet of paper, write a letter to Addy Viser's advice column. Describe a
problem and ask for advice. In your letter, use at least one belief modal in the past, at
least two social modals in the past, and at least one modal in the progressive form.

> Example: *Dear Addy Viser,*
> *Last week, my husband and I invited our friends to come to our new*
> *house. We were supposed to go out to dinner and to a movie with them.*
> *They should have arrived at about six o'clock. At seven thirty they still*
> *hadn't come . . .*

TOEFL TIME

Allow yourself twelve minutes to complete the 20 questions in this exercise. Questions 1 through 10: Circle the letter of the one word or phrase that best completes each sentence.

1. Although the U.S. Congress passed a law in 1974 that the Navaho _____ from the Big Mountain area in Arizona, many have refused to leave their land.
   (A) had to move
   (B) couldn't move
   (C) must have moved
   (D) might have moved

2. In the mid 60s, scientists considered the possibility that astronauts _____ die when they returned from the weightlessness of space.
   (A) can
   (B) must
   (C) might
   (D) should

3. Twenty years from now, Iceland could _____ liquid hydrogen, rather than fossil fuels, to power land and water vehicles.
   (A) be to use
   (B) be using
   (C) have used
   (D) to use

4. People believe scientists _____ to find a cure for the common cold by now.
   (A) could
   (B) must be able
   (C) should have been able
   (D) had to be able

5. A careful reevaluation of the terminal illness suffered by Edgar Allen Poe has led doctors to believe that this American author _____ from rabies.
   (A) may have died
   (B) might be dying
   (C) could die
   (D) should have died

6. Partly because a Florida anti-smoking campaign _____ the ideas and energies of teenagers, it was called the most effective such campaign of the late 1990s.
   (A) can use
   (B) ought to use
   (C) had better use
   (D) was able to use

7. Without an establishment such as the World Trade Organization to settle disputes, nations may _____ into protectionism.
   (A) retreat
   (B) retreated
   (C) retreating
   (D) to retreat

8. Although they _____ the armed forces when the draft ended in the 70s, many young people enlisted for the benefits, which included education and health care.
   (A) mustn't join
   (B) mustn't have joined
   (C) didn't have to join
   (D) couldn't join

Go on to the next page ➡

135

9. Recognizing that disabled children

    _____ have good access to playground
    facilities, one nonprofit organization builds areas
    where children in wheelchairs can participate
    more easily.

    (A) mustn't
    (B) can't
    (C) ought to
    (D) better

10. Because of federal laws, Alaskan fishermen who
    are licensed to catch cod and pollack

    _____ other species of fish that they
    catch by accident.

    (A) can't have kept
    (B) can't keep
    (C) might not have kept
    (D) might not keep

Questions 11-20: Circle the letter of the underlined part of the sentence that is incorrect.

11. The National Aeronautics and Space Administration <u>was able</u> <u>to test</u> such
                                                    A   B

    things as rendezvous in space with the Gemini project, so without Gemini, the

    Apollo mission to the moon <u>might</u> never <u>be happening</u>.
                                        C   D

12. The Komodo dragon, which <u>can</u> <u>grow</u> to over ten feet in length, produces a pro-
                                 A B

    tein molecule that scientists soon <u>may</u> <u>be able</u> use to synthesize a new antibi-
                                      C   D

    otic.

13. Actress Mira Sorvino <u>must</u> <u>have returned</u> to China after she graduated from
                        A   B

    Harvard, but she <u>couldn't</u> <u>make</u> the trip and so went into acting instead.
              C   D

14. As a child, horror author R. L. Stine <u>was not allowed</u> <u>to buy</u> horror comic books,
                             A   B

    but he <u>could</u> to <u>read</u> them at the local barber shop.
         C   D

15. A female black widow spider <u>will</u> eats her mate; she <u>may</u> <u>be able to</u> <u>consume</u> up
                     A   B   C   D

    to 25 males a day.

16. Motivational speakers often advise that people <u>mustn't</u> <u>give up on</u> dreams;
                             A   B

    instead they <u>should</u> <u>have tried</u> to use every opportunity they can.
        C   D

Go on to the next page

136

17. Although global warming <u>may</u> <u>coming</u> soon, some researchers believe that a
                                            A   B

    past era of warming <u>might</u> <u>have been</u> beneficial to humans.
                              C   D

18. Police <u>could</u> take a long time to respond to a call, especially where they may
             A

    <u>must</u> cover a considerable distance or where the roads <u>might</u> <u>not</u> be in good
    B   C   D

    condition.

19. By using a laser, doctors <u>should be able to</u> deal with some chronic ear infections
                                   A   B

    that in previous treatments <u>might not have</u> <u>respond</u> to antibiotics.
                                  C   D

20. Finding a new drug <u>may</u> <u>taking</u> an average of $600 million dollars, so pharma-
                            A   B

    ceutical companies feel that they <u>must</u> <u>protect</u> their most valuable assets:
                                       C   D

    patents.

Answers for Chapter 14, Exercise 5

1. True. More weddings occur in New York than in any other state. Florida is in second place, and California is third.

2. Not true. The average couple is engaged for 11 months before they marry.

3. Not true. June is the most popular month for weddings. January is the least popular.

4. True.

5. Not true. In the late 1990s, the average first-time bride was 24.5 years old and the average first-time groom was 26.7 years old.

6. True.

7. Not true. The average number of children in an American family is about 2.1.

Unit Eight

Passives

chapter 16

Passive Overview

☐ Forming Passive Sentences

Frank is a sports announcer. Frank doesn't seem to be able to get anything correct today. Write two sentences in the passive, one in the negative using the object of the active sentence and one with the words given to correct Frank's mistakes. Include the subject of the active sentence in a *by* phrase.

1. *Frank:* Elvis Presley sang the National Anthem. (an Elvis impostor)

   <u>The National Anthem wasn't sung by Elvis. It was sung by an Elvis impostor.</u>

2. *Frank:* The governor is throwing out the opening pitch. (the mayor)

   _____

3. *Frank:* Jay White is going to pitch the first inning. (Mark Erikson)

   _____

4. *Frank:* Bill Watson hits the ball into right field. (left field)

   _____

5. *Frank:* The outfielder, Sam Jacobs, will catch it. (a fan in the stands)

   _____

6. *Frank:* Bill Watson has hit the last run of the game. (first)

   _____

☐ Passive Sentences with Verbs in Different Tenses

Use the words in parentheses to complete the passive sentences. Use appropriate verb tenses. Use contractions with negatives.

The International Olympic Committee (IOC) <u>was founded</u> (found) in 1894,
(1)

and two years later the first modern Olympic games _____ (hold) in
(2)

Athens, Greece. These early games later evolved into the Summer Olympics.

The Winter Olympics _____ (not, initiate) until 1924. From then until
(3)

1994, the Summer and Winter Olympics took place in the same year every four

years. From 1994 until the present they _____ (hold) in alternate
(4)

even-numbered years. The Olympics _____ (not, hold) in 1916, 1940, and
                                        (5)
1944 because of the World Wars.

    In 1896, 42 events _____ (schedule) in nine sports, and 285 athletes
                            (6)
participated. In 1992 in Barcelona, Spain, 28 sports _____ (include) in the
                                                          (7)
games and over 10,600 athletes participated. Since 1896, the dreams of more and

more athletes _____ (realize), many athletic records _____
                    (8)   (9)
(break), and many medals, gold, silver, and bronze _____ (win).
                                                        (10)

    The site for the Olympics _____ (usually, choose) six years in
                                    (11)
advance. Many nations vie for the chance to host these special events. Even though

Berlin _____ (choose) as the site for the Olympics long before 1916, the
            (12)
games there _____ (cancel) because of the First World War. Many of the
                (13)
sites for the Olympics have been surrounded by controversy. Some people believe

that the 1936 Olympics in Berlin _____ (should, not, hold). But, athletes
                                        (14)
believe that politics _____ (can, keep) out of the games. Nowadays, there
                            (15)
is less controversy of a political nature, and Olympic games _____
                                                                    (16)
(attend) by teams from more countries. Which site _____ (will, choose)
                                                        (17)
next? When it is time to pick a new site, the nations in the running will wait eagerly

to hear the announcement of the winner.

    The Olympics open with an elaborate ceremony. All the athletes file into the sta-

dium. They _____ (lead) by the Greek athletes. The host nation's athletes
                (18)
are the last to enter. Then, the Olympic hymn _____ (play) and the
                                                    (19)
Olympic flag _____ (raise). The runner enters carrying the Olympic
                (20)
torch that _____ (light) by the rays of the sun in Olympia, Greece
                (21)
and _____ (carry) from there by a series of runners. Imagine the thrill
        (22)
of watching as the Olympic flame _____ (light) by the last runner.
                                        (23)

3   Transitive and Intransitive Verbs

Change active sentences to passives or write *No change*. Include the subject of the active sentence in a *by* phrase.

1. Nagano, Japan, hosted the 1998 Winter Olympics.

   The 1998 Winter Olympics were hosted by Nagano, Japan.

2. Many exciting events took place there.

   No change.

3. Both news reporters and sports announcers of a major U. S. television network covered the event.

   _____

4. They were wearing the Nike logo on their jackets during their broadcasts.

   _____

5. Were these news reporters and sports announcers endorsing Nike?

   _____

6. Reporters shouldn't wear the logo.

   _____

7. Many viewers appeared to believe this.

   _____

8. The major television network agreed with them about the news reporters.

   _____

9. Now, news reporters can't wear corporate logos.

   _____

10. But, the network allows the sports announcers to wear corporate logos.

    _____

11. Are sports announcers different from news reporters?

    _____

12. This seems a contradiction to some viewers.

    _____

4 Direct and Indirect Objects as Subjects of Passive Sentences

Complete each sentence with an appropriate passive form of the verb in parentheses.
Circle the indirect object. Rewrite the sentence using the indirect object as the subject
of the passive sentence.

1. In the first modern Olympics, medals __were awarded__ (award) (to athletes) in
   42 events.

   In the first modern Olympics, athletes were awarded medals in 42 events.

2. By 1992, Olympic medals _____ (give) to athletes in 28 sports.

   _____

3. In 1972, gold medals _____ (present) to Mark Spitz, a U.S. swimmer, a
   record-setting seven times.

   _____

4. At the 1976 Summer Olympics, a perfect score of ten _____ (give)
   to Romanian gymnast Nadia Comaneci for her performance on the uneven
   parallel bars.

   _____

5. How many medals _____ (award) to world-class athletes in future
   Olympic competitions?

   _____

GRAMMAR PRACTICE 2: Function of Passive Sentences

5 Meaning of Passive Sentences

Read the passage. Then put a check next to the sentence in each pair that gives the
information that is in the passage.

Most football teams in the United States have their team logos on both sides of

their team helmets, but the logo of the Pittsburgh Steelers is painted on only one

side. In 1962, the logo was created for the Steelers by the United States Steel

Corporation (U.S. Steel). At that time, the public's reaction to the logo couldn't be

determined, so it was put on only one side of the helmets in case the Steelers

decided to change it. Over the years, the team has often been asked about their

helmets. To keep people talking about the logo and the team, the logo is still only

painted on one side of Steeler helmets.

1. _____ The Pittsburgh Steelers paint the logo on their own helmets.

   ___✓___ Someone paints the logo on the Pittsburgh Steelers' helmets.

2. _____ The Steelers designed the logo.

   _____ U.S. Steel designed the logo.

3. _____ The team knew that the public liked the logo.

   _____ The team didn't know if the public liked the logo.

4. _____ The players asked questions about the helmets.

   _____ People asked the players questions about the helmets.

5. _____ Players still wear the logo.

   _____ Players used to wear the logo, but now they don't.

6 **Receivers in Active and Passive Sentences**

Underline the receiver of the action of each **boldfaced** verb. Circle the performer of
the action, if it is given.

The most remarkable growth of a sport in the twentieth century **wasn't made** by
basketball or baseball. Soccer **achieved** this increase. This fast-growing sport **was**
originally **played** by amateurs in British-influenced countries, but now it **is dominated** by professionals world-wide. Much of the growth occurred in the second half
of the century, and three reasons **can be given** for the spread of soccer.

First, the World Cup **is televised** throughout the world. During the Cup, work
schedules **are rearranged** so that millions of people **can watch** the games.

Second, the growth of the game **was influenced** by the high-level play of the
club teams. The best players from all over the world **are recruited** to keep the clubs
competitive with one another, and the careers of these players **are followed** by the
fans in their home countries.

Third, the fans **are** also **playing** soccer. Youth clubs **have been organized**
throughout the world, and children **are starting** their practice sessions at ages four,
five, and six. In the last fifty years, soccer has truly become the world's game.

7 Omitting the *By* Phrase

Circle the verbs in the following passive sentences. (Some sentences have more than
one verb.) Cross out *by* phrases that aren't important or necessary. Leave in any *by*
phrase that has important or necessary information.

1. He was honored by sportswriters before his third birthday.

2. One of his records may never be broken by anyone.

3. He was named Secretariat by his owner, and he was voted Horse of the Year by
   people in both of his competitive years.

4. In 1973, horse racing's Triple Crown hadn't been won by a horse in 25 years.

5. The Triple Crown is awarded by racing officials to any horse winning the
   Kentucky Derby, the Preakness, and Belmont Stakes all in the same year.

6. The 1973 Triple Crown was won by Secretariat in grand style.

7. The Kentucky Derby was run by Secretariat in world record time.

8. Secretariat's record-making run in the Belmont Stakes has never been equaled
   by another horse.

9. Secretariat won the Belmont Stakes by 31 lengths, a distance so great that the
   images of Secretariat and the next closest horse couldn't be captured at the
   same time by TV cameras.

8 The *By* Phrase

Make passive sentences with the information given. Include the agent in a *by* phrase if
the agent is important or provides necessary information. Do not include a *by* phrase if
the agent is not important. Use appropriate tenses.

Swimming

Agent	Action	Receiver	Additional Information
1. people	enjoy	the sport of swimming	today
2. the Japanese	set up	swimming competitions	in the first century B.C.
3. the ancient Greeks and Romans	use	this sport	to train warriors

1. _The sport of swimming is enjoyed today._

2. _Swimming competitions were set up by the Japanese in the first century B.C._

3. _____ .

Table tennis

Agent	Action	Receiver	Additional Information
4. the English	play first	table tennis	on dining room tables
5. people	also called Ping-Pong	table tennis	since the early 1900s
6. the U.S. Table Tennis Association	govern	tournaments in the United States	since the 1930s

4. _____.

5. _____.

6. _____.

Mountain Climbing

Agent	Action	Receiver	Additional Information
7. athletes	start	the sport of mountain climbing	in eighteenth-century Europe
8. Edmund Hillary and Tenzing Norgay	conquer	Mt. Everest	in 1953
9. climbers	not climb	many of the highest mountains in South America	yet

7. _____.

8. _____.

9. _____.

Ice skating

Agent	Action	Receiver	Additional Information
10. people	first use	ice skates	as transportation
11. the people from the Netherlands	hold	speed races	in the Netherlands in the fifteenth century
12. the Dutch	develop	"clap skates"	in 1997 so that skaters could go faster

10. _____.

11. _____.

12. _____.

🕘 Passives in Academic Writing—Guided Writing

On a separate sheet of paper, write a paragraph on a scientific or other academic topic of your choice. Use at least five passive sentences in your paragraph. Try to use more than one tense and at least one negative. Give your paragraph to your teacher for correction.

> Example: The muscles in the calf of the leg are attached to the heel bone by the Achilles tendon, a powerful, cordlike structure. If this tendon is torn, normal use of the foot and leg is lost. Eighty-three percent of these injuries are suffered by men between the ages of 30 and 40. Achilles tendon injuries are often caused by a lack of regular conditioning and by overloading the tendon. In other words, the tendon is often injured when it hasn't been exercised properly and when too much stress is placed on it. Some degeneration of the tendon is experienced by many athletes regardless of their conditioning, and the problem can be worsened by inappropriate footwear.

More about Passives

chapter 17

GRAMMAR PRACTICE 1: *Get* Passives; Passive Causatives

▐ Get Passives

Despite high expectations for the team by their new owner, the local baseball team has been having a bad season and needs to change their luck. A sports announcer is interviewing the team owner. Complete each sentence with the words in parentheses. Use the *get* passive in an appropriate tense.

Sports announcer: Why are you having this bonfire rally?

Owner: We hope to change our luck by get-

ting rid of the things that are bring-

ing us bad luck. A bonfire rally

seemed a good way to do that.

Sports announcer: What kinds of things ___have already gotten thrown___ (already,
(1)

throw) into your bonfire?

Owner: Well . . ., several bats _____ (burn) and caps
(2)

_____ (toss) in by several players.
(3)

Sports announcer: What about the manager? Did he add anything to the fire?

Owner: A pair of old shorts _____ (pitch) in by the manager,
(4)

who participated in spite of thinking it was pretty weird. Look,

right now shoes and gloves _____ (put) in by the
(5)

pitcher and catcher. All kinds of sports souvenirs

_____ (add) by our fans, too.
(6)

Sports announcer: What happens if your luck doesn't change?

Owner: We'll have another bonfire. Things _____ (burn) until
(7)

our luck changes.

Sports announcer: But, what if the bonfire rallies don't help?

     Owner: Well, I certainly hope they do, but if they don't, then I guess I'll

     have to consider other things. Players _____ (trade).
             (8)

     Managers _____ (fire). The team _____
           (9)   (10)

     (may, sell).

2 Guided Writing

On a separate sheet of paper, write a sentence with the *get* passive and the past
participle for each verb in the list. Use the *get* passive in different tenses. Give your
sentences to your teacher for correction.

Example: <u> They haven't gotten finished with the work yet. </u>

1. finish   6. worry

2. excite   7. prepare

3. scare   8. pay

4. confuse   9. pack

5. lose   10. do

3 Passive Causatives

The United States Women's Soccer Team enjoys some privileges today, but that hasn't
always been true. Look at the statements in the Early Days column. Then use the words
given to write sentences with passive causatives in the Later Days column. Use *the
players* as the subject of each sentence. Do not include a *by* phrase if the agent is not
important.

Early Days	Later Days
1. The players were served food they couldn't eat.	1. Team chefs prepare their food. <u>The players have/get their food prepared by</u> <u>team chefs.</u>
2. The players carried their own luggage.	2. Someone carries their bags.
3. The players bought their own practice gear.	3. Someone buys their practice gear for them.
4. The players stayed in cheap hotels.	4. Someone books their rooms in nice hotels.
5. Few people knew the players.	5. Someone sent a postcard of the team to a late-night TV program for publicity.
6. The players didn't have many endorsements.	6. Agents handle their many contracts for them.

Unit Wrap-up

Error Correction

Find and correct the errors in the following passage. Some errors may be corrected in more than one way. Including the example, there are nine errors.

                                      dominate

Every year, four tournaments ~~are dominated~~ the men's professional golf season.

They are called The Majors and define the best players in the sport. The

tournaments—the Masters, the U.S. Open, the British Open, and the PGA—are

considered to be challenging and pressure-filled. No player can called great unless

he has won a Major.

In 1953, three of the four tournaments—the Masters, the U.S. Open, and the

British Open—were won by the same man, Ben Hogan. That year, Hogan was

become the only golfer to have won these three tournaments in the same year.

Hogan didn't enter the PGA, partly because it was held too soon after the British

Open and partly because Hogan hadn't really been recovered from a near-fatal

accident in 1949. Perhaps, too, Hogan didn't enter the PGA because it hasn't ever

been giving the same respect as the other tournaments. Yet, golf great Arnold

Palmer, who has won the other Majors, regrets not having won this tournament.

A "magic" number in the sport of golf is 18, the number that represents the most

Major tournaments that have been won a single individual: Jack Nicklaus. This

record, which hasn't approached by any other competitor, may never get broken.

Nicklaus made it clear that these four tournaments were the ones he was training to win. Because Nicklaus was the best golfer of his era, he was copied by other

professional golfers, and the Majors truly became the tournaments to win.

After the PGA tournament, the last of the Majors, gets finished in August other

tournaments on the professional tour still play. Competition isn't stopped, but for

another year, the winners of the Majors have been decided, and the losers have had

their hopes crush. The best of the pros may already have gotten started looking

ahead to the next year.

Guided Writing

On a separate sheet of paper, write a paragraph about a product, service, or natural
resource you are familiar with. Write at least five passive sentences in different tenses,
including modals. Include the agent in a *by* phrase where necessary. Use *get* passives and
passive causatives.

> Example: *Thousands of pairs of sports shoes are produced each year by
> companies such as Nike and Reebok. Many different styles have been
> designed for various activities and sports. These shoes get purchased by
> both professional and amateur athletes. Many professional athletes have
> special shoes designed for them by these big companies. In turn, the shoes
> are endorsed by the famous athletes with the result that more shoes can
> be sold by these companies . . .*

TOEFL TIME

Allow yourself twelve minutes to complete the 20 questions in this exercise. Questions 1 through 10: Circle the letter of the one word or phrase that best completes each sentence.

1. The entire plot of *Dr. Jekyll and Mr. Hyde*

_____ in a dream by the author, Robert Louis Stevenson, before he wrote the novel.

(A) had seen
(B) had been seeing
(C) had been seen
(D) had it seen

2. In order to cut costs, the United States

Government often _____ by outside contractors rather than by civil servants.

(A) gets work done
(B) has done work
(C) gets worked
(D) has been worked

3. In 1609, corn _____ for the first time by Virginia colonists.

(A) planted
(B) was planting
(C) was planted
(D) has planted

4. The Globe Theater, where Shakespeare's plays

_____, was opened in Southwark, London in 1599.

(A) were performing
(B) were performed
(C) performed
(D) had performed

5. A three-month area-specific on-line dating service

_____ cost a lot of money.

(A) was
(B) could be
(C) has been
(D) could

6. In 1939, Hollywood film companies

_____ produced every day.

(A) were an average of two movies
(B) got an average of two movies
(C) an average of two movies
(D) an average of two movies got

7. The height of the Statue of Liberty

_____ more than 93 meters.

(A) is measured
(B) is measuring
(C) measures
(D) has been measured

8. Before 1804, the candidate who _____ second place in a presidential race automatically became vice president.

(A) had been earned
(B) had earned
(C) had it earned
(D) got earned

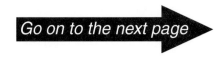

Go on to the next page

151

9. The amount of land lost to forest fires in the

   United States _____ from 32 million
   acres in 1944 to an average of 3.7 million acres
   today.
   (A) had it reduced
   (B) has reduced
   (C) has been reduced
   (D) was reducing

10. People in the United States were shocked when

    Princess Diana died while she _____
    driven through Paris.
    (A) was being
    (B) been
    (C) had been
    (D) has been

Questions 11 through 20: Circle the letter of the underlined part of the sentence that is
incorrect.

11. One theory about why the dinosaurs <u>were disappeared</u> is that the earth <u>was</u> <u>hit</u>
                                                  A   B C

    <u>by a comet</u> around 65 million years ago.
        D

12. Navy SEALs <u>are</u> <u>expected</u> to be in top physical shape, and they <u>get</u> trained
               A   B   C

    their <u>instructors</u> to work together as a team under adverse conditions.
        D

13. The tragic sinking of the Titanic <u>was</u> <u>happened</u> at a time when the ship <u>was</u>
                                 A   B   C

    <u>believed</u> to be impossible to sink.
        D

14. Tomatoes <u>were</u> <u>introducing</u> in England in 1596, where they <u>were</u> <u>grown</u> as orna-
              A   B   C   D

    mental plants.

15. About 24 billion tons of topsoil <u>are</u> <u>lost</u> every year to wind and water erosion,
                                   A B

    <u>indicating</u> that one-third of the world's arable land <u>will</u> depleted in twenty years.
        C   D

16. Trees that <u>have</u> <u>lined</u> rural roads for over a century are <u>be</u> cut down because
                 A   B   C

    they <u>have been</u> called a danger to motorists.
        D

17. If hydrogen that is <u>used</u> for power can itself <u>be created</u> through renewable
                      A   B

    energy sources, urban air quality <u>should</u> be <u>improve</u>.
                                     C   D

Go on to the next page

18. The Black Death, which <u>was</u> killed 20 million people in fourteenth-century
                          A

   Europe, <u>is</u> now <u>being</u> <u>rivaled</u> by AIDS as the most destructive infectious disease.
          B   C   D

19. More than 90 books <u>have</u> <u>been</u> emerged from a small room which <u>is</u> inhabited
                   A   B   C

   <u>by English writer</u> Dick King-Smith.
       D

20. Advances in genetic engineering <u>are</u> <u>being</u> <u>made</u> at such a fast pace that the
                                    A   B   C

   ethical dilemmas surrounding the technology <u>are appeared</u> unanswerable.
                                              D

Unit Nine

Conditionals

Conditionals

chapter 18

GRAMMAR PRACTICE 1: Overview of Conditionals; Factual Conditionals; Future Conditionals

▯ Factual Conditionals

Complete the sentences so that each sentence has an *if* clause and a result clause. Put *if* in the appropriate place in the sentence. Use *then* where possible. Punctuate carefully.

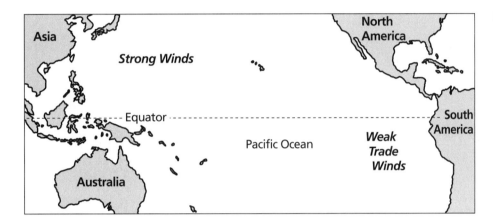

El Niño

1. With Present Tense Verbs

   a. Trade winds are blowing in normal patterns. (cause)

      <u>If trade winds are blowing in normal patterns, then</u> they maintain a balance between warm western Pacific water and cool eastern Pacific water.

   b. Warm water in the western Pacific flows east. (result)

      <u>Warm water in the western Pacific flows east if</u> easterly trade winds decrease, causing a condition we call El Niño.

   c. Cooler, nutrient-rich water is pushed deeper. (result)

      _____

      there is an El Niño condition, and sea life suffers from lack of food.

   d. El Niño conditions exist. (cause)

      _____

      they produce extreme weather such as heavy rainfall and flooding.

2. With Past Tense Verbs

   a. They built new cities. (cause)

   Because the Inca of Peru knew about the effects of El Niño,

   _____

   they put them on the tops of hills.

   b. They built on the coast. (cause)

   _____ they didn't build near rivers.

3. With Modals

   a. Scientists can get a wide range of accurate information on the Pacific. (result)

   _____

   they use information gathered by buoys anchored along the equatorial
   Pacific, statistical data, and climate modeling.

   b. Scientists understand El Niño better. (cause)

   _____ they may be able to
   predict the effects so people can prepare for the extreme weather conditions.

2 Future Conditionals—Form and Function

Use the words given to write future conditionals. Write the words in the order that
they are given. *El Niño* is always the cause in each sentence.

1. Another El Niño / come / weather / change all over the world

   If another El Niño comes, weather will change all over the world.

2. it / be / an El Niño year / Peru and parts of the United States and Europe / suffer
   from damaging floods

   _____

3. Indonesia, Australia, and India / experience / drought / El Niño / happen

   _____

4. Many countries / have / flash floods / more rain / fall as a result of El Niño

   _____

5. El Niño / occur / the next year / be / a La Niña year

   _____

6. Countries / have / drought during El Niño / they / have / too much rain during
   La Niña

   _____

3 Guided Writing

On a separate sheet of paper, write a paragraph on the causes and results of a severe
weather condition you are familiar with. Use factual conditionals with present and past
tense verbs, and modals, and the future conditional. Give your paragraph to your
teacher for correction.

> Example: If it's a late summer day, storm clouds are probably gathering over
> Denver. If you hear thunder, then lightning will follow . . .

GRAMMAR PRACTICE 2: Present Unreal Conditionals

4 Present Unreal Conditionals—Form

Complete the present unreal conditional sentences, using the words in parentheses. Use
would in the result clause. Use contractions with negatives.

1. If we ____counted____ (count) the number of lightning strikes on earth every

   second, the number ____would be____ (be) about 100.

2. If lightning _____ (not, be) dangerous, hundreds of people

   _____ (not, get) hurt or killed by it every year.

3. A meteorologist _____ (answer) "lightning and floods" if we

   _____ (ask) about the most life-threatening weather hazards in the
   USA.

4. If the amount of lightning-caused property damage in a year in the USA

   _____ (be) calculated, the result _____ (be) in the millions
   of dollars.

5. If people _____ (want) to talk about other problems caused by lightning,

   they _____ (not, forget) fires and injuries to animals.

5 Present Unreal Conditionals—Function

Read each sentence and mark the sentences that follow it **T** (true) or **F** (false).

1. If lightning weren't dangerous, we wouldn't have to be careful in a thunder-storm.

   ___F___ a. Lightning didn't use to be dangerous.

   ___T___ b. Lightning is dangerous.

2. If air were a good conductor of electricity, the forces that produce lightning wouldn't have to be as powerful as they are.

   _____ a. Air is a good conductor of electricity.

   _____ b. Powerful forces produce lightning.

3. We could swim safely in a thunderstorm if lightning didn't travel well through water.

   _____ a. It's not safe to swim during a thunderstorm.

   _____ b. Lightning travels well through water.

4. If a woman were on a bicycle in a thunderstorm, she wouldn't be safe from lightning.

   _____ a. This sentence talks about something that happened in the past.

   _____ b. It's safe to ride a bike in a thunderstorm.

6 Factual versus Unreal Conditions

Complete the factual conditionals and unreal conditionals with the correct form of the verbs in parentheses. Use *would* in the result clause of the unreal conditionals. Use contractions with negatives.

1. Lightning sometimes strikes people. If someone _____gets_____ (get) hit by

   lightning and survives, he or she _____is_____ (be) likely to suffer serious long-term effects from it.

2. Lightning kills more people every year than any other weather-related event. If

   lightning _____ (not, hurt) anyone we _____ (still have) other disasters.

3. Eighty to ninety percent of lightning strike victims survive. If no one

   _____ (live) after getting hit by lightning, we _____ (respect) this weather phenomenon more.

4. People are better electricity conductors than air and trees are. Lightning

_____ (not, hit) people so often if they _____ (be) bad conductors.

5. Staying outside in a thunderstorm isn't a good idea. If people _____

(go) inside a building, they _____ (be) safer.

7 Guided Writing

A thunderstorm just started. On a separate sheet of paper, write advice for the following situations. Use *If I were you,*... Give your sentences to your teacher for correction.

All of my windows are open.	I am on a small boat on a lake.
My computer is on.	I am playing golf.

Example: *If I were you, I'd close your windows.*

GRAMMAR PRACTICE 3: Past Unreal Conditionals

8 Past Unreal Conditionals—Form

Use the words in parentheses to complete the past unreal conditionals. Use *would, might,* or *could* in the result clause to express the indicated meaning. In cases where two forms are possible, write both forms. Use contractions with negatives.

1. In 1790, Kilauea, a volcano in Hawaii, erupted, killing 80 people marching

across it. If those people ___*hadn't been walking*___ (not, walk) on the volcano,

they ___*might not have been*___ (not, be) killed.
  _{possibility}

2. In 1912, Novarupta, a volcano in Alaska, was the site of the largest eruption of

the twentieth century. It _____ (cause) incredible damage if it
  _{certainty}

_____ (erupt) in a populous area.

3. The eruption of Mount St. Helens in the state of Washington in 1980 shot ash

twelve miles into the air. This eruption _____ (take) scientists by
  _{possibility}

complete surprise if there _____ (not, be) earlier earthquakes and minor eruptions.

4. Before 1980, Mount St. Helens had not erupted for 123 years. If anyone

   _____ (see) it erupt, he/she _____ (tell) others about it.
                                                        ability

5. The eruption of Mount St. Helens killed 57 people. If it _____ (happen)

   on Monday instead of Sunday, several hundred loggers at work on the mountain

   _____ (die) in the explosion.
        certainty

🌋 Past Unreal Conditionals—Function

Read each sentence and mark the sentences that follow it *T* (true) or *F* (false).

1. The eruption that formed the volcano Paricutin started in 1943. Today's scientists wouldn't have learned so much about volcanoes if Paricutin hadn't erupted recently.

   ___F___ a. Scientists didn't learn anything from Paricutin's eruption.

   ___T___ b. Paricutin didn't form thousands of years ago.

2. Paricutin was born in Mexico. If Paricutin hadn't developed on land, scientists wouldn't have been able to see the new volcano form.

   _____ a. Scientists observed Paricutin as it grew.

   _____ b. Paricutin developed in the ocean.

3. If the volcano hadn't formed in the middle of a cornfield, it might have caused more damage.

   _____ a. Paricutin didn't cause as much damage as possible.

   _____ b. The volcano formed in an agricultural area.

4. If the owner of the cornfield, Dominic Pulido, hadn't watched the volcano form, he would have missed an historic event.

   _____ a. The owner of the cornfield missed seeing the volcano form.

   _____ b. The forming of the volcano was an historic event.

5. The Pulidos heard something like underground thunder before the volcano erupted. Smoke and ash came from the ground, trees shook, and Pulido could smell sulfur. Pulido might have realized what was happening if he had been a volcanologist.

   _____ a. Pulido was a scientist that studies volcanoes.

   _____ b. Pulido knew what was happening when he smelled the sulfur.

🔟 Past Unreal Conditionals

Read the passage about a very destructive volcano. Then use the information given to write past unreal conditionals. Use the clauses in the order that they are given.

In 1883, the Indonesian volcano Krakatau exploded dramatically. For several days before the explosion, there were eruptions, raining ash and blocks of lava into the surrounding area. The volcano chamber that this ash and lava were coming from was under the sea. On August 28, the chamber collapsed. Millions of tons of ocean water and two-thirds of the volcano fell into the molten lava in the chamber. The resulting explosion was the loudest noise on earth in recorded history. It was heard over 3000 km away in Australia; 5000 km away, a British army officer thought it was distant gunfire. Wind created in the explosion circled the earth seven times before it finally died out.

1. There were eruptions before the explosion. As a result, there wasn't enough material in the chamber to support it. ___If there hadn't been eruptions before the___

___explosion, there would have been enough material in the chamber to support it.___

2. Because the chamber wasn't above sea level, ocean water rushed into it.

_____

3. The volcano didn't remain standing because it collapsed in the explosion.

_____

4. The explosion was so loud that people in Australia could hear it.

_____

5. The wind from the explosion didn't circle the earth more times because the force of the explosion dissipated.

_____

▋▋ Guided Writing

On a separate sheet of paper, write affirmative and negative statements about your life
and activities. Give your paper to your teacher for correction.

1. Write three factual statements about your life and activities now. Then write a
    present unreal conditional sentence about each statement.

    Example: I'm taking organic chemistry. I could go out more often if I weren't
    taking organic chemistry.

2. Write three factual statements about your life and activities in the past. Then
    write a past unreal conditional sentence about each statement.

    Example: I didn't have a job last year. If I had had a job, I might not have
    had time to study.

GRAMMAR PRACTICE 1: Other Forms in Conditionals

🔳 Conditionals with Conditions and Results in Different Times

Use the conditions and results given to write sentences about natural forces. Use the clauses in the order that they are given.

1. Factual Conditionals—Past Time Condition, Present Time Result

   a. condition: A fire burned all the grass and trees in an area of Yellowstone.

      result: There is nothing left to burn.

      <u>If a fire burned all the grass and trees in an area of Yellowstone, there is</u>

      <u>nothing left to burn.</u>

   b. condition: A louder noise than the explosion of Krakatau occurred.

      result: We have no record of it.

      _____

      _____

   c. result: People pay attention to hurricane warnings.

      condition: They lived through a strong hurricane when they were young.

      _____

      _____

2. Unreal Conditionals—Past Time Condition, Present Time Result

   a. condition: Rapid Creek destroyed homes and businesses along its banks.

      result: There is a bike path along the waterway.

      <u>If Rapid Creek hadn't destroyed homes and businesses along its banks,</u>

      <u>there wouldn't be a bike path along the waterway.</u>

   b. result: The oceans are as deep as they are now.

      condition: Many glaciers have melted since the last Ice Age.

      _____

      _____

   c. condition: Erosion from the Colorado River didn't stop.

      result: The Grand Canyon exists.

      _____

      _____

3. Unreal Conditionals—General Condition, Past Time Result

   a. result: Alferd Packer was trapped in the Colorado mountains.

      condition: Blizzards come up unexpectedly.

      Alferd Packer wouldn't have been trapped in the Colorado mountains if

      blizzards didn't come up unexpectedly.

   b. condition: The weather can't be controlled.

      result: The 1999 drought wasn't avoided.

      _____

   c. condition: People adapt to their environments.

      result: Eskimos adjusted to living in very cold places.

      _____

2 *Should (Happen To) and Were To*

Use the conditions given to complete sentences about the future with *should happen to* or *were to*. Use the clauses in the order that they are given.

1. condition: The next El Niño / be particularly strong

   result: there / be extensive damage

   (should happen to) ___ *If the next El Niño should happen to be particularly strong,*

   there will/would be extensive damage.

2. condition: A tsunami / threaten a populated area

   result: Many people / be / evacuated

   (should happen to) _____

3. condition: A wildfire / start in an isolated area

   result: it / probably / be allowed to burn

   (were to) _____

4. condition: A volcano / send a huge amount of ash into the atmosphere

   result: Global temperature may drop

   (should happen to) _____

5. condition: Another Ice Age occur

   result: The climate / change dramatically

   (were to) _____

3   Inverted Conditionals

Rewrite each conditional sentence as an inverted conditional. Use the clauses in the order that they are given.

1. If you should live on a volcano, you ought to have an evacuation plan.

   Should you live on a volcano, you ought to have an evacuation plan.

2. If you should live on a fault line, you might also live close to a volcano.

   _____

3. You would have heard quite an explosion if you had been near Krakatau in 1883.

   _____

4. You would see lava glowing if you were to fly over the island of Hawaii at night.

   _____

4   *If So* and *If Not*

Read the following passage. If a condition clause can be replaced with *if so* or *if not*, cross it out and write *if so* or *if not* above it. If the clause can't be replaced, write *NC*.

Do you know what to do in a tornado? ~~If you don't know what to do in a tornado~~,
If not,
this is a good time to learn. First, know whether your community has a warning

system. If your community has a warning system, make sure that you know what

the warning is. If your community doesn't have a warning system, make sure that

you have a radio so that you can find out what is happening. Then look at your

home. If you have a basement, that is the best place to be in a tornado. If you don't

have a basement, the next best place is an interior room with no windows.

5   Guided Writing

On a separate sheet of paper, write a paragraph about what you think would happen if volcanologists detected a volcano that was going to create the most powerful explosion ever witnessed by humans. Use *should happen to* and *were to*, inverted conditionals, and conditionals with *if so* and *if not*. Give your paragraph to your teacher for correction.

> Example: If scientists should happen to know about such a volcano, they
> would start looking for ways to prevent the explosion. If they were to find a
> way to stop the explosion, they would need to act fast . . .

GRAMMAR PRACTICE 2: Sentences with *Wish* or *Hope*

6 *Wish* and *Hope* About the Present and Future

Complete the sentences by using the correct forms of the words in parentheses to express wishes or hopes about the present and future. Where more than one form is possible, use any appropriate form. Use contractions with negatives.

Host: Thanks for talking with me today. I hope we ___can/will find___ (find) out
(1)

more about wildfires and firefighting policies. Are all wildfires caused by

natural forces?

Scientist: I wish that only nature _____ (start) fires, but, unfortunately,
(2)

human beings still cause wildfires as well, often through carelessness with

cigarettes or campfires.

Host: Lightning from thunderstorms sometimes causes fires, too, right? When

you see a thunderstorm, do you hope that the lightning from it

_____ (not, start) a fire?
(3)

Scientist: I wish things _____ (be) that easy. Fires have beneficial effects,
(4)

so when I see a thunderstorm, I hope that it _____ (cooperate)
(5)

with us. For example, lightning from a thunderstorm may start a fire

tomorrow. We hope that the fire _____ (burn) the dry, old vege-
(6)

tation that has accumulated.

Host: Can't people clean out the dead vegetation?

Scientist: We wish they _____ (can), but we're talking about millions of
(7)

acres in National Parks and Forests.

Host: What about fire-fighting policies in the future?

Scientist: We will always fight fires to protect lives. We hope we _____
(8)

(also, save) property. We wish we _____ (can) protect every-
(9)

one's property, but we know we can't. We hope that people

_____ (work) with us to keep everyone safe.
(10)

7   *Wish* and *Hope* About the Past

Complete the sentences by using the correct forms of the words in parentheses to express wishes or hopes about the past. Use contractions with negatives.

Host: Tell me about the 1988 Yellowstone Fire. I wish I __had been__ (be)
$\underset{(1)}{}$

there to see it.

Scientist: The 1988 fires were the worst I have ever seen. I hope they

_____ (be) the last fires ever of that magnitude in the Park.
$\underset{(2)}{}$

Host: Were all the fires caused by lightning?

Scientist: I wish that lightning _____ (start) all the fires, but one was
$\underset{(3)}{}$

caused by a cigarette.

Host: The fires were originally allowed to burn, right?

Scientist: Yes, that's right. We wish we _____ (know) that nature was
$\underset{(4)}{}$

going to work against us. We wish we _____ (not, wait) so long
$\underset{(5)}{}$

to step in.

Host: What happened?

Scientist: We wish it _____ (rain) sooner after the fires started. In previ-
$\underset{(6)}{}$

ous years, rains had put out the fires, so we were expecting the same thing

in 1988.

Host: Is there anything else that worked against you?

Scientist: I wish that we _____ (not, have to) fight so many fires at once.
$\underset{(7)}{}$

Host: Was there anything good that came out of the fires?

Scientist: Oh, sure. We hope we _____ (learn) something we can share
$\underset{(8)}{}$

with others. We wish we _____ (be able to) learn these things
$\underset{(9)}{}$

through other means, but sometimes experience is the best teacher.

8 Guided Writing

On a separate sheet of paper, write two sentences about your hopes for the present or future, two wishes about the present or future, two hopes about the past, and two wishes about the past. Give your paper to your teacher for correction.

> Example: I hope that I see a tornado someday because I've always been
> fascinated by them. I wish I could go to the moon.

GRAMMAR PRACTICE 3: Alternatives to *If;* Implied Conditions

9 Alternatives to *If*—Form and Meaning

Use the expressions given to write conditional sentences that express the meaning of the underlined information. Use negatives if needed. Use the clauses in the order that they are given. Use each expression once.

even if	only if	✓provided that	unless	☆whether or not

1. Snow is experienced by the majority of Americans every year. <u>If they live in a snow region, they will probably see snow.</u>

   Provided that they live in a snow region, they will probably see snow.

2. Snow can be dangerous. <u>Our having sophisticated technology doesn't matter. We can't control snow.</u>

   a. _Whether or not we have sophisticated technology, we can't control snow._

   b. _____

3. <u>We prepare for snowstorms. That is the only way we can lessen their damage.</u>

   a. _____

   b. _____

as long as	even if	providing	whether or not	unless

4. Blizzards often produce conditions called "white outs," where no one can see very far. <u>Maybe you haven't seen "white out" conditions; in that case, it's hard to believe that visibility could be so poor.</u>

   _____

5. People in a blizzard may know an area well, but they can still get lost.

a. _____

b. _____

6. Stay home. If you are warm and have food and water, you should survive a blizzard.

a. _____

b. _____

10 Implied Conditions

A. Write sentences that state the conditions that are implied in the sentences given.

1. Avalanches involve complex relationships among a number of changing conditions. Otherwise, they would be easy to predict and control.

   If avalanches didn't involve complex relationships among a number of changing

   conditions, they would be easy to predict and control.

2. Without heavy, dense snow, avalanches are less likely to occur.

   _____

3. With the right conditions, an avalanche can travel two miles.

   _____

4. Vegetation often holds the snow. Otherwise, an avalanche could more easily start.

   _____

5. Backcountry skiers need to be aware of avalanche conditions, or they may find themselves in a dangerous predicament.

   _____

B. Use the sentences and expressions given to write sentences with implied conditions. If more than one verb form is possible, use any appropriate form.

1. If the snow in an avalanche is dry, it can travel up to 100 miles per hour. (with)

   With dry snow, an avalanche can travel up to 100 miles per hour.

2. Dry snow avalanches go around trees. If the snow isn't dry, avalanches push trees out of their way. (otherwise)

   _____

3. If avalanche crews didn't compact snow with machines above avalanche zones, there might be more avalanches. (without)

   _____

4. If they use explosives, crews can start a small avalanche to avoid a bigger one. (with)

   _____

5. Avalanche crews must train carefully. If they don't train carefully, they may endanger themselves. (or else)

   _____

Unit Wrap-up

Error Correction

Find and correct the errors in the following passage. Some errors can be corrected in more than one way. Including the example, there are seven errors.

                                                without
It's hard to talk about natural disasters ~~or else~~ talking about economics. If that weren't true, the Weather Bureau, which often predicts weather-related disasters, didn't move from the Department of Agriculture to the Department of Commerce in the 1940s.

Most Americans don't know that two people died in the Great Plains blizzard of 1886. If they know anything about that blizzard, they usually remember that 90% of the cattle on the ranges of the Great Plains died. Ranchers wouldn't have lost so many cattle if the weather wouldn't have been so severe.

In the 1988 Yellowstone Park fires, one principle concern was for the businesses around the park. In the event that fires threaten private property or Old Faithful, the Park Service would always try to put them out, but that year there was another concern. Business people were concerned that if too much of the Park burned, tourists didn't come to the area. In fact, people came to Yellowstone after the fires just to see the damage. They wished that the fires hadn't happened, but they were curious to see what had changed. Otherwise, they wouldn't come.

Despite the risks, people continue to build on lands that are susceptible to natural disasters. Unless we make good judgments about using sensitive areas, we would continue to pay for mistakes in natural resources, property, and lives.

Guided Writing

Imagine that you live in a house in a forest. A forest fire is approaching. You can rescue only four possessions. On a separate sheet of paper, write a paragraph about what you would choose to save. Use unreal conditionals, *wish* or *hope*, an alternative to *if*, and an implied condition. Give your paragraph to your teacher for correction.

> Example: If I had to escape quickly, I would save my photograph albums. I wouldn't be able to replace them if they burned . . .

TOEFL TIME

Allow yourself twelve minutes to complete the 20 questions in this exercise.

Questions 1 through 10: Circle the letter of the one word or phrase that best completes each sentence.

1. Adults should have their eyes checked annually;

   _____, conditions such as glaucoma and cataracts might go undiagnosed.
   (A) even if
   (B) if so
   (C) unless
   (D) otherwise

2. As long as current trends _____, four million Americans will receive blood transfusions next year.
   (A) continue
   (B) will continue
   (C) continued
   (D) had continued

3. If the Empire State Building _____, the Chrysler Building would have been the world's tallest building for longer than nine months.
   (A) hadn't built
   (B) hadn't been built
   (C) wasn't built
   (D) weren't built

4. _____ Earth Day be celebrated through the year 2070, it will have existed for over one hundred years.
   (A) If
   (B) Should
   (C) Had
   (D) Were

5. If the paperback book hadn't been widely produced and circulated, fewer books

   _____ in the hands of the reading public today.
   (A) are
   (B) would be
   (C) were
   (D) would have been

6. The Internet cannot take the place of actual travel

   _____ it becomes more widely available to people worldwide.
   (A) even if
   (B) only if
   (C) if not
   (D) or else

7. Solar power would probably be more popular today if its cost in the early part of the twentieth

   century _____ so high.
   (A) isn't
   (B) wasn't
   (C) hadn't been
   (D) weren't

8. _____ a tsunami is about to strike, coastal waters recede to the horizon.
   (A) If
   (B) Only if
   (C) Or
   (D) Without

9. If a motorist _____ the island of Hawaii, she encounters eleven different climates.
   (A) circles
   (B) has circled
   (C) were to circle
   (D) had circled

10. _____ medieval laws not prohibited ordinary people from wearing linen and lace, buttons might not have become status symbols in the fourteenth century.
    (A) If
    (B) Were
    (C) Should
    (D) Had

Go on to the next page

172

Questions 11 through 20: Circle the letter of the underlined part of the sentence that is incorrect.

11. Medicine <u>has</u> fewer weapons in its arsenal <u>today</u> <u>had</u> Alexander Fleming not
         A   B   C

    <u>discovered</u> penicillin in 1928.
        D

12. <u>Without</u> volunteers, the 2159-mile Appalachian Trail probably <u>wasn't</u>
       A   B

    <u>constructed</u> and <u>couldn't</u> be maintained.
        C   D

13. Baseball fans <u>heard</u> the first radio broadcast of a game if their radios <u>would be</u>
             A   B

    <u>tuned</u> to Pittsburgh station KDKA, which <u>transmitted</u> the game in 1921.
      C   D

14. Newspaper readers <u>might</u> <u>enjoyed</u> doing a crossword puzzle; <u>if so</u>, they <u>have</u>
                  A   B   C   D

    journalist Arthur Wynne to thank for creating them.

15. <u>If only</u> <u>the moon</u> completely <u>blocks</u> the sun does a total eclipse <u>occur</u>.
      A   B   C   D

16. The passive resistance tactics of Mahatma Gandhi <u>were effective</u>; <u>otherwise</u>,
                                                 A   B

    they <u>might not have</u> so greatly <u>influence</u> the struggle for civil rights in the
           C   D

    United States.

17. If settlers on the Great Plains <u>didn't move</u> to river valleys where Rocky Mountain
      A   B   grasshoppers <u>laid</u> their eggs, the
    grasshoppers <u>might</u> not have become extinct.   C
                     D

18. <u>Even if</u> Jack London's writings <u>are often dismissed</u> by American critics, <u>do</u> they
      A   B   C

    <u>remain</u> popular overseas.
      D

19. The U.S. policy on dams <u>will</u> <u>be accepted</u> by a large majority of citizens <u>only</u>
                        A   B   C

    <u>if can</u> opposing views be reconciled.
      D

20. The zipper <u>was developed</u> in the early 1900s; <u>unless</u>, clothing <u>would</u> certainly
               A   B   C

    <u>look</u> different today.
      D

Unit Ten

Noun Clauses

Noun Clauses

chapter 20

GRAMMAR PRACTICE 1: Noun Clauses

1 Noun Clauses

Use the verb in parentheses in an appropriate tense to complete each noun clause for the situation given. Underline the verb or *be* + adjective in the main clause and circle the word that introduces the noun clause.

1. In the beginning, the heroine <u>was sure</u> (that) the man of her dreams

   ___didn't love___ (not, love) her. (situation at the same time)

2. She wondered why he _____ (look) at her strangely when she told him of her plan to leave. (earlier situation)

3. The detective believed that the murderer _____ (reveal) himself eventually. (later situation)

4. The murderer realized that the clever detective _____ (have) the evidence he needed to prove his guilt. (situation at the same time)

5. The young people were horrified that the door of the mansion _____ (lock) behind them. (earlier situation)

6. They wondered if the monster _____ (appear) like people said it would on a night with a full moon. (later situation)

GRAMMAR PRACTICE 2: Types of Noun Clauses

2 Forming Sentences with *That* Clauses

Combine the two sentences to form a sentence with a *that* clause. Include *the fact* when necessary. Do not omit any words other than *this*.

1. Readers expect this. Certain elements will occur in romance books.

   ___Readers expect that certain elements will occur in romance books.___

2. This is well known. Emotional risk and conflict are basic to the romance genre.

   _____

3. Romance writers insist on this. Their readers are intelligent.

   _____

4. Romance writers don't pretend this. Their books are fine literature.

_____

5. They believe in this. They write extremely well-crafted, balanced entertainment.

_____

3 Guided Writing

On a separate sheet of paper, write a paragraph which gives your opinions about genre
fiction. Answer the following questions: Who should read genre fiction? When should
readers read it? Where should it be read? How often should people read it? Is it
literature? Which genre do you prefer? Use noun clauses with verbs such as *agree*,
believe, *suppose*, and *think*, and adjectives such as *clear*, *convinced*, *positive*, and *sure* to
express your opinions. Give your paragraph to your teacher for correction.

> Example: I believe that genre fiction is good for everyone. It is a fact that it
> is very popular. I believe that people should read it for fun, but not all the
> time. . . .

4 Responding with *So* or *Not*

Complete the responses in the dialogue between a writer of genre fiction and an
interviewer. Use *so* and *not*.

Interviewer: Do you agree that people enjoy reading genre fiction?

Author: I ___believe so.___ (believe). My last book sold over a million copies.
      (1)

Interviewer: Is genre fiction fine literature?

Author: I _____ (not, think) But, it is well written, and the stories are
        (2)

ones the reader can relate to, aren't they?

Interviewer: Yes, I _____ (suppose). Readers of genre fiction identify with
           (3)

the heroes and heroines, don't they?

Author: Yes, it _____ (seem). That's why believable characters are so
        (4)

important.

Interviewer: Do all writers of genre fiction write as much as you?

Author: I _____ (not, be afraid). I'm one of the more prolific writers
        (5)

of genre fiction at present.

Interviewer: Do you plan to continue to write ten books a year?

Author: I _____ (hope). As long as I have story ideas, I'll keep writ-
                    (6)

ing. My readers expect it and it pays the bills.

Interviewer: Thank you for talking to me today. We'll look forward to your next
book.

5 Noun Clauses with *Wh*-Words

A detective is asking a suspect some questions. Use each of his questions as a noun
clause to complete the sentences.

1. Where did you find the knife?

   Can you tell me _____ *where you found the knife?* _____

2. Why aren't your fingerprints on it?

   Can you explain _____?

3. Why did you wipe it off?

   I don't understand _____.

4. What time was it when you found it?

   Do you remember _____?

5. We believe your wife was murdered at about 9:00 last night. Where were you at
   the time of the murder?

   Do you know _____?

6. You say you were sleeping then. When do you usually go to bed?

   I'd like to know _____.

7. Why did you go to bed early that night?

   Can you tell me _____?

8. The maid told me that she saw you go out about an hour before the murder took
   place. You couldn't have gone to bed when you say. Why have you lied to me?

Would you please tell me _____?

6 Noun Clauses with *Wh*-Words; Expressing Uncertainty

A group of frightened teens are talking to the police about a horrible creature they just encountered in the woods near their neighborhood. Use the questions to complete the sentences with noun clauses.

1. You say you saw a monster in the woods. What did the creature look like?

   We're not sure __what the creature looked like__, but it was horrible!

2. How tall was it?

   We're not certain _____, but it was taller than we are.

3. Who else has seen the creature?

   We don't know _____. We just know that it is there.

4. Where did you first spot it?

   We didn't notice _____. We were too busy looking at it.

5. When did you see it?

   We can't be sure _____ because nobody was wearing a watch.

6. What did the creature do when it saw you?

   We don't know _____ because we didn't wait around to find out.

7. How did you escape?

   We don't know _____, either, but we know we were lucky.

8. I'll need to check your story out. Who will go to show me the place you saw the monster?

We can't decide _____ because we're all too afraid!

7 Noun Clauses with *if / whether*

A. Use the questions to complete the sentences with noun clauses with *if* or *whether*. If both *if* and *whether* are possible, use *if*.

1. Can he forgive me for leaving?

   I wonder ___if he can forgive me for leaving_____.

2. Is he looking for me?

   _____ is something I will never know.

3. Did he see me following him to her house yesterday?

   I can't be sure _____.

4. Have I done the right thing?

   I wonder _____.

5. Does he love me?

   I have thought so much about _____.

6. Will I ever find another love like him?

   The question is _____.

B. Add *or not* to the sentences in Part **A**. Put *or not* within the noun clause if possible. If this is not possible, put it at the end of the noun clause.

> or not.
> Example: *I wonder if he can forgive me for leaving* ∧

8 Guided Writing

What do you wonder about? What questions would you like to have answered? On a separate sheet of paper, write sentences and questions with noun clauses. Use the words given with question words or *if* or *whether* to introduce each noun clause. Give your sentences to your teacher for correction.

1. I wonder	4. I have often wondered
2. I'm not sure	5. I would like to know
3. I don't understand	6. Can you tell me

> Example: I wonder if there is life on other planets in other solar systems.
> I'm not sure what I will be doing 10 years from now.

Noun Clauses in Reported Speech; Quoted Speech

GRAMMAR PRACTICE 1: Overview of Quoted Speech and Reported Speech

▯ Punctuating Quoted Speech and Identifying Reported Speech

A. Add the missing punctuation to the following quoted speech.

"Hello, Doctor." a woman's voice said. "My name is Margo."

Hello, Margo I replied. I can't see you. The video must not be on

Oh, I know. I'd like to use audio only for a while if that's OK Margo said.

Fine. So what's the problem I asked.

It's my son she said. He says that he's in love with a hologram.

I thought to myself Oh, great. Another one. The third this week

He told me he's found his life partner, but I want him to spend more time with

biological beings she continued

Do you know why he doesn't have more biological friends I asked

Well, we're a little isolated she said He doesn't have much exposure to biological

beings, and he says he doesn't like them. My husband and I try to spend time with

him, but we're very busy

B. Underline the sentences in Part **A** that include reported speech.

② Quoted Speech; Verbs Used to Introduce Speech

Rewrite the dialogue as quoted speech. Fill in the blanks with the words that introduce each quote. Use the past tense, and use *to* before the object pronoun if necessary. Punctuate carefully.

1. I, ask, her

   ___I asked her, "___ Have you met any of his hologram friends?"

2. Margo, replied

   Hugo, that's my son, used to introduce me to his holograms _____ He told me that he understood them better than biological beings. His father and I are, well, intellectuals, so it's no surprise that he is, too.

3. I, suggest

   Well, I think you and your husband should encourage Hugo to develop his physical side, not just his intellect. Swim. Go for a walk. Do things together

   _____

4. Margo, answer, me

   Doctor, I think I'd better turn on the video now _____. There's something you should know.

5. I, tell, myself

   Oh, great _____ I wonder what this means.

6. Margo, explain

   You see, Doctor, we are computers _____ We took some of my programming and some of my husband's and put them together to form Hugo. We had to have technicians put together the physical components, but Hugo is our son.

7. I, exclaim

   Well, this is a surprise! _____ So why did you contact me?

8. she, reply

   _____ I picked your name out of a database of psychologists. I thought that if I could get a human's perspective, I could figure out what to do about Hugo.

9. I, ask, her

   Then you know nothing about me? _____ Because I'm not human, either. I'm an experimental program in an artificial intelligence institute at a major research university.

3 Guided Writing

Choose one of the following topics, and, on a separate sheet of paper, write a conversation. Each participant in the conversation should speak at least three times. Use quoted speech and punctuate carefully. Give your conversation to your teacher for correction.

1. Continue the conversation in Exercise 2.

2. Write a conversation between one of the computers and another being.

3. Write a conversation between two characters you create.

> Example: "Dave! Dave!" cried Margo. "You'll never believe what just happened!"
>   "You're probably right," said Dave. "But tell me anyway."

GRAMMAR PRACTICE 2: Reported Speech

4 Changes in Verb Tense in Reported Speech

A. It was a dry, dusty day on the plains of Kansas. Mrs. Donovan had talked earlier with the deputy. The deputy is now telling the sheriff about their conversation. Finish changing the speech to reported speech by filling in the verbs in the appropriate tenses and the pronouns. Make all changes possible, including those that are optional. Where a change is not possible, fill in the verb or pronoun as given in the original speech.

1. *Mrs. Donovan:* I want to talk to the sheriff. My husband is missing.

   She said that ___she wanted___ to talk to the sheriff and that ___her___

   husband ___was missing___.

2. *Mrs. Donovan:* He has been gone for about a week, but he had planned to be gone for only a couple days.

   She said that _____ _____ for about a week, but that

   _____ _____ to be gone for only a couple days.

3. *Mrs. Donovan:* My husband planned to meet someone here in town.

   She said that _____ husband _____ to meet with someone here in town.

4. *Mrs. Donovan:* Someone was interested in our land and wanted to talk to us.

   She said that someone _____ interested in _____ land and

   _____ to talk to _____.

5. *Mrs. Donovan:* I hoped you had seen my husband.

   She said that _____ hoped _____ _____

   _____ husband.

6. *Deputy:* I'm sorry, but I haven't seen him. If I had seen him, I would have told you.

   I told her that _____ _____ sorry, but _____

   _____ _____. I told her that if _____

   _____ _____, _____ _____

   _____.

7. *Mrs. Donovan:* I'm going to the stable to take care of my horses.

   She said _____ _____ to the stable to take care of

   _____ horses.

8. Just then, a man ran by the sheriff's office yelling, "Fire! There's a fire at the horse stable!"

   That man just said that there _____ a fire at the stable!

5 Changes in Modals in Reported Speech

The sheriff and the deputy ran to the stable. The sheriff pulled the stable owner, John McVee, out of the flames while the deputy helped to put out the fire. Mrs. Donovan wasn't there, but McVee had seen Mr. Donovan earlier in the week. Now he is telling the sheriff about their conversation. Finish changing the speech to reported speech by filling in each modal + verb and the pronouns. Make all changes, including those that are optional. Where a change is not possible, fill in the modal + verb or pronoun as given in the original speech.

1. *Mr. Donovan:* I know that it's raining, but I have to go to Sharon Springs.

   He said _____ he _____ knew that _____ it _____ was raining, but that

   _____ he _____ had to go _____ to Sharon Springs.

2. *Mr. Donovan:* I must leave now. I can't wait.

   He said _____ _____ then and that _____

   _____ wait.

3. *Mr. Donovan:* I'm going to be back in a few hours. I shouldn't be gone long.

   He said _____ _____ back in a few hours and that

   _____ _____ gone long.

4. *Mr. Donovan:* I think that the rain might stop. If it doesn't, I may not be able to cross the creek.

   He said that _____ thought that the rain _____ stop and

   that if _____ didn't, _____ _____ the creek.

5. *Mr. Donovan:* I should have written a letter to my wife. I could have had you deliver it if something goes wrong.

   He said _____ _____ a letter to _____ wife.

   _____ _____ _____ deliver _____ if

   something went wrong.

6. *Mr. McVee:* I'll tell your wife if anything happens.

   I told him that _____ _____ _____ wife if anything happened. McVee started coughing even though the fire was almost out. Suddenly a woman screamed. It sounded as if it had come from the hotel. They searched the town, but Mrs. Donovan was nowhere to be found.

6 Changes in Time and Place Words in Reported Speech

Two days later, Rob Honeywell rode into town. He had seen Mrs. Donovan the day before and went to tell the sheriff about their conversation. Complete the reported speech by filling in time and place words. Make appropriate changes (some words could be changed in several ways). If no change is needed, fill in the words as they appear in the original speech.

1. *Mrs. Donovan:* If you want to help me, you can ride into town and bring a horse
   back here.

   She said that if I wanted to help her, I could ride into town and bring a horse

   back _____there_____.

2. *Mrs. Donovan:* I found my husband this morning. He's OK now, but he can't walk
   to town.

   She said that she had found her husband _____ _____. He

   was OK _____, but he couldn't walk to town.

3. *Mrs. Donovan:* When he gets there, he will need to see a doctor.

   She said that when he got _____, he would need to see a doctor.

4. *Mrs. Donovan:* He hurt his ankle two days ago, and his horse ran away.

   She said that he had hurt his ankle _____ _____

   _____, and his horse had run away.

5. *Mr. Honeywell:* I should be there tomorrow. I'll bring horses for you and your
   husband.

   I told her that I should be _____ _____. I said I would
   bring horses for her and her husband.

7 Changes That Occur in Reported Speech

After the Donovans returned to town, they talked to the doctor. The doctor then went to the sheriff's office and told him about their conversation. Rewrite the sentences as reported speech. Make all possible changes.

1. *Mrs. Donovan:* When I realized my danger at the hotel, I turned and ran.

   _____Mrs. Donovan said (that) when she realized her danger at the hotel, she turned_____

   _____and ran._____

2. *Mrs. Donovan:* I must have screamed after that man grabbed me.

   _____

   _____

3. *Mrs. Donovan:* He made my horse run so that I couldn't jump off.

_____

4. *Mrs. Donovan:* If he hadn't tried to cross the river, his horse might not have thrown him off.

_____

5. *Mrs. Donovan:* He couldn't swim, and I couldn't help him.

_____

6. *Mrs. Donovan:* I'm happy to be here in your office, but I'm very tired.

_____

7. *Mrs. Donovan:* I have to get some sleep now, but I'll talk to the sheriff later.

_____

8 Guided Writing

Finish the story on a separate sheet of paper. Use reported speech to tell what the Donovans said to the sheriff. What happened to Mr. Donovan? Who was the man in the hotel? Why was Mr. Donovan missing? Where and how did Mrs. Donovan find him? Give your paper to your teacher for correction.

> Example: The Donovans went to talk to the sheriff about what had happened. Mr. Donovan said that he had gotten a message changing the meeting to Sharon Springs. However, shortly after he started out . . .

GRAMMAR PRACTICE 3: Questions, Commands, and Requests in Reported Speech; Noun Clauses after Verbs or Adjectives of Urgency

9 Questions, Commands, and Requests in Reported Speech

It's Mitzi's first day as a librarian. She has to ask her supervisor for information about the library. Rewrite the sentences as reported speech. Make all possible changes.

1. *Woman:* Do you have any books by Ray Bradbury?

   This woman inquired if we have/had any books by Ray Bradbury.

2. *Patron:* Where are the Westerns?

   Someone asked _____

3. *Teenager:* What time does the library close?

   Someone else asked _____

4. *Child:* What should I do to get a library card?

   This girl wants to know _____

5. *Young woman:* Put my name on the list to reserve the next Tony Hillerman novel.

   A woman asked me _____

6. *Father with young children:* Would you keep some books for me for a few minutes?

   A man wanted me _____

7. *Young man:* Has anyone turned in my wallet?

   That man asked _____

8. *Another librarian:* Don't worry. It will get easier.

   Arthur told me _____ It will get easier.

10 ● Noun Clauses after Verbs or Adjectives of Urgency

Complete the sentences with the correct form of the verbs in parentheses. Use negatives where indicated. Use passives where appropriate.

1. Publishers of paperback romance fiction understand that book covers

   _____are_____ (be) important in selling the books.

2. They think it is desirable that the book cover ____catch____ (catch) a reader's eye.

3. Readers of romance agree that a good cover _____ (attract) readers and that a poor one may doom an otherwise successful book.

4. Is it imperative that a cover _____ (tell) the reader what the book is about?

5. A long-time reader of romance advises that a cover _____ (have) an element from the story.

6. She feels that some covers _____ (be) poor because they feature the characters (a handsome man and a beautiful woman, of course) too prominently.

7. She also prefers that male models _____ (not, use) when they don't match the author's description of the character.

8. Finally, most readers of romance are now demanding that the cover

   _____ (not, embarrass) them when they are reading the book in public.

Unit Wrap-up

Error Correction

Find and correct the errors in the passage. Some errors can be corrected in more than one way. Including the example, there are nine errors.

             that
No one would disagree ~~if~~ reading is important for teenagers. Diana Tixier

Herald, author of *Teen Genreflecting,* believes that good readers be avid readers and

often these avid readers are readers of genre fiction. She knows that genre fiction

doesn't always get much respect. Nevertheless, Herald contends that escapist read-

ing of genre fiction is an ideal outlet for teens, who have different needs from people

of other age groups. That the teen years are a time of self-discovery is clear. She

argues if genre fiction fits the needs of teen readers. She asks herself that teens can

divide the world into more manageable parts by selecting and reading a type of

genre fiction that appeals to them.

    For her book, Herald wanted to know how do teens select genre fiction. As a

librarian, she wondered if or not teens would read more if a library organized the

books in a different way. She had noticed that teens pay attention to the labels on

the books they read. She believes that they are the only readers who ask for books,

not by author and title, but by the imprint (specific publisher). She recommends

that a library offers genre collections, clearly identified as such, to make books more

accessible to teens.

    Herald also thought about if the books should be displayed differently. She feels

that it is important that teens are given the opportunity to see the covers, too. She

says that making the books more accessible to teens will encourage them to become

avid, and thus good, readers.

Guided Writing

From a fiction novel of your choice, select a passage that contains dialogue. It should
have at least five lines of quoted speech. On a separate sheet of paper, rewrite the
quoted speech as reported speech. Make all the possible changes. Give your paper and
a copy of the dialogue from your fiction novel to your teacher for correction.

> Example: Brent grabbed his coat and, glancing at his watch, told Tom that
> he was leaving. He said that he had told his clients that they could reach him
> the next day . . . (*Grammar Links 3* Student Book, page 386)

TOEFL TIME

Allow yourself twelve minutes to complete the 20 questions in this exercise.

Questions 1 through 10: Circle the letter of the one word or phrase that best completes the sentence.

1. Although they have theories, scientists aren't certain why _____.
   (A) did dinosaurs disappear
   (B) dinosaurs disappeared
   (C) would dinosaurs disappear
   (D) dinosaurs disappear

2. Meteorologists wonder _____ or not El Niño conditions will increase in intensity in the future.
   (A) that
   (B) when
   (C) if
   (D) whether

3. People are surprised about _____ Pablo Casals worked until the end of his life.
   (A) that
   (B) the fact that
   (C) if
   (D) when

4. Ancient sea-going cultures _____ the position of the moon and stars could be used to navigate.
   (A) were aware that
   (B) were aware of
   (C) were aware if
   (D) were aware about

5. Population experts agree that it is urgent that we _____ prepared for a world with 8 billion people in it by the year 2010.
   (A) to be
   (B) will be
   (C) be
   (D) are

6. When a hurricane threatens coastal areas, authorities ask residents _____.
   (A) that they will evacuate
   (B) the fact that they evacuate
   (C) to evacuate
   (D) if they evacuate

7. Stock market analysts wonder when _____ a downward trend.
   (A) that the stock market is going to start
   (B) is the stock market going to start
   (C) is the stock market to start
   (D) the stock market is going to start

8. Politicians are often asked _____ if they are elected to office.
   (A) that they will do
   (B) what will they do
   (C) what they will do
   (D) about the fact that they do

9. The American artist Philemona Williamson believed _____.
   (A) art should be magical
   (B) whether art should be magical
   (C) that should art be magical
   (D) should art be magical

10. _____ was a meat-packer from New York is a matter of legend.
    (A) The original "Uncle Sam"
    (B) That the original "Uncle Sam"
    (C) Originally, "Uncle Sam"
    (D) If the original "Uncle Sam"

Questions 11 through 20: Circle the letter of the underlined part of the sentence that is incorrect.

11. If the computing capability of the Apollo space missions <u>was</u> less than <u>that</u> of a

A (under "If")   B   C
    common hand-held organizer <u>is surprising</u>.

D

12. Scientists <u>don't agree</u> <u>about</u> <u>if</u> there was ever life on Mars <u>or not</u>.

        A   B   C   D

13. It is interesting <u>that</u> many people <u>believe</u> <u>that</u> strange things are happening

        A   B   C D
    in an area of the Atlantic Ocean called the Bermuda Triangle has been

    documented in several books.

14. John F. Kennedy <u>told</u> people <u>not ask</u> what their country could do for them, but

               A   B
    rather <u>what</u> they <u>could do</u> for their country.

     C   D

15. The mother of pop singer Jewel Kilcher <u>advised</u> that she <u>didn't have</u> a plan to fall

                                 A   B
    back on when she started her singing career because she believed <u>that</u> she

                                              C
    <u>wouldn't succeed</u> if she did.

     D

16. Former Surgeon General C. Everrett Koop <u>recommends</u> <u>that</u> every American

                                  A   B
    <u>takes</u> charge of his or her own health and <u>not be</u> afraid to ask questions about a

 C   D
    medical condition.

17. <u>The possibility</u> <u>that</u> the sleep-deprived mind <u>be</u> prone to "microsleeps," lapses

      A   B   C
    of consciousness so brief <u>that</u> the subject may not be aware of them, has been

                   D
    suggested in recent studies.

18. Albert Einstein is reported to have said <u>that</u> the single most important decision

                              A
    any of us will ever make is <u>if or not</u> to believe <u>that</u> the universe <u>is</u> friendly.

                        B   C   D

19. Scientists think <u>if</u> cheetahs evolved in the area <u>that</u> <u>is</u> now the western United

             A   B C
    States and then they later <u>spread</u> into Europe, Asia, and Africa.

                       D

20. The Mattel toy company <u>says</u> <u>that</u> an average American girl <u>have</u> ten Barbie

                        A   B   C
    dolls and that every second, two <u>are</u> sold somewhere in the world.

                              D

Unit Eleven

Adverb Clauses and Phrases; Connecting Ideas

Adverb Clauses and Phrases

chapter

22

GRAMMAR PRACTICE 1: Adverb Clauses

① Identifying Adverb Clauses

The following passage contains five adverb clauses, including the example. Read the passage. Underline each adverb clause and circle its subordinating conjunction. Indicate which question each clause answers by writing *when, where, why,* or *how* above it.

Successful business owners need to know the reasons behind people's purchases

why

(so that) they can meet the needs of their clients or customers. While they are

thinking about starting a new business, owners need to budget time and money for

market research. They need to know the likelihood of the success of their business

before they invest a lot of time and money. Starting a business where it won't do well

can be frustrating and expensive, so they try to find out as much as possible about

their potential customers. In the end, they hope that they have the right information

to make good decisions, and they proceed as if they are going to succeed.

GRAMMAR PRACTICE 2: Types of Adverb Clauses

② Adverb Clauses of Time and Reason

Use the subordinating conjunctions given to complete the sentences. Use each one once. Put commas where they are needed.

whenever	until	since	✓as

1. _____As_____ she drinks her AWAKE coffee, Margie comes to life.

2. _____ she started drinking AWAKE Margie used to be sleepy all day.

Copyright © Houghton Mifflin Company. All rights reserved.   193

3. She has had much more energy _____ she started drinking AWAKE.

4. Try AWAKE. _____ you drink it you'll have more energy, too!

because	as long as	as soon as	before

5. End your day with a smooth cup of Assured Herbal Tea. _____ you take a sip you'll feel calm and relaxed.

6. Even _____ you finish the cup you'll feel warm and secure.

7. You'll enjoy Assured _____ we use only the freshest herbs.

8. _____ she can remember, Evelyn has ended her day with Assured. You can, too.

3 Adverb Clauses of Time and Reason

Underline the adverb clause in each sentence. Then write **T** for time or **R** for reason to indicate what kind of adverb clause each sentence contains.

1. <u>Because I was interested in this TV program</u>, I started to watch it.   **R**

2. We've seen seven commercials since we started watching this program.   _____

3. Just as the program was getting more exciting, they broke for a commercial.   _____

4. I'm starting to lose interest in sitting here as I can't stand commercials.   _____

5. Once this happens, I start to think about food.   _____

6. Since the program isn't on, I might as well get a sandwich.   _____

7. Television can be dangerous as it can make you get fat.   _____

4 Adverb Clauses of Result

The following are people's responses to telephone survey questions about TV commercials. Combine the sentences using *so . . . that* or *such . . . that*.

1. The message was confusing. I didn't understand the commercial.

   The message was so confusing that I didn't understand the commercial.

2. I didn't understand the commercial. It was a confusing message.

   It was such a confusing message that I didn't understand the commercial.

3. I paid attention to the beautiful model. I didn't notice the name of the product.

_____

4. It's an expensive car. I can't afford to buy it.

_____

5. I've seen many commercials recently. I can't remember any of them.

_____

6. I haven't seen those commercials. I have few opportunities to watch television.

_____

5 **Direct Contrast or Opposition**

Use the words given to write sentences with *whereas* and *while*. Each sentence can be
written in more than one way.

1. most teens / follow / fads
   some teens / be / influencers

   While most teens follow fads, some teens are influencers. OR Whereas some teens are influencers, most

   teens follow fads. OR Most teens follow fads, while some teens are influencers. OR Some teens are

   influencers, whereas most teens follow fads.

2. teens in the past / not be / the main shoppers in the family
   teens today / make / many of the shopping decisions

   _____

   _____

3. adults / often buy / a product / for practical reasons
   teens / usually choose / a product / because it's cool

   _____

   _____

4. teens in the past / not have / much money to spend
   teens today / spend / an average of $99.00 per week

   _____

   _____

6 Reason versus Weaker Contrast and Opposition

Use one of the subordinating conjunctions given to complete the sentences. Use each conjunction only once. There is more than one possible answer in some sentences.

| although   ✓because   despite the fact   since |

_____Because_____ they are surveyed so often and studied so much, teens are
     (1)

claiming that they no longer set fads. _____ small groups of hip teens
                        (2)

used to think up something new and different and watch it spread to the

mainstream, teens today may be under the influence of marketing firms that

influence what the trends will be. _____ the marketers are in control,
                                (3)

teens wonder if they are being coerced into wearing, watching, and eating what the

adult marketers want them to. _____ that teens of today may be just
                         (4)

followers, they continue to buy what is currently cool.

| as   because   in spite of the fact   though |

_____ businesses want to sell more and more products to teens, they keep
    (5)

coming up with new fads. _____ that they are not setting the trends, teens
                (6)

today are still savvy shoppers who know what they want. _____ they may
                                           (7)

be influencing teens, marketers know they must work to keep teens interested in their

products. _____ Levi Strauss did not stay in tune with what teens want, the
         (8)

company lost customers to smaller brands of jeans considered more 'cool' by teens.

7 Adverb Clauses of Purpose

Combine the given sentences to form one sentence with an adverb clause of purpose.
Use *can* for ability. Otherwise, use *will*.

1. Marketing research firms look for teens who are trendsetters. They want to
   identify teens that they call "influencers." (so that)

   Marketing research firms look for teens who are trendsetters so that they

   can identify teens that they call "influencers."

2. The firms seek out influencer teens. They want to get their opinions on the
   latest trends in fashion and other areas. (in order that)

   _____

3. They survey influencer teens. They want to find out what's hip in the minds of a teen. (so that)

_____

4. Teen responses are analyzed. The firm wants to make recommendations to companies like Nike and Pepsi. (in order that)

_____

5. Companies pay for market research. They want their products to be successful with teens. (so that)

_____

8 Adverb Clauses of Manner

Write sentences with the words in parentheses using *as if* or *as though*.

1. Do they have a lot of money?

   It's possible that they do. They spend money _____*as if OR as though they have a*_____

   _____*lot of it.*_____

2. Is he a professional athlete?

   I don't know, but he dresses _____.

3. Are you really hungry?

   I'm not starving, but I know I'm eating _____.

4. Is she a famous actress?

   It's possible that she is. She acts _____.

5. Do they need more clothes?

   No, they don't, but they are buying clothes _____.

9 Guided Writing

On a separate sheet of paper, write a paragraph about yourself as a consumer. What do you buy? How much do you spend? Do you follow trends? What is your purpose for the things you buy? How do you spend money? Use the following subordinating conjunctions in your paragraph:

    1) contrast or opposition – *whereas/while, although/though/even though;*

    2) purpose – *so that* and *in order that;*

    3) manner – *as if/as though.*

Give your paragraph to your teacher for correction.

> Example: Although I know I should save some money, I often spend all the money I have. Because I like to wear the latest fashions, I spend a lot of money on clothes. But, even though I like to look stylish, I don't always follow the latest trends. Sometimes I buy an outfit so that I'll look different from others. My father used to say I spent money as if it grew on trees . . .

GRAMMAR PRACTICE 3: Adverb Phrases

10 Identifying Adverb Clauses and Adverb Phrases

Underline the adverb clauses once and the adverb phrases twice. Put a **T** above the
clauses and phrases of time, an **R** above the clauses and phrases of reason, and a **C**
above the clauses and phrases of contrast and opposition.

Paco Underhill, managing director of Envirosell, has been called a retail
                                    R
anthropologist because he has been recording and analyzing what customers do in
                              R
stores for the last 20 years. Having spent hours studying video tapes of shoppers, he
is an expert on shopper behavior. He knows that although the merchandise in a
store is important, the layout of the physical space of a store can make or break that
store. When he enters a store, he quickly evaluates where and how the merchandise
is displayed. Observing the movement of shoppers, Paco Underhill is able to advise
his clients on how to set up their stores for success.

11 Adverb Phrases of Time and Reason

Paco Underhill has made the following observations about the behavior of shoppers.
Reduce the adverb clause in each sentence to an adverb phrase if possible. Otherwise,
write **NR**. More than one reduced form may be possible.

1. When they walk, people in the United States tend to keep to the right.

   When walking, people in the United States tend to keep to the right.

2. Before shoppers decide to enter a store, the store must catch their attention. _NR_

3. When they prepare display windows, retailers should angle them to the left.

   _____

4. As they are walking along, shoppers will be able to see the merchandise in the
   display windows.

   _____

5. As they enter a store, shoppers are walking at a fast pace.

   _____

6. Because they are walking fast, they need time to slow down.

   _____

7. Since she is moving too fast, a shopper will miss anything in the first fifteen to twenty feet of the store.

_____

8. As a shopper is going too fast to really see the merchandise, retailers shouldn't put anything of value in the first fifteen feet of the store.

_____

9. Because he has studied thousands of hours of videotape of customers entering stores, Paco Underhill also believes in the invariant right.

_____

10. This means that after they enter the store, shoppers invariably turn to the right.

_____

11. When a store knows this, the display department won't put anything of value to the left of the door where customers won't see it.

_____

12 Adverb Phrases of Contrast and Opposition

Paco Underhill has also observed gender differences in shopping behavior. In each sentence contrasting men and women shoppers, reduce the adverb clause to an adverb phrase if possible. Otherwise, write **NR**. More than one reduced form may be possible.

1. Although men shop, too, women are still the target market for retailers. ___NR___

2. While men stay an average of nine minutes in a store, women stay over 12 minutes.

_____

3. Though they both need to be enticed to buy accessories, men and women buy them at different times and places.

_____

4. Although men will pick up accessories when they pick up pants to try on, women will look for accessories after they've tried on the pants.

_____

5. While they are able to make choices in style and size, men prefer help in matching colors.

_____

chapter 23 · *Connecting Ideas*

GRAMMAR PRACTICE 1: Connectors

1 Coordinating Conjunctions—Punctuating Sentences; Parallel Structures

Some of these sentences contain one or more errors in punctuation and/or with parallel structures. Other sentences contain no errors. Use commas where necessary to punctuate the sentences. Correct the errors in parallel structure. If a sentence contains no errors, write **NC**. Some errors can be corrected in more than one way.

1. Every product has to stand out or ~~looking~~ *look* different from its competitors.

2. Personal computer (PC) manufacturers found that many of their products were similar to their competitors' products, so they needed to differentiate their products.

3. They tried to show both that they had a good product and good service.

4. The PC companies "sold" their computers their knowledge and they helped with problems.

5. Customers could either buy a prepackaged system or they could put together their own systems.

6. They could ask for help or they could use their own judgment.

7. The customers were supported while buying the computers and after the sale.

8. Selling after-the-sale service seemed to be effective and success for many PC customers appreciated the extra help.

2 Omitting Words

Combine the sentences into one sentence with *and*. Make the content in each sentence parallel. Make all sentences as concise as possible—that is, omit repeated words.

1. Personal computer (PC) companies promoted security. PC companies promoted compatibility. PC companies promoted service.

   Personal computer (PC) companies promoted security, compatibility, and service.

2. The company that made Macintosh computers had a different approach. The company that made Macintosh computers had a unique approach.

   _____

3. Macintosh advertised that it was fun. Macintosh advertised that it was for individuals. Macintosh advertised that it was easy to use.

   _____

4. Macintosh computers came out in different colors. Macintosh computers were sold to many young people.

_____

5. Macintosh computers have supporters and detractors. PC's have supporters and detractors.

_____

3 Punctuating Sentences Connected by Transitions

Use commas, semicolons, and periods to punctuate the following sentences. Add capital letters where necessary. There may be more than one way to punctuate the sentences.

In the late 1990s, one of the most popular investments was in companies associated with the Internet; however, (OR . However,) since many of these companies weren't making a profit, their values were hard to assess. Many investors saw the Internet as a new way of doing business they therefore didn't want to be left out of any important future developments in addition buying Internet stocks became trendy, despite the lack of dividends. Other investors recognized the potential of an accelerating trade in Internet stocks consequently they were able to buy low and sell high. One company more than tripled its initial opening price on the first day that it was traded for example.

GRAMMAR PRACTICE 2: Relationships Expressed with Connectors— Addition and Time

4 Addition with Paired Coordinating Conjunctions and Transitions

A. Combine the sentences into one sentence using the connectors in parentheses.

1. (not only . . . but also) When wearing our shoes, you'll look sophisticated. When wearing our shoes, you'll feel terrific.

   When wearing our shoes, you'll not only look sophisticated but also feel terrific.

2. (both . . . and) Our shoes support your feet. Our shoes make your legs look elegant.

   _____

3. (either . . . or) You'll be satisfied. You'll get your money back.

   _____

4. (neither . . . nor) You're not going to be disappointed in our shoes. Your friends aren't going to be disappointed in our shoes.

_____

B. Connect the second sentence to the first using the connectors in parentheses. Put the connector in the second sentence in the position indicated in the parentheses.

1. (*moreover* / beginning) Your dog will be healthier. You'll spend less time and money at the veterinarian's office.

   Your dog will be healthier. Moreover, (OR ; moreover,) you'll spend less time and

   money at the veterinarian's office.

2. (*furthermore* / beginning) HealthyDog dog food tastes great. HealthyDog dog food is good for your dog's health.

   _____

3. (*in addition* / middle) Your dog's coat will be shiny. Your dog will be more active.

   _____

4. (*also* / end) HealthyDog will change the way your dog feels. It'll make you happy.

   _____

5 Time Connectors

Connect the ideas in the following paragraph by inserting time connectors at the beginning of sentences where they are appropriate. Use the connectors in parentheses.

1. (first, after that) I'm going to address two aspects of consumer behavior in the
            First,   **After that,**
   United States. I'll speak about planned obsolescence. I'll address need versus want.

2. (meanwhile, in the end) The products we buy are designed to wear out. Models and parts change. We have to buy something new because we can't repair our "old" stuff.

3. (then, finally) Often, before we buy something, advertisers have tried to convince us that we not only want but need their products. We ourselves begin to believe that we need the products. We buy what we want, not necessarily what we need.

6 Guided Writing

On a separate sheet of paper, write a paragraph about a time you went shopping. What happened? What did you buy? Use at least two connectors of addition and two connectors of time. Give your paragraph to your teacher for correction.

> Example: One time when I went Christmas shopping, I was looking for a gift for my nephew. It was crowded; in addition, I was tired and hungry . . .

GRAMMAR PRACTICE 3: Other Relationships Expressed with Connectors

7 Reason and Result Connectors

Use the connectors given to complete the sentences. Use each connector once.

✓because   so   therefore

1. _____Because_____ the logo of this product is well known, consumers recognize the product.

2. The logo of this product is well known; _____, consumers recognize the product.

3. The logo of this product is well known, _____ consumers recognize the product.

as a result   for   on account of

4. The ad was effective. _____, company sales increased.

5. _____ the ad's effectiveness, company sales increased.

6. Company sales increased, _____ the ad was effective.

because of   consequently   so

7. The company used a multimedia campaign, _____ it reached a wider audience.

8. _____ using a multimedia campaign, the company reached a wider audience.

9. The company used a multimedia campaign; _____, it reached a wider audience.

8 Contrast and Opposition Connectors

Combine the two sentences using each of the connectors given. Use the sentences in
the order they are given. In some cases, more than one way to combine the sentences is
possible. Punctuate carefully.

1. People remember the jingle. They don't remember the product.

   a. while _While people remember the jingle, they don't remember the product._

   OR People remember the jingle, while they don't remember the product.

   b. but _____

   c. however _____

2. Famous people are often used in ads. They sometimes have a negative effect on
   the product.

   a. although _____

   b. yet _____

   c. nevertheless _____

3. The slogan is recognizable. The company may stop using it.

   a. despite the fact that _____

   b. nonetheless _____

   c. yet _____

4. This company's logo is good. Its slogan is poor.

   a. whereas _____

   b. in contrast _____

   c. on the other hand _____

9 Guided Writing — Exemplification

On a separate sheet of paper, write sentences that give examples for each of the
statements. Use *for example* or *for instance*. Give your sentences to your teacher for
correction.

1. I buy clothes that are comfortable.	4. That company sells cars that are sporty.
2. I buy jeans that are stylish.	5. That company sells snacks that are delicious.
3. I buy shoes that are practical.	6. That company sells games that are fun.

   Example: I buy clothes that are comfortable. For instance, I only buy loose
   fitting T-shirts made of soft cotton.

Unit Wrap-up

Error Correction

Correct the errors in the underlined segments in the following passage. Some errors may be corrected in more than one way.

_As_
<u>Though</u> fiber-optic, digital, and satellite technologies advance in the next ten years, they will give advertisers new tools to use television and the Internet interactively. <u>Such that</u>, advertisers will be able to target very specific markets. For instance, custom-made ads will target such specific markets as a particular age group or a specific zip code. Whereas advertisers' messages were delivered to large general audiences before, <u>so they'll</u> be delivered to the narrow audiences most interested in the product or service. For example, advertisers can target sports fans or dog lovers. Thus, micro-marketing will replace mass marketing. Furthermore, the technology will give consumers the power to order products <u>in addition</u> information instantly. Whenever they want a product, consumers will have only to click a button to get it.

Several companies are working on ways to blend Internet and television advertising. A viewer will be able to not only view the product on a television ad, <u>and</u> also split his TV screen and click on the web site for more information. Although <u>is coming</u>, the evolution of interactive television and Internet advertising will be a slow process. <u>Consequently</u>, there is also technology which will allow consumers to block advertising and control what advertising they watch. Interactive advertising will give both advertisers and consumers more choice, convenience, and control. But, privacy issues must be addressed. Advertisers must control who gets access to information and <u>using</u> it. Either the advertising industry will regulate itself to protect consumer privacy <u>nor</u> it will lose the trust of the consumer.

Guided Writing

Choose two ads from a magazine, or a newspaper—one that is effective and one that is
not. On a separate sheet of paper, write a paragraph in which you compare and contrast
them. Give reasons why one works and the other doesn't. Use subordinating
conjunctions, coordinating conjunctions, and transitions of addition, result and reason,
and contrast and opposition in your paragraph. Give your ads and your paragraph to
your teacher for correction.

> Example: I prefer this ad for jeans that shows an active woman wearing
> them to that one because it doesn't show the jeans. Whereas this one lets
> me see the product, that one tries to appeal to young people who like a par-
> ticular type of music . . . .

TOEFL TIME

Allow yourself twelve minutes to complete the 20 questions in this exercise.

Questions 1 through 10: Circle the letter of the one word or phrase that best completes the sentence.

1. _____ with a live virus, the Salk polio vaccine is safer than the Sabin polio vaccine.
   - (A) Instead of making it
   - (B) Because of not making
   - (C) As it isn't made
   - (D) In addition

2. In the fall, gardeners are advised to cover their outdoor plants at night _____ the plants won't be killed by an early frost.
   - (A) however
   - (B) in order to
   - (C) for instance
   - (D) so that

3. _____, artist David Hollowell creates images of the game.
   - (A) After loving baseball
   - (B) Whereas he loves baseball
   - (C) Yet he loves baseball
   - (D) Loving baseball

4. Akitas tend to be fairly big dogs with well-defined muscles, _____ they used to hunt bears.
   - (A) for
   - (B) when
   - (C) therefore
   - (D) whereas

5. A bacterium may produce chemicals that cut viral DNA into pieces _____ it can protect itself from the DNA.
   - (A) in order
   - (B) so that
   - (C) for
   - (D) therefore

6. Being smart and cautious, _____.
   - (A) sagebrush sometimes hides cattle
   - (B) sagebrush is sometimes hidden behind by range cattle
   - (C) range cattle sometimes hide behind sagebrush
   - (D) range cattle hidden behind sagebrush

7. The National Transportation Safety Board investigates _____.
   - (A) whereas a plane crashes
   - (B) after a plane crashes
   - (C) consequently, a plane crashes
   - (D) yet a plane crashes

8. _____ has become a leading Internet subject.
   - (A) Looking up genealogy
   - (B) Although looking up genealogy
   - (C) While looking up genealogy
   - (D) As looking up genealogy

9. _____ they are mammals, bears are warm-blooded.
   - (A) Also
   - (B) Not only
   - (C) Consequently
   - (D) Because

10. The human body needs salt, _____ most Americans consume too much.
    - (A) however
    - (B) yet
    - (C) thus
    - (D) or

Go on to the next page

Questions 11 through 20: Circle the letter of the underlined part of the sentence that is incorrect.

11. In autumn, not only chlorophyll no longer is produced in trees, but other
    <u>A</u>   <u>B</u>   <u>C</u>
    pigments in the leaves are exposed.
                       <u>D</u>

12. High-level chess matches are such strenuous activities that professionals train
                              <u>A</u>   <u>B</u>
    for them if they were athletes.
           <u>C</u>   <u>D</u>

13. Both excitement and if you are afraid produce rapid heart rates and
    <u>A</u>   <u>B</u>
    increased adrenaline flow; in addition, they both produce stress.
            <u>C</u>   <u>D</u>

14. There are other benefits of higher education in addition to increasing
                                              <u>A</u>
    knowledge; for instance, educated people usually both earn more money and
    <u>B</u>   <u>C</u>
    self-confidence.
    <u>D</u>

15. Because only a fraction of our communication being verbal, our bodies often
            <u>A</u>   <u>B</u>
    convey a message; the tone of our voices can carry meaning, as well.
                                          <u>C</u>   <u>D</u>

16. Although Roger Maris' single-season home-run record was thought to be
    <u>A</u>   <u>B</u>
    untouchable, nevertheless, both Mark McGuire and Sammy Sosa broke his
                 <u>C</u>   <u>D</u>
    record in 1998.

17. Because arthroscopic surgery has not only reduced the recovery time and also
    <u>A</u>   <u>B</u> <u>C</u>
    decreased the chance of infection, knee surgery patients can start rehabilitation
    <u>D</u>
    sooner.

Go on to the next page ➡

18. Having waited for the Mars Climate Orbiter to reach Mars, the loss of the craft
    $\underline{}$ $\underline{}$
    A   B

    was a big disappointment both to the engineers who built it and
                            $\underline{}$
                            C

    to the astronomers who were waiting to receive its data.
    $\underline{}$
    D

19. Though botox contains a highly purified neurotoxin, it is used both to control
                                                      $\underline{}$ $\underline{}$
                                                      A   B

    severe muscle spasms and smoothing out wrinkles; furthermore, it can relieve
                            $\underline{}$ $\underline{}$
                            C   D

    headaches.

20. Cormorants, which are diving birds, have neither external nostrils or any other
                                                $\underline{}$ $\underline{}$
                                                A   B

    way to breathe when their mouths are closed.
               $\underline{}$ $\underline{}$
               C   D

ANSWER KEY

Unit One

Chapter 1: Simple Present and Present Progressive

GRAMMAR PRACTICE 1:
Simple Present and Present Progressive

1 Simple Present—Form and Function

A. 2. Do people schedule   3. don't think   4. Does the human body follow   5. run   6. don't use

B. 2. a   3. a   4. b   5. b   6. a

2 Present Progressive—Form and Function

A. 2. 're always complaining   3. 'm trying
4. 'm sleeping   5. 'm eating   6. Are you listening
7. isn't telling OR 's not telling

B. 2. c   3. b   4. b   5. a   6. a   7. a

3 Time Expressions with Simple Present and Present Progressive

2. Do you exercise on the weekends?

3. They aren't watching a lot of TV these days.

GRAMMAR PRACTICE 2:
Verbs with Stative Meaning

7 Verbs with Stative Meaning and Verbs with Active Meaning

A.   My husband has a busy schedule. He stays up late to watch TV programs that he doesn't really hear because he's tired after a hard day. He rarely exercises and looks tired all the time. He says he's being lazy, but he isn't lazy. He's really a morning person, so when he stays up late, he seems unwell in the morning. He knows his schedule is making him unhappy and he wants to do something about it.

Nowadays, I'm listening to my body's internal clock. I'm also paying attention to natural time and my natural work cycle. I usually work best early in the day. These days, I'm going to work early and leaving early, too. I go to bed when my body tells me I'm tired, so I don't mind getting up early now. I like my new schedule. I'm feeling great.

4. He goes to bed at ten o'clock.

5. Are you working at this time?

6. She doesn't eat dinner in the evening.

4 Simple Present and Present Progressive— Time Expressions

2. He often gets up at sunrise in the morning.   3. Nowadays we are eating a big breakfast before work.   4. John is working a flexible schedule this year.   5. They relax at home on weekends.   6. Are you studying or working more at present?
7. Briana doesn't exercise regularly every day.

5 Guided Writing: Simple Present and Present Progressive

Answers will vary.

6 Simple Present and Present Progressive

2. do they do   3. move / are moving   4. observe and record   5. measure / are measuring   6. determine / are determining   7. studies   8. think   9. are trying / try
10. is asking   11. do we remember   12. don't remember
13. does time run / is time running

<u>Do</u> you <u>like</u> your schedule? At present, are you following your natural cycle or are you

following clock time?

B.   's being   'm feeling   is thinking

8   Verbs with a Stative and an Active Meaning

2. a. are looking b. looks 3. a. have b. 're having
4. a. are weighing b. weigh 5. a. are feeling b. feels
6. a. are   b. are being

Chapter 2: Simple Past and Past Progressive

GRAMMAR PRACTICE 1:
Simple Past and Past Progressive

1   Simple Past—Form and Pronunciation

A. 2. did he do   8. set up   14. did he play
   3. wanted   9. rolled   15. put
   4. increased   10. was Galileo   16. hit
   5. fell   11. needed   17. took
   6. dropped   12. didn't have   18. got
   7. What was   13. knew   19. demonstrated

B. /t/   /d/   /id/
   increased   used   wanted
   dropped   rolled   needed
                                 demonstrated

2   Simple Past and Past Progressive—Function

A. 2. SP 3. PP 4. PP 5. PP 6. SP 7. PP 8. SP

B. 2. was attending 3. was discussing 4. were arguing
   5. started 6. pulled 7. forgot 8. fought
   9. were fighting 10. cut off 11. wore

3   Simple Past and Past Progressive

2. died 3. was studying 4. broke out 5. closed
6. stayed 7. was waiting / waited 8. thought / was thinking
9. was sitting 10. fell 11. helped 12. became
13. was working / worked 14. made 15. was

4   Guided Writing: Simple Past and Past Progressive

Answers will vary.

GRAMMAR PRACTICE 2:
Simple Past and Past Progressive in Time Clauses

5   Simple Past and Past Progressive in Time Clauses

3. [In the 1880s, when the United States was thinking about instituting standardized time,

   the railroads were very powerful.]

4. Farmers and factory owners needed to get their products to the railway station before the

   train arrived. Knowing at what time the train arrived became very important.

5. After the farmers and factory owners started paying attention to clock time, other busi-

   ness owners and professionals began using it, too.

6. While clock time was taking over the business world, natural time remained important in

   the personal world.]

7. [For about forty years, workers chose their own activities when they had free time.]

8. This changed after radios became popular and programs came on at a certain time.

9. Families often checked the radio schedules before they made plans for their free time.

10. After most families had radios, clock time became important in our personal lives.

6 Simple Past and Past Progressive in Time Clauses

2. After Lauren went to work, Paul got up. OR Paul got up after Lauren went to work.   3. While Lauren was working, Paul got up. OR Paul got up while Lauren was working.   4. Paul got up before Lauren ate lunch. OR Before Lauren ate lunch, Paul got up.   5. When Lauren left work, Paul went to work. OR Lauren left work when Paul left work. OR Paul went to work when Lauren left work. OR When Paul went to work, Lauren left work.   6. Lauren left work before Paul ate dinner. OR Before Paul ate dinner, Lauren left work.
7. Lauren went to bed while Paul was working. OR While Paul was working, Lauren went to bed.   8. After Lauren went to bed, Paul met friends. OR Paul met friends after Lauren went to bed.   9. Lauren was sleeping when Paul came home. OR When Paul came home, Lauren was sleeping. OR When Lauren was sleeping, Paul came home. OR Paul came home when Lauren was sleeping.

GRAMMAR PRACTICE 3:
Used To

7 *Used To-* Form

A. 2. didn't use to have   3. Did your teacher use to play   4. used to use   5. did you use to check   6. used to check   7. used to help   8. used to help

B. 3. Would your teacher play   4. would use   5. would you check   6. would check   7. would help   8. would help

8 Guided Writing: *Used To* and *Would*

Answers will vary.

Unit Wrap-up

Error Correction

1. invented
Long before people ~~were inventing~~ clocks, they would look up at the sun to tell time.

2. reaches
Because the sun ~~is reaching~~ the highest point in the sky about once every twenty-four hours,

it is a convenient marker of time passing from one day to the next. However, the earth doesn't

3. move
~~moves~~ around the sun on a consistent basis. It varies from day to day by as much as sixteen

4. followed
minutes. This variation wasn't noticeable until more and more people ~~follows~~ clock time

instead of natural time.

5. realize
Nowadays we seldom ~~realizing~~ that clock time and sun time don't match. We make

appointments by our watches, not by the position of the sun in the sky. Watches also help us

agree on the time, with enough precision to satisfy most of our needs.

To satisfy their needs, scientists developed much more accurate and precise methods of

6. are depending / depend
measuring time. They ~~are depend~~ on mathematical measurements of the motion of the sun

and stars. They are also using an atomic clock, which relies on the change of cesium atoms

from one state to another.

Although scientists are now measuring time with great accuracy and precision for any

7. know

one place, we ~~are knowing~~ that time itself is not constant. Albert Einstein's theory of relativity

8. affect

predicted that motion and gravity ~~are affecting~~ time. An experiment in 1971 tested his theory.

9. was

While one airplane was traveling west carrying an atomic clock, another ~~is~~ traveling east with

another atomic clock. The atomic clock on the plane traveling east gained time while the one

on the plane going west lost time.

Are our lives changing because we know more about the nature of time? Probably not.

Have we lost something with our reliance on clock time? Who knows? Only time can tell!

Guided Writing: Present and Past, Simple and Progressive

Answers will vary.

TOEFL TIME

Questions 1–10

1. C   2. D   3. C   4. A   5. B   6. D   7. A   8. B   9. B
10. B

Questions 11–20

11. D (*omit*)   12. C (building)   13. D (creates)
14. D (refused OR were refusing)   15. C (used to think OR thought)   16. D (used to)   17. B (died)   18. C (when)
19. C (cost)   20. C (opened)

Unit Two

Chapter 3: Present Perfect and Present Perfect Progressive

GRAMMAR PRACTICE 1:
Present Perfect and Present Perfect Progressive

1 Present Perfect—Form

2. hasn't given   3. 've invented   4. haven't done   5. has happened   6. hasn't technology saved   7. has our time gone   8. have needed   9. have spent   10. have made
11. have wanted   12. haven't changed

2 Present Perfect Progressive—Form

2. haven't been enjoying   3. have been feeling   4. have they been feeling   5. 've been trying   6. have we been doing   7. 've been speeding up   8. 've been doing
9. 've been using   10. 've been working   11. 've been trying
12. have we been getting   13. we haven't

3 Present Perfect and Present Perfect Progressive

2. e   3. b   4. d   5. c

4 Present Perfect versus Present Perfect Progressive

2. I have written /(have been writing) a movie script for two years.

3. I (have gone)/ have been going to six writers' conventions in the last two years.

4. (I haven't watched)/ (haven't been watching) TV since I started writing the script.

5. My children and husband (haven't seen)/ (haven't been seeing) much of me lately either.

6. I (have traveled)/ have been traveling overseas, and I'd like to do that again.

7. I (have made a decision)/ have been making a decision to relax more when I finish this script.

8. (Have you had)/ Have you been having time for all the things you want to do recently?

9. Is there anything that you (haven't done)/ (haven't been doing) lately because you have no time?

5 Guided Writing

A and **B**: Answers will vary.

GRAMMAR PRACTICE 2:
Present Perfect versus Simple Past

6 Present Perfect and Simple Past—Function

2. became; c 3. has lived; b 4. have had; a
5. have been; a 6. saw; d 7. has painted; b 8. saw; d

7 Present Perfect versus Simple Past

2. read 3. 've been 4. Have you ever driven 5. drove
6. haven't driven 7. 've always wanted 8. 've never had
9. started 10. Have you saved 11. 've saved

8 Guided Writing: Present Perfect versus Simple Past

Answers will vary.

9 Present Perfect, Present Perfect Progressive, and Simple Past

A. 2. 've lived / 've been living 3. moved 4. did you leave
5. were 6. didn't have 7. Have your lives been
8. 've lived / 've been living 9. has been building
10. hasn't finished 11. 've taught / 've been teaching
12. 've had 13. has spent / has been spending
14. 's caught 15. 's been writing 16. Have you been
17. 've been 18. were

Chapter 4: Past Perfect and Past Perfect Progressive

GRAMMAR PRACTICE 1:
Past Perfect and Past Perfect Progressive

1 Past Perfect

A. 2. Before he came to the United States, he had (driven) a car.

3. Before he came to the United States, he had (caught) a fish.

4. Before he came to the United States, he had (made) many friends.

5. Before he came to the United States, he had (ridden) a horse.

6. (left)

7. Before he came to the United States, he hadn't (slept) in a tent.

8. Before he came to the United States, he hadn't (gone) skiing.

9. Before he came to the United States, he hadn't (heard) a coyote howl.

10. Before he came to the United States, he hadn't (written) e-mail to his parents.

11. Before he came to the United States, he hadn't (read) a novel in English.

12. Before he came to the United States, he hadn't (had) so much fun.

B. Miami, Florida

2 Past Perfect versus Simple Past

2. In 1885, Karl Benz invented the automobile. OR Karl Benz invented the automobile in 1885. 3. When Karl Benz invented the automobile, Etienne Lenoir had already built the first internal combustion engine. OR Etienne Lenoir had already built the first internal combustion engine when Karl Benz invented the automobile.
4. Henry Ford didn't mass produce the Model T until 1908. OR Henry Ford hadn't mass produced the Model T until 1908. OR Until 1908, Henry Ford didn't mass produce the Model T. OR Until 1908, Henry Ford hadn't mass produced the Model T.
5. Humans had used the wheel for thousands of years before Nicholas-Joseph Cugnot invented the steam-powered tricycle. OR For thousands of years before Nicholas-Joseph Cugnot invented the steam-powered tricycle, humans had used the wheel. OR Before Nicholas-Joseph Cugnot invented the steam-powered tricycle, humans had used the wheel for thousands of years. 6. By 1904 the Wright brothers had achieved powered flight. OR The Wright brothers had achieved powered flight by 1904. 7. Charles Lindbergh flew the first transatlantic solo flight after Paul Cornu had designed the first helicopter. OR After Paul Cornu had designed the first helicopter, Charles Lindbergh flew the first transatlantic solo flight. 8. The first supersonic jet passenger service hadn't begun until 1976. OR Until 1976, the first supersonic jet passenger service hadn't begun.
9. Frank Whittle had performed a test flight on the first jet engine before the first supersonic jet service began. OR Before the first supersonic jet service began, Frank Whittle had performed a test flight on the first jet engine.
10. The Wright brothers had already achieved powered flight when Paul Cornu designed the first helicopter. OR When Paul Cornu designed the first helicopter, the Wright brothers had already achieved powered flight.

3 Past Perfect versus Simple Past

2. asked, had stored   3. had sung, (had) danced, had
worked   4. didn't have, had played   5. had been, wasn't
able to   6. thought about, had done, gathered   7. made,
had requested   8. picked up, threw   9. realized, hadn't
used   10. begged, didn't change

4 Past Perfect Progressive

2. had been playing, hadn't been gathering   3. Had the ants
been doing   4. had been working, had been searching
5. had the ants been looking   6. had been looking

5 Past Perfect and Past Perfect Progressive

2. had been looking   3. Had the clock struck
4. had gotten   5. had been climbing   6. had struck
7. had struck, had never heard   8. Had it been feeling
9. hadn't been thinking

6 Past Perfect, Past Perfect Progressive, and Simple
Past

2. bragged, teased   3. had been telling   4. challenged
5. hadn't run, had run   6. accepted   7. were   8. took
9. had danced, had been dancing   10. had gone   11. got
12. realized   13. crossed, had crossed   14. didn't stop,
hadn't stopped

Unit Wrap-up

Error Correction

              1. read
Recently I ~~had read~~ a book about people who use their time well. I had been looking for

                     2. found
role models and trying to be more like them when I ~~have found~~ this book about CEOs.

Herb Kelleher, CEO of Southwest Airlines, is one such role model. During an interview,

someone asked him, "What does a typical day look like for you now?" He said that he didn't

               3. looked
know. He said, "I have never ~~look back.~~ I have always tried to remain directed forward." He has

                4. set
decided what is important and has ~~been setting~~ his priorities based on those decisions.

             5.
      Several years ago, he ~~has~~ delegated control of his schedule to his executive vice president,

Colleen Barrett. Why did he do that? Herb Kelleher said that before Colleen began handling

his appointments, scheduling his day took up too much of his time. When he spent time on

           6. didn't focus
scheduling, he ~~hasn't focused~~ on other important matters.

            7. (omit)
Colleen Barrett had been ~~being~~ Herb Kelleher's secretary before she became his executive

vice president. When she worked as his secretary, she learned a lot about the business and her

          8. was
boss, so it ~~had been~~ easy for her to take over this duty. Since then, Herb has concentrated on

running the company, while she has managed his daily activities.

9. has been

So far, Herb Kelleher ~~was~~ a good role model for me while I have been trying to use my

10. have

time well. I ~~had~~ been managing my time better since I finished the book. There is just one

problem. I don't have an executive vice president to schedule my day!

Guided Writing

Answers will vary.

TOEFL TIME

1. A 2. C 3. D 4. B 5. A 6. D 7. C 8. B 9. B
10. D 11. A (have been) 12. A (*omit* had) 13. C (for)
14. C (confirmed) 15. B (had) 16. B (had)
17. B (already OR *omit*) 18. B (when OR after)
19. D (won) 20. B (has)

Unit Three

Chapter 5: Future Time

GRAMMAR PRACTICE 1:
Will and *Be Going To*

1 *Will*—Form and Function

A. 2. will we ride 3. 'll try 4. will be 5. won't be
6. will we go on 7. will be 8. 'll be 9. 'll take care
10. won't leave 11. 'll ride 12. won't ride
13. will you wave

B. 2. 2, 13 3. 3, 9 4. 5, 12

2 *Be Going To*—Form and Function

A. 2. is going to carry 3. is going to dive 4. 're going to
reach 5. 're going to experience 6. aren't going to return
7. is going to take 8. are you going to ride

B. First line: All sentences except the last one are expectations.
Second line: Which one are you going to ride next?

3 *Will* and *Be Going To*—Function

2. prediction 3. expectation 4. offer 5. prediction
about immediate future 6. request 7. expectation
8. refusal

4 Expressing the Future in Sentences with Time
Clauses

A. 2. is going to dive, reaches 3. travel, 're going to
experience 4. go, are going to proceed 5. is, are going
to travel 6. arrives, are going to be

B. 2. After you experience the first drop of 188 feet, you will
go into the first vertical loop. OR You will go into the first
vertical loop after you experience the first drop of 188 feet.
3. Before the train enters a high-speed 180 degree turn, it
will go through two more vertical loops. OR The train will
go through two more vertical loops before it enters a
high-speed 180 degree turn. 4. As soon as it goes
through the loops, it will fly up a hill. OR The train will fly
up a hill as soon as it goes through the loops.
5. When you go through the classic corkscrew inversion,
you will finish the ride. OR You will finish the ride when
you go through the classic corkscrew inversion.

5 Guided Writing

Answers will vary.

GRAMMAR PRACTICE 2:
Expressing the Future with the Present
Progressive, the Simple Present, and
Be About To

6 Expressing the Future with Present Progressive,
Simple Present, and *Be About To*

2. c 3. b 4. a

7 Expressing the Future with Present Progressive
and Simple Present

A. 2. action on a schedule 3. planned event 4. plan
5. planned event 6. prediction 7. planned event
8. plan 9. prediction

B. 2. opens 3. 'm packing 4. 'is going OR goes
5. 'll probably be OR will probably be 6. are we visiting
OR do we visit 7. 'm bringing 8. isn't going OR
doesn't go 9. 'll be OR will be

8 Expressing the Future with Present Progressive,
Simple Present, and *Be About To*

1. b. 'm about to call c. are you going d. 'll know e. closes
2. a. 'll be b. 'm telling c. 're going d. 're making
e. 'm about to pick up f. 'm going

9 Guided Writing

Answers will vary.

Chapter 6: Future Progressive, Future Perfect, and Future Perfect Progressive

GRAMMAR PRACTICE 1:
Future Progressive

1 Future Progressive with *Will* and *Be Going To*—Form

A. 2. won't be carrying   3. will they be doing   4. will be carrying out   5. 'll be going   6. 'll be traveling   7. 'll be passing   8. will be helping

B. 2. 's also going to be researching   3. is going to be taking on   4. are going to be carrying out   5. are going to be saving   6. are these scientists going to be doing   7. 're going to be devoting

2 Future Progressive versus Future

A. 2. will be   3. will fly, will be flying   4. will be waiting   5. will cheer, will be cheering   6. Are you going to ride, Will you be riding   7. will depart, is going to be departing   8. Will you be

B. 5

3 Future Progressive in Sentences with Time Clauses

2. drive, will be using   3. drive, will be controlling   4. use, won't be causing   5. will be riding, install   6. have, will be living   7. build, won't be commuting

GRAMMAR PRACTICE 2:
Future Perfect and Future Perfect Progressive

4 Future Perfect with *Will* and *Be Going To*—Form

A. 2. will we have solved   3. 'll have found   4. 'll have put   5. will have discovered   6. won't have changed   7. Will anything have changed   8. 'll have gotten   9. will have learned

B. 2. are going to have gone   3. is going to have returned   4. are going to have studied   5. is going to have mapped   6. 're going to have learned   7. Are scientists going to have collected   8. 're going to have looked   9. Are they going to have found

5 Future Perfect Progressive with *Will* and *Be Going To*

A. 2. will have been blowing, 21   3. will have been running, 10   4. won't have been blowing   5. will have been writing, 21   6. will have been reading, 7   7. will have been reading, 5   8. will Ron have been looking at   9. 'll have been observing

B. 2. is going to have been blowing,   3. is going to have been running,   4. isn't going to have been blowing   5. is going to have been writing   6. is going to have been reading   7. is going to have been reading   8. is Ron going to have been looking at   9. 's going to have been observing

6 Future Perfect and Future Perfect Progressive with *Will* and *Be Going To*

2. a, b   3. a   4. a, b   5. a, b   6. a, b   7. a

7 Time Clauses, Future Perfect, and Future Perfect Progressive

A. 2. Before he begins plans for a moon base, he will have worked on the Mars missions for three years. OR He will have worked on the Mars missions for three years before he begins plans for a moon base.   3. When he goes into space, he will have trained as an astronaut for two years. OR He will have trained as an astronaut for two years when he goes into space.   4. By the time he goes into space, he won't have worked at NASA for ten years. OR He won't have worked at NASA for ten years by the time he goes into space.

B. 2. Before he starts working on the moon base, he will have been working on the Mars mission for three years. OR He will have been working on the Mars mission for three years before he starts working on the moon base.   3. When he starts working on the moon base, he will have been working for NASA for five years. OR He will have been working for NASA for five years when he starts working on the moon base.   4. By the time he goes into space, he will have been working at NASA for six years. OR He will have been working at NASA for six years by the time he goes into space.

8 Guided Writing

Answers will vary.

Chapter 7: Phrasal Verbs; Tag Questions

GRAMMAR PRACTICE 1: Phrasal Verbs

1 Phrasal Verbs Without Objects

A.

B. 2. started out
3. came back OR have come back
4. will go on OR am going to go on
5. broke down
6. set in
7. turned out OR had turned out
8. showed up

2   Phrasal Verbs; Placement of Pronoun Object

2. Q: pull along his sled?   A: pulled it along.

3. Q: carry out his plan   A: carried it out

4. Q: did keep up the pace   A: kept it up

5. Q: did try out the parasail   A: didn't try it out

6. Q: held up Borge Ousland   A: held him up

7. Q: make up the time   A: make it up

8. Q: took off his skis   A: took them off

3   Phrasal Verbs—Meaning

2. on   3. off   4. (a) out (b) off   5. up   6. (a) up (b) off
7. down

GRAMMAR PRACTICE 2:
Verb-Preposition Combinations; Phrasal Verbs with Prepositions

4   Verb-Preposition Combinations

2. depend on   3. plan for   4. learned from
5. protected . . . from   6. (has) happened to   7. worry
about / think about   8. think about / worry about   9. suffered from   10. recovered from   11. come from   12. care
about   13. write about   14. will talk about   15. will pay
for OR am going to pay for   16. will read about

Unit Wrap-up

Error Correction

                                                          1. will land / will be landing
   In the future, robots and other devices that ~~will be land~~ on Mars and other celestial

bodies will probably have gone to Antarctica before they ever leave Earth. Scientists will be

using this cold continent more and more as they design devices for Mars exploration. They

                                       2. them out
want to take the machines there and try ~~out them~~ because of the similarities in climate

between Mars and Antarctica. Both of these places have frozen soil, and Antarctic lakes

                                       3. sets
resemble the Martian lakes of long ago. Before anyone ~~will set~~ foot on Mars, scientists are

going to have been exploring Lake Hoare in Antarctica for many years. They will have been

looking at the algae that live at the bottom of the ice-covered lake. They want to

    4. about it   5. will search / are going to search
know ~~it about~~ because it is a very simple form of life. In the future they ~~search~~ for similar algae

under the surface of Mars in what they think are old lake beds. The water dried up long ago,

5   Phrasal Verbs with Prepositions

A. 2. f   3. a   4. g   5. b   6. h   7. d

B. 2. get back from   3. put up with   4. get down to
5. come up with   6. put up with / watch out for / get
along with   7. meet up with

6   Guided Writing

Answers will vary.

GRAMMAR PRACTICE 3:
Tag Questions

7   Tag Questions—Form

2. Q: didn't they   A: they did
3. Q: did it   A: it didn't
4. Q: wasn't he   A: he was
5. Q: had they   A: they hadn't
6. Q: don't they   A: they do
7. Q: haven't they   A: they have
8. Q: aren't they   A: they are
9. Q: won't we   A: we will
10. Q: are there   A: there aren't
11. Q: doesn't it   A: it does
12. Q: aren't I   A: you are

but the remains of the algae, if there are any, might still be there. By 2010, a spacecraft is going

      6. returned   **7. back**

to have ~~been returning~~ to Earth with soil samples. When the spacecraft comes ~~off~~, scientists

will find algae fossils in the soil, won't they? Maybe, but regardless of what they find, scientists

                                         8. on

aren't going to give up their search for life too easily. They will keep ~~in~~ looking looking in other

                        9. won't

places until they close in on their goal, ~~don't~~ they?

Guided Writing

Answers will vary.

TOEFL TIME

Questions 1–10

1. A   2. D   3. A   4. A   5. C   6. B   7. D   8. C   9. A
10. B

Questions 11–20

11. B (have figured out)   12. D (completes)   13. A (will have)   14. C (*omit*)   15. C (get it out)   16. C (are)   17. B (get along with)   18. B (succeed in)   19. B (is about to)
20. C (used them up)

Unit Four

Chapter 8: Nouns and Determiners

GRAMMAR PRACTICE 1:
Types of Nouns and Determiners

1 Proper and Common Nouns

Conquest, travel, and trade have helped spread different kinds of food and methods of

                                          R

cooking throughout the world. For example, romans redesigned the

gardens of the countries they conquered, and Christian soldiers returned from religious wars

   M   **E**   **N**   **A**   **M**

in the middle east and north africa with new ingredients and recipes. The travels of marco

P   **V**   **I**   **C**   **I**   **E**

polo of venice, italy, helped establish trade with china and india, which gave europeans tea,

                                          C

spices, and the practice of heating the cooking pot with coal. When columbus and other

                   E   **A**

explorers returned to europe from america, they brought new food and recipes with them.

     I   **T**

Then, italians traded these things with turks, who in turn traded with other Eastern

E   **E**

europeans, thereby helping to spread new food throughout most of europe.

2 Using Articles with Proper Nouns

3. the   4. the   5. NA   6. NA   7. the   8. the   9. NA
10. the   11. the   12. the   13. NA   14. the   15. the
16. NA   17. NA   18. NA   19. the   20. NA   21. the
22. NA

3 Proper Nouns Acting as Common Nouns

2. ND   3. the   4. The   5. a   6. ND   7. a   8. two   9. ND
10. ND   11. a   12. the   13. ND

4 Count and Noncount Nouns

                                                  C   N

The Internet has also been instrumental in spreading **ideas** about **cooking**. Many on-line

C

bookstores have a **section** for **cookbooks** that includes **reviews** about the **books**. Television

C

and radio **programs** often have corresponding **websites** that give **recipes** and further

N

information and **advice** about different **kinds** of **food**. Some **companies** use the Internet to

C

give **consumers help** with their **products**. For example, one **company** that sells frozen

C

turkeys has a very popular **website** about the Thanksgiving **holiday**.

5 Count Nouns versus Noncount Nouns; Plural
Count Nouns

A. 2. bosses   3. work   4. advice   5. parties   6. Fun
7. husbands   8. wives   9. children   10. vegetables
11. life   12. Flies   13. enemy OR enemies   14. Mice
15. teeth   16. bacteria   17. health   18. customers
19. money   20. men   21. tomatoes   22. crates
23. garlic   24. boxes   25. heads

B. The boxes will break, and the heads of garlic will fall out
and roll on the floor.

6 Subject-Verb Agreement

2. have   3. enters   4. have   5. plays   6. rests   7. aren't
8. looks   9. is

7 Nouns Used as Count and Noncount Nouns

2. a business   3. A pressure   4. pressure   5. a chance
6. chance   7. a fire

GRAMMAR PRACTICE 2:
Definite and Indefinite Articles

8 The Definite Article—Function

2. e   3. b   4. g   5. a   6. c   7. f

9 The Indefinite and [0] Article

2. a   3. e   4. c   5. d

10 Definite and Indefinite Articles

2. a   3. [0]   4. the   5. an   6. the   7. the   8. the   9. a
10. [0]   11. [0] OR a   12. [0]   13. [0]   14. a   15. the
16. the   17. a   18. The   19. [0]   20. the   21. a   22. [0]
23. the

11 Definite and Indefinite Articles

2. [0] / some   3. a   4. the   5. the   6. the   7. the
8. [0] / some   9. [0]   10. the   11. the   12. a   13. the
14. the   15. some / the   16. the

12 Generic Statements

A and B. 2. a. The/An   b. [0]   c. The
                 3. a. [0]   b. a   c. The/A
                 4. a. The   b. [0]   c. the / a

13 Guided Writing

Answers will vary.

GRAMMAR PRACTICE 3:
Quantifiers

14 Numbers and Measure Phrases

1. b. a bunch of   c. a bag of   d. a slice of   e. a bottle of
2. a. a pair of   b. a couple of   c. a half pound of   d. a can of
   e. either f. both

15 *Much* and *Many*

2. How many   3. How much   4. How much
5. How much   6. How many

16 Quantifiers

2. thousands of   3. no   4. quite a few   5. one of   6. years
7. several   8. a great deal of   9. none   10. All
11. several / some   12. each / every   13. Plenty of / Lots of
14. not all   15. none   16. some   17. many / most

17 Guided Writing

Answers will vary.

Chapter 9: Modifiers, Pronouns, and Possessives

GRAMMAR PRACTICE 1:
Modifiers

1 Modifiers

A. Every good (cook) knows that even a great (recipe) isn't going to result in a delicious (dish) without quality (ingredients). Professional (chefs) use only fine, fresh (produce). They usually prefer to buy healthy organic (fruit) and (vegetables) at small farmer-owned (stands) at local (markets) instead of in large grocery (stores). For example, they select dark green leafy (lettuce) and smooth , round (tomatoes) at the peak of freshness for their summer (salads). They pick ripe red (strawberries) sweet Persian (melons) and exotic tropical (fruit) for luscious, light (desserts).

B. *Opinion:* great OR delicious OR quality OR fine OR luscious
Appearance: leafy / smooth
Shape: round
Color: green / red
Origin: Persian
Find a noun used as a modifier: grocery OR summer
Find a compound modifier: farmer-owned

2 *-Ing* and *-ed* Adjectives

2. -ed . . . , -ing   3. -ed   4. -ing   5. -ing   6. -ed . . . , -ing
7. -ing

3 Noun Modifiers; Compound Modifiers

A. 2. Bread Machine   3. Clay Pot   4. Chili Sauce

B. 2. Four-Course Meals   3. Award-Winning Recipes
4. Twenty-Minute Meals   5. Three Hundred-Calorie Meal

4 Order of Modifiers

2. authentic old Southern   3. great American food
4. famous art   5. modern nonstick   6. French herb
7. very interesting regional   8. delicious international coffee

5 Guided Writing

Answers will vary.

GRAMMAR PRACTICE 2:
Pronouns

6 Reflexive and Reciprocal Pronouns

2. by myself   3. himself   4. by yourself   5. yourself
6. each other   7. by ourselves   8. each other   9. him
10. one another   11. itself   12. us   13. each other

7 Indefinite Pronouns

2. anything OR something

3. anything

4. Someone OR Somebody (was)

5. No one OR Nobody (has)

6. Everyone OR Everybody (wants)

7. anything

8. nothing

9. anyone OR anybody

10. anything

11. something

8 Forms of Other

2. another   3. another   4. Another   5. The other
6. others   7. the others   8. others

GRAMMAR PRACTICE 3:
Possessives

9 Possessives

A. 2. In the 1500s, European <u>traders'</u> <u>ships</u> carried the chiles to other places.

3. The <u>length</u> <u>of a century</u> was the time needed for chiles to spread throughout the world.

4. A Hungarian cook has <u>her</u> <u>recipes</u> for chile peppers, and a Chinese cook has <u>his</u>, too.

5. <u>Mexico's</u> chile <u>peppers</u> are especially famous for <u>their</u> <u>flavor</u> and <u>heat</u>.

6. The chile <u>pepper's</u> <u>seeds</u> and <u>ribs</u> make it hot.

7. If <u>your</u> <u>skin</u> is as sensitive as <u>mine</u> is, wear gloves when handling hot chiles.

B.

Form	Function
2. singular possessive noun: *Mexico's* OR *pepper's*	1. ownership: *traders'* OR *her* OR *his* OR *your* OR *mine* OR *their*
3. plural possessive noun: *traders'*	2. amount: *of a century*
4. possessive pronoun: *his* OR *mine*	3. part of a whole: *pepper's*
5. possessive phrase: *of Mexico* OR *of a century*	4. origin: *of Mexico* OR *Mexico's*

10 Possessive Determiners, Possessive Pronouns, and Possessive Nouns

2. China's   3. their   4. theirs   5. South Carolina's
6. the world's   7. people's   8. its   9. Asians'   10. my
11. Her   12. my   13. family's   14. Our   15. hers

11 Possessive Nouns versus Possessive Phrases

2. center of the house's activities   3. stove's warmth OR warmth of the stove   4. gossip of the neighborhood and wider community   5. my parents' house   6. smells of cooking holiday food   7. my uncles' funny stories

Unit Wrap-up

Error Correction

The cultivation of cacao is very precarious: the trees won't produce fruit if they are too far

      1. Earth's
from the ~~Earth~~ equator. They also won't grow in high altitudes if the temperature falls below

          2. are
60° F (about 16° C). The growing trees require year-round moisture and ~~is~~ sensitive

3. a number of
to ~~a number~~ diseases. Squirrels, monkeys, and rats tend to eat the soft pulp that surrounds the

      4. a seed OR the seeds
trees' hard, bitter seeds, and a ~~a seeds~~ will promptly die without the proper humidity and tem-

perature.

      5. much-loved
The seeds, though, are valued for producing a ~~much-loving~~ product: chocolate.

      6. another
Researchers disagree with one ~~one other~~ about the exact origins of chocolate, but they tend to

      7. the tree OR the trees
agree that the first domestication of ~~tree~~ was in the low-lying forests of what is now Mexico, at

8. Mayans

least 3000 years ago. The ~~mayans~~, who lived there, probably spread their chocolate-

drinking habits to others in Central America, eventually reaching the Aztecs in the highlands

9. means

of Mexico. The Native Americans had several ways, not just a single ~~mean~~, of preparing

10. their   11. chili

~~his~~ processed chocolate, including flavoring it with ~~chilies~~ peppers.

The Aztecs valued the caffeine-rich seeds so highly that they used them as currency.

Because of this, only royalty and the upper-class consumed the rich, bitter chocolate drinks.

12. himself   13. last Aztec OR Aztecs' last

Montezuma ~~by himself~~, one of the ~~Aztec last~~ rulers, probably gave chocolate to Hernán

14. chocolate   15. Europe

Cortés, a Spanish explorer. The Spanish introduced some ~~some chocolate~~ into ~~the Europe~~,

where the bitter drink was first mixed with sugar. Nowadays, people from all over the world

enjoy this treat from the Americas.

Guided Writing

Answers will vary.

TOEFL TIME

Questions 1–10

1. C 2. D 3. A 4. A 5. B 6. C 7. D 8. A 9. B
10. A

Questions 11–20

11. A (Some archeologists) 12. D (a shorter stay)
13. C (furniture) 14. B (interesting) 15. D (the Western world) 16. D (sunflowers) 17. C (the person) 18. A (her)
19. C (*omit*) 20. B (other)

Unit Five

Chapter 10: Adjective Clauses

GRAMMAR PRACTICE 1:
Adjective Clauses; Subject and Object Pronouns

1 Forming Adjective Clauses; Subject Relative Pronouns

2. who OR that is adventurous 3. who OR that are talkative
4. which OR that is dangerous 5. which OR that are stressful

2 Forming Adjective Clauses; Object Relative Pronouns

2. who OR whom OR that OR [0] we consider enterprising
3. who OR whom OR that OR [0] we consider conscientious
4. which OR that OR [0] we consider exciting
5. which OR that OR [0] we consider important

3 Relative Pronouns

2. who/that 3. which/that 4. which/that
5. who/whom/that/[0] 6. which/that 7. who/that
8. who/that 9. who/that 10. who/that
11. which/that/[0] 12. which/that

4 Forming Adjective Clauses; *Someone, Everybody, Something*

2. someone who/whom/that/[0] 3. something which/that
4. everybody who/that 5. Someone who/that
6. something which/that/[0]

5 Combining Sentences to Form Sentences with Adjective Clauses

2. They are personality tests which OR that indicate a person's traits. 3. People who OR that have the right personality traits for a certain job will probably succeed. 4. These are traits which OR that OR [0] we consider important for a particular job. 5. Someone who OR that doesn't have these traits probably won't be happy at a job.

6 Guided Writing

Answers will vary.

GRAMMAR PRACTICE 2:
Relative Pronouns as Objects of Prepositions; Possessive Relative Pronouns

7 Adjective Clauses with Prepositions

2. For a short time you can probably do a job that your personality isn't well suited for. which your personality isn't well suited

for / [0] your personality isn't well suited for / for which your personality isn't well suited

3. In the long run, however, you will be better off if you do a job that you are happy at. which you are happy at / [0] you are

happy at / at which you are happy

4. A person that you can talk with honestly may help you decide on a good career. who you can talk with honestly / whom you

can talk with honestly / [0] you can talk with honestly / with whom you can talk honestly

8 Combining Sentences; Clauses with *Whose*

2. An immediate response on these tests is preferred to a later response whose accuracy may be decreased by too much thought.   3. People whose responses are slow may answer as they wish they were, not as they really are.
4. Answers based on wishes will not help a person whose personality is actually quite different.   5. A person whose answers tend toward a specific trait has a strong preference in one aspect of work.   6. For example, a person whose responses indicate an outgoing personality probably prefers to work with other people.

9 Relative Pronouns as Objects of Prepositions; Possessive Relative Pronouns

2. which/that/[0] 3. whose 4. whom 5. which
6. whose 7. which/that/[0] 8. who/whom/that/[0]

10 Relative Pronouns

2. which/that/[0] 3. which/that/[0] 4. who/that
5. whom 6. whose 7. which 8. which/that 9. who/that
10. which/that/[0]

Chapter 11: More About Adjective Clauses; Adjective Phrases

GRAMMAR PRACTICE 1:
Adjective Clauses with *Where* and *When*

1 Adjective Clauses with *Where*

A. 2. The place where John eats is at a small table alone. OR The place at which John eats is a small table alone. OR The place which John eats at is a small table alone.
The place where George eats is a large round table with friends. OR The place which George eats at is a large round table with friends. OR The place at which George eats is a large round table with friends.
3. The place where John relaxes is home with a good book. OR The place at which John relaxes is home with a good book. OR The place which John relaxes at is home with a good book.

The place where George goes is a lively night spot. OR The place to which George goes is a lively night spot. OR The place which George goes to is a lively night spot.
4. The place where John feels comfortable is a small group of close friends. OR The place in which John feels comfortable is a small group of close friends. OR The place which John feels comfortable in is a small group of close friends.
The place where George feels comfortable is a large noisy crowd. OR The place in which George feels comfortable is a large noisy crowd.OR The place which George feels comfortable in is a large noisy crowd.

B. introvert: John   extrovert: George

2 Adjective Clauses with *When*

A. 2. when we feel confused or frustrated   3. when an employee feels nervous   4. when students feel many emotions   5. when an artist feels creative   6. when you felt bored

B. 2. in which we feel confused or frustrated   3. in OR at which an employee feels nervous   4. in which students feel many emotions   5. in OR at which an artist feels creative
6. in OR at which you felt bored

3 Guided Writing

Answers will vary.

GRAMMAR PRACTICE 2:
Restrictive vs. Nonrestrictive Adjective Clauses

4 Nonrestrictive Adjective Clauses

2. Howard Gardner, who is a professor at Harvard University, has studied human development for over 30 years.
3. Gardner, who did research on artistic talents in children, developed theories on intelligence.   4. He proposed that intelligence, which can be measured in many different ways, is made up of many different aspects.   5. These aspects, which Gardner called "multiple intelligences," work together to form a person's intellect.   6. Gardner studied the relationship between types of intelligence and creativity, which both come in many different forms.

5 Restrictive versus Nonrestrictive Clauses

2. Freud, <u>whom Gardner called "linguistic" and "logical"</u>, was interested in psychology.

3. Picasso, <u>whose "intelligences" were "spatial" and "bodily"</u>, was known for his painting.

4. Both men were considered creative because of the innovations <u>which they made in their fields.</u>

5. The places <u>where they spent most of their lives</u> were in western Europe.

6. Freud died in 1931, the year <u>when Picasso turned 50 years old</u>.

7. The traits of the people <u>he studied</u> helped Gardner develop ideas about creativity.

6 Restrictive versus Nonrestrictive Clauses; All or Some? One or More?

2. a   3. b   4. b   5. a

7 Nonrestrictive and Restrictive Clauses—Pronouns and Punctuation

2. , which . . . "creativity tests",   3. whose   4. where
5. which/that/[0]   6. which   7. when   8. , which . . . tests,
9. which/that

GRAMMAR PRACTICE 3:
Adjective Phrases

8 Forming Adjective Phrases

A. Along with Freud and Picasso, Gardner studied other famous creators ~~who lived~~ *living*

at approximately the same time. Albert Einstein, ~~who was~~ the most famous physicist of the

20th century, and Igor Stravinsky, ~~who was~~ an innovative composer, were two more of

Gardner's subjects. T.S. Eliot and Martha Graham, ~~who were~~ both born in the United States,

were a poet and a dancer, respectively. Gardner's seventh subject reflected "interpersonal

intelligence," ~~which relates~~ *relating* to human interactions, and is credited with developing nonvi-

olent, passive resistance in political struggles. That person was Mahatma Gandhi.

B. However, other people ↑ ~~sharing~~ these traits aren't so successful. What's the difference? *who OR that share*

Is it something something ↑ ~~running~~ in a family? Or is it the method *which OR that runs*

↑ used to raise a "creator"? *which OR that is*

The facts ↑ ~~answering~~ these questions aren't clear. *which OR that answer*

9 Guided Writing

Answer will vary.

Unit Wrap-up

Error Correction

For hundreds of years, people have been noticing that human beings tend to have differ-

1. who
ent personality types. Plato, ~~that~~ was a Greek philosopher, wrote about four kinds of

2. which OR that[O]
character ~~who~~ humans have. Because Plato was interested in the societal role that these types

of character played, he focused on the actions and characteristics that each type

3. displayed
~~displayed them~~. He wrote about artisans, guardians, idealists, and rationals.

Aristotle, Plato's student, defined four types of people, also, but he defined them on the

4. whose
basis of happiness. Someone ~~which~~ happiness came from sensual pleasure was different from

5. who OR that
someone ~~whom~~ wanted to acquire assets. Others found happiness in acting in a moral fash-

ion, while Aristotle's fourth type of person enjoyed logic.

6. when . . . alive, OR that . . . alive,   OR [O] . . . alive, OR which . . . alive in, OR in which . . . alive,
During the time ~~when~~ Plato was alive ~~in~~,

7. Hippocrates, a . . . physician,
~~Hippocrates a Greek physician~~ proposed that people have distinct temperaments from the

day that they are born. He identified, in about 370 B.C., four personality types based on bodily

8. Galen, who was a . . . OR Galen, a . . .
fluids: eagerly optimistic, doleful, passionate, and calm. Galen, ~~was~~ a Roman physician in the

second century A.D., furthered Hippocrates' ideas. These two physicians looked for reasons for

our thoughts and actions from within our bodies, not from our surroundings. That our physi-

9. personality
ology helped to determine our ~~personality, which~~ was new to Western thought.

10. which OR that [O]
The four personality temperaments ~~whose~~ Hippocrates and Galen described comple-

mented Plato's four descriptions of social actions. Hundreds of years later, others interested in

personality types also found four types. Perhaps our personalities haven't changed much in

the last 2000 years.

Guided Writing

Answers will vary.

TOEFL TIME

Questions 1–10

1. C   2. B   3. A   4. B   5. B   6. C   7. B   8. D
9. C   10. D

Questions 11–20

11. A (that/which is called OR called)   12. D (*omit*)   13. D (which hang down)   14. A (including)   15. B (that/which have)   16. B (*omit*)   17. D (*omit*)   18. C (whose)   19. D (which)   20. B (River)

Unit Six

Chapter 12: Gerunds and Infinitives

GRAMMAR PRACTICE 1:
Overview of Gerunds and Infinitives; Gerunds

1 Overview of Gerunds and Infinitives

One result of <u>launching</u> Music Television (MTV) in 1981 was that both the television and the music industries took off in new directions. Before this time, it was unusual (to see) music videos, but <u>televising</u> them 24 hours a day became a winning formula for <u>attracting</u> young viewers. News and documentaries about music and performers were included on the broadcasts (to supplement) the videos. Young "VJ's", or Video Jockeys, hosted the programs and recommended <u>listening</u> to artists that they liked (to hear). By <u>promoting</u> rock concerts and by <u>holding</u> interviews with artists, MTV not only attracted viewers but also exposed those viewers to a wide variety of performers.

2 Gerunds as Subjects, Objects of Verbs, and Objects of Prepositions

A.   ~~Appear~~ *Appearing* on television helped the career of musician Ricky Martin. At the 1999 Grammy Awards, ~~sing~~ *singing* "The Cup of Life" earned Martin a standing ovation. He certainly must have been happy about ~~receive~~ *receiving* this recognition of his music, and he also must have enjoyed ~~accept~~ *accepting* the award for Best Latin Pop Performance. After his appearance on the Grammys, Martin's fame kept ~~increase~~ *increasing*. His song, "Livin' La Vida Loca", soared to the top of the pop charts, and people looked forward to ~~buy~~ *buying* his album. From ~~grow~~ *growing* up in San Juan, Puerto Rico, to ~~live~~ *living* the crazy life, Martin has always loved ~~sing~~ *singing*.

B. subject of a sentence: singing
object of a verb: accepting, increasing, singing
object of a preposition: buying, growing, living
be + adjective + preposition: receiving

3 Gerunds; *By* + Gerund; *Go* + Gerund

       becoming
A. By ~~become~~ famous, Ricky Martin increased both his problems and his pleasures. If he

    dancing   blending   approaching
goes ~~dance~~ or on a date, he has a problem ~~blend~~ into the crowd. Fans can't help ~~approach~~ him

           Maintaining
for an autograph. ~~Maintain~~ his private life is hard. On the other hand, he is having a good

    performing   exposing
time ~~perform~~. When he goes out on stage, he finds himself ~~expose~~ his thoughts and feelings to

              shopping   drawing   reminding
his fans. Perhaps he can't go ~~shop~~ by himself without ~~draw~~ attention, but by ~~remind~~ himself

of the line between his personal life and his private life, he may be able to live quite well with

his fame.

B. *by* + gerund: reminding
go + gerund: dancing, shopping
subject: Maintaining
object of a preposition: drawing
gerunds used with other expressions: blending,
approaching, exposing, performing

4 Guided Writing

Answers will vary.

GRAMMAR PRACTICE 2:
Infinitives

5 *It* + Infinitive, Infinitive as Subject

A. 2. It takes time to learn about all the programs.   3. It is
difficult to decide what to watch.   4. It is a good idea not
to waste time on programs that don't interest you.

B. 2. To have a remote control is necessary.   3. To see how
quickly you can become interested in each program is
interesting.   4. Not to channel surf when someone else
is trying to watch a program is a good idea. OR To channel
surf when someone else is trying to watch a program isn't
OR is not a good idea.

6 Verb + Infinitive Patterns

2. to rescue   3. to take   4. to take care of   5. to let   6. to
know   7. them to put   8. them not to work   9. them to do
10. to do   11. to keep up   12. to wrap   13. to give up
14. to keep   15. to fire

7 Adjectives Followed by Infinitives

2. were ashamed to admit   3. were stunned to learn
4. were delighted to hear   5. will you be surprised to hear

8 Infinitive of Purpose

2. (In order) To figure out if they are lying   3. (in order) to
conceal his or her guilt   4. (In order) To fool us   5. (in
order) to arrest the murderer   6. (in order) to find out who
committed the crime

9 Infinitives with *Too* and *Enough*

A. 2. Jon is too young to watch an R-rated movie at a theater
alone.   Matt is old enough to watch an R-rated movie at
a theater alone.   3. Jon is young enough to buy a child's
ticket to a movie   Matt is too old to buy a child's ticket to
a movie

B. 2. Matt has enough money to go to a concert.   3. Matt
has enough sense not to spend all day playing video
games.   4. Jon doesn't have enough money to buy a lot
of music CDs.

10 Guided Writing: Infinitives as Adjectives

Answers will vary.

11 Guided Writing

Answers will vary.

Chapter 13: More About Gerunds and Infinitives

GRAMMAR PRACTICE 1:
Gerunds versus Infinitives

1 Verbs Taking Only Gerunds or Only Infinitives

2. to earn   3. attaining   4. feeling   5. hearing   6. to say
7. to thank   8. speaking

2 Verbs Taking Gerunds and Infinitives

2. searching   3. to explore   4. to see   5. to examine
6. to be   7. believing

3 Verbs That Take Both Gerunds and Infinitives

2. going   3. to go   4. seeing   5. holding   6. to repair
7. to meet   8. to join   9. moving   10. turning   11. to tell
12. opposing   13. to enjoy

4 Guided Writing

Answers will vary.

GRAMMAR PRACTICE 2:
Performers of Gerunds and Infinitives; Progressive Infinitives; Perfect Gerunds and Infinitives

5 Performers of Gerunds and Infinitives

3. for the audience to recognize   4. watching   5. the humans' looking   6. us to believe   7. Woody's feeling
8. Buzz's becoming   9. (for) popular actor Tom Hanks to do
10. for him to make   11. for Tim Allen to do   12. these two actors to bring

6 Progressive Infinitives; Perfect Gerunds and Infinitives

A. 2. to be turning   3. to be vanishing   4. to be growing
5. to be creating

B. 3. to have turned   4. to have grown   5. having experienced   6. having stood

7 Sensory Verbs and Causative Verbs

1. b. disappear   2. a. grow / growing   2. b. appear
3. a. battle / battling   3. b. create   3. c. create
4. a. fire/firing   4. b. to add

8 Guided Writing

Answers will vary.

Unit Wrap-up

Error Correction

                                  1. playing
Eric Clapton earned his fame through ~~play~~ his guitar, but he may have kept his solo

career alive because of his singing. As a teenager, Clapton took up playing the guitar, and he

later started performing in public. Practicing the guitar improved his music but left little time

                           2. going   **3. to pursue**
for schoolwork, so he stopped ~~to go~~ to school ~~for pursuing~~ a career in music. After he joined

                          4. being
The Yardbirds, he became known for ~~be~~ one of the best blues guitarists playing at that time. As

his reputation grew, Clapton seemed to be moving from one band to another, often because

                                                    5. his
the musicians' egos were too big to keep the band together. Within ten years of ~~him~~ having

dropped out of school, Clapton was considered to be a leading rock guitarist. He was

6. famous enough
~~enough famous~~ to be invited to play with many other musicians. However, he didn't appreci-

7. having

ate ~~to have~~ become so well-known, and at one time he seemed to be trying to hide in an

unknown band. Clapton's popularity faded for a while, but he continued to record albums.

8. Clapton OR Clapton's

The soundtrack of the 1992 film Rush included ~~for Clapton~~ singing "Tears in Heaven," a trib-

ute to his son, who had recently died. Clapton's performance of "Tears in Heaven" and other

9. to reach

songs on a special television program made it possible for him ~~reaching~~ a new audience. This

10. release   **11. kept on singing OR continued to sing**

success let him ~~to release~~ another album, and he ~~kept on to sing~~ in other movies.

Guided Writing

Answers will vary.

TOEFL TIME

Questions 1–10

1. B   2. C   3. A   4. D   5. A   6. C   7. C   8. D   9. C
10. A

Questions 11–20

11. A (stampede)   12. D (waking up)   13. D (to master)
14. C (was)   15. B (seeing)   16. A (To prepare)
17. D (diversifying)   18. C (to work)   19. B (people to eat
OR eating)   20. D (not loud enough)

Unit Seven

Chapter 14: Modals

GRAMMAR PRACTICE 1:
Overview of Modals; Ability Modals

1   Overview of Modals

Tony's Tips for Meeting People

(Can) you walk into a room full of people and start talking immediately? You

✓

ought to try it sometime. All of us <u>are supposed to</u> <u>be able to</u> meet new people, but some of us

find that a little hard. Try my tips and start making new friends today!

■ You (must) show confidence! If you think you are worth knowing, other people (will) agree!

   You (could) try saying to yourself, "I am an interesting person!" Believe it.

■ You (should) look people in the eye! People <u>aren't going to</u> speak to you if you look at their

   shoes!

   ✓

■ Of course, you ought to smile! You (may) <u>be able to</u> get someone else to speak with just a

   nice smile. Try it and see!

■ You have got to say something! "Hi!" is a good start! You are allowed to keep your remarks

   simple. You don't have to be funny; just be sincere!

                                                                 ✓
■ You (must) not talk only about yourself! In fact, you had better let the other person talk more

   than you do. You (might) learn interesting things if you just listen.

So, what do you think? Are you going to be able to do these simple things? Of course you are!

Start today! You (should) see results soon!

2 Present, Future, and Past Ability

2. were not able to / couldn't   3. were able to / could
4. was able to / could   5. were able to   6. was able to
7. were able to / could   8. isn't able to / can't
9. are able to / can   10. is able to / can   11. will be able to
12. won't be able to   13. are able to / can
14. won't be able to / aren't able to/ can't

GRAMMAR PRACTICE 2:
Belief Modals

3 Belief Modals–Degrees of Certainty About the Present

2. may OR might OR could   3. may OR might OR could
4. may OR might OR could   5. may OR might   6. should
OR ought to   7. must OR could   8. must OR have to OR
have got to   9. should OR ought to   10. should

4 Belief Modals–Degrees of Certainty About the Future

2. should / ought to   3. may   4. will we   5. might / could
6. may / might   7. should   8. may / could   9. might
10. may   11. will

5 Guided Writing

Answers will vary.

GRAMMAR PRACTICE 3:
Social Modals

6 Permission, Requests, and Offers

1. b. will OR could   c. Shall   d. could OR will
2. a. May OR Can   b. Can OR May   c. Would

7 Guided Writing: Permission, Requests, and Offers

Answers will vary.

8 Suggestions, Expectations, Advice, and Necessity

2. must OR have to OR have got to   3. is supposed to OR is to
4. mustn't OR must not OR cannot OR can't OR can not OR
are not allowed to   5. doesn't have to OR does not have to
6. could OR might   7. don't have to OR do not have to
8. should OR ought to   9. should OR ought to   10. must
OR has to OR has got to   11. should OR ought to
12. had better

9 Guided Writing

Answers will vary.

Chapter 15: More About Modals

GRAMMAR PRACTICE 1:
Perfect Modals; Belief Modals in the Past

1 Perfect Modals—Form

2. may not have been   3. could have been   4. might have
married   5. shouldn't have told   6. must have gotten
7. couldn't have been   8. could have had   9. must have
said   10. ought to have told   11. shouldn't have raised
12. might not have chosen

2 Belief Modals in the Past

1. b. couldn't have / mustn't have
1. c. should have / ought to have
1. d. must have / had to have / has to have / has got to have
2. a. may have / might have / could have
2. b. couldn't have / mustn't have
2. c. must have / had to have / has to have / has got to have
2. d. may have / might have / could have
3. a. may have / might have / could have
3. b. mustn't have / couldn't have

3 Guided Writing

Answers will vary.

GRAMMAR PRACTICE 2:
Social Modals in the Past

4   Social Modals in the Past

2. should have OR ought to have   3. shouldn't have
4. had better not have   5. couldn't   6. could have OR
might have   7. was to have OR was supposed to have
8. might have OR could have   9. didn't have to
10. should have OR ought to have

5   Belief and Social Modals in the Past

2. must   3. might / could   4. couldn't   5. mustn't have had
6. had to   7. couldn't talk   8. might / could   9. shouldn't
10. didn't have to accept   11. must / had to   12. was supposed to call

Unit Wrap-up

Error Correction

                                      1. find
Anthropologists have seldom been able to ~~finding~~ a society in which men and women

don't marry, even though when and how they marry might vary. In some cultures, couples are

                                2. may
supposed to marry as soon as they reach adulthood. In others, couples ~~may be~~ delay marriage

                               3. should
until they want children. But, most cultures believe that couples ~~should to~~ marry.

    Types of marriage also vary. The most prevalent practice is monogamy, a marriage

between one husband and one wife. There are also polygamous societies. In these, a man may

            4. doesn't have to   **5. may not /can't/ mustn't**
have more than one wife, but he ~~but he~~ ~~must not~~. A wife, however ~~mayn't~~ have more than one

husband. Polyandry, in which a wife can have more than one husband, is extremely rare,

occurring in only one percent of the world population.

          6. can make OR have made OR make
Young people in many cultures ~~can have made~~ their own decisions about marriage, but

freedom to choose one's spouse is a fairly recent development in the history of marriage. In

the past, marriages had to be arranged in most cultures. Although arranged marriages may

have been more common in the past, they still occur today where people believe that mar-

riage ought to maintain family ties or social bonds. Nowadays, even in these cultures, young

6   Guided Writing

Answers will vary.

GRAMMAR PRACTICE 3:
Progressive Modals and Perfect Progressive Modals

7   Progressive and Perfect Progressive Modals

2. should be doing OR should have been doing   3. might
have been sitting   4. shouldn't have been thinking
5. must have been talking   6. might have been fighting
7. couldn't have been feeling   8. ought to have been looking
9. must have been playing   10. may be taking
11. might be making   12. should be choosing
13. must not be accepting

people may be choosing their own mates. When they do, their families often believe they

7. shouldn't
~~mustn't~~ have.

        8. Will you OR Will you be able to OR Can you
Will you marry? ~~Will you can~~ choose your own mate? Many societies are changing, and

attitudes about marriage should be changing along with them. It is unlikely, however, that

            9. is going to OR will
marriage, in some form, ~~is going to be~~ disappear any time soon.

Guided Writing

Answers will vary.

TOEFL TIME

Questions 1–10

1. A   2. C   3. B   4. C   5. A   6. D   7. A   8. C   9. C
10. B

Questions 11–20

11. D (have happened)   12. D (be able to)   13. A (might OR would)   14. C (was able)   15. A (*omit*)   16. D (try)
17. B (come OR be coming)   18. B (*omit*)   19. D (responded)   20. B (take)

Unit Eight

Chapter 16: Passive Overview

GRAMMAR PRACTICE 1:
Form of Passive Sentences

1   Forming Passive Sentences

2. The opening pitch isn't / is not being thrown out by the governor. It's / It is being thrown out by the mayor.
3. The first inning isn't / is not going to be pitched by Jay White. It's / It is going to be pitched by Mark Erikson.
4. The ball isn't / is not hit into right field by Bill Watson. It's /

It is hit into left field by Bill Watson.
5. It won't / will not be caught by the outfielder, Sam Jacobs. It'll / It will be caught by a fan in the stands.
6. The last run of the game hasn't / has not been hit by Bill Watson. The first run of the game has been hit by Bill Watson.

2   Passive Sentences with Verbs in Different Tenses

2. were held   3. weren't initiated   4. have been held
5. weren't held   6. were scheduled   7. were included
8. have been realized   9. have been broken   10. have been won   11. is usually chosen   12. was chosen   13. were cancelled   14. shouldn't have been held   15. can be kept
16. are attended   17. will be chosen   18. are led   19. is played   20. is raised   21. was lit (lighted) OR has been lit (lighted)   22. is carried OR was carried OR has been carried
23. is being lit (lighted)

3   Transitive and Intransitive Verbs

3. The event was covered by both news reporters and sports announcers of a major U.S. television network.   4. The Nike logo was being worn by them on their jackets during the broadcast.   5. Was Nike being endorsed by these news reporters and sports announcers?   6. The logo shouldn't be worn by reporters.   7. No change.   8. No change.
9. Now, corporate logos can't be worn by news reporters.
10. But, the sports announcers are allowed to wear corporate logos by the network.   11. No change.   12. No change.

4   Direct and Indirect Objects as Subjects of Passive Sentences

2. were given (athletes) By 1992, athletes were given Olympic medals in 28 sports.

3. were presented (Mark Spitz) In 1972, Mark Spitz, a U.S. swimmer, was presented gold medals a record-setting seven times.

4. was given (Romanian gymnast Nadia Comaneci) At the 1976 Summer Olympics, Romanian gymnast Nadia Comaneci was given a perfect score of 10 for her performance on the uneven parallel bars.

5. will be awarded (world-class athletes) How many world-class athletes will be awarded medals in future Olympic competitions?

GRAMMAR PRACTICE 2:
Function of Passive Sentences

5 Meaning of Passive Sentences

2. _____✓_____ U.S. Steel designed the logo.

3. _____✓_____ The team didn't know if the public liked the logo.

4. _____✓_____ People asked the players questions about the helmets.

5. _____✓_____ Players still wear the logo.

6 Receivers in Active and Passive Sentences

The most remarkable growth of a sport in the twentieth century **wasn't made** by (basketball or baseball.) (Soccer) **achieved** this increase. This fast-growing sport **was** originally **played** by (amateurs in British-influenced countries,) but now it **is dominated** by (professionals) world-wide. Much of the growth occurred in the second half of the century, and three reasons **can be given** for the spread of soccer.

First, the World Cup **is televised** throughout the world. During the Cup, work schedules **are rearranged** so that (millions of people) **can watch** the games.

Second, the growth of the game **was influenced** by (the high-level play) of the club teams. The best players from all over the world **are recruited** to keep the clubs competitive with one another, and the careers of these players **are followed** by (the fans) in their home countries.

Third, (the fans) **are** also **playing** soccer. Youth clubs **have been organized** throughout the world, and (children) **are starting** their practice sessions at ages four, five, and six. In the last fifty years, soccer has truly become the world's game.

7 Omitting the *By* Phrase

2. One of his records (may) never (be broken) ~~by anyone~~.

3. He (was named) Secretariat by his owner, and he (was voted) Horse of the Year ~~by people~~ in both of his competitive years.

4. In 1973, horse racing's Triple Crown (hadn't been won) ~~by a horse~~ in 25 years.

5. The Triple Crown (is awarded) ~~by racing officials~~ to any horse winning the Kentucky Derby, the Preakness, and Belmont Stakes all in the same year.

6. The 1973 Triple Crown (was won) by Secretariat in grand style.

7. The Kentucky Derby (was run) by Secretariat in world record time.

8. Secretariat's record-making run in the Belmont Stakes (has) never (been equaled)

~~by another horse~~.

9. Secretariat (won) the Belmont Stakes by 31 lengths, a distance so great that the images of

Secretariat and the next closest horse (couldn't be captured) at the same time by TV cameras.

8 The *By* Phrase

3. This sport was used by the ancient Greeks and Romans to train warriors.   4. Table tennis was first played on dining room tables by the English.   5. Table tennis has also been called ping pong since the early 1900s.   6. Tournaments in the U.S. have been governed by the U.S. Table Tennis Association since the 1900s.   7. The sport of mountain climbing was started in eighteenth century Europe. 8. Mt. Everest was conquered in 1953 by Edmund Hillary and Tenzing Norgay.   9. Many of the highest mountains in South America haven't been climbed yet.   10. Ice skates were first used as transportation.   11. Speed races were held in the Netherlands in the fifteenth century.   12. "Clap skates" were developed by the Dutch in 1997 so that skaters could go faster.

9 Passives in Academic Writing — Guided Writing

Answers will vary.

Chapter 17: More About Passives

GRAMMAR PRACTICE 1: Get Passives; Passive Causatives

1 *Get* Passives

2. have gotten burned   3. have gotten tossed   4. got pitched   5. are getting put   6. are getting added OR will get added   7. will get burned OR are going to get burned 8. will get traded OR are going to get traded   9. will get fired OR are going to get fired   10. may get sold

2 Guided Writing

Answers will vary.

3 Passive Causatives

2. The players have OR get their bags carried.   3. The players have OR get their practice gear bought for them. 4. The players have OR get their rooms booked in nice hotels.   5. The players had OR got a postcard of the team sent to a late-night TV program for publicity.   6. The players have OR get their many contracts handled for them by agents.

Unit Wrap-up

Error Correction

                     1. dominate
Every year, four tournaments ~~are dominated~~ the men's professional golf season. They are

called The Majors and define the best players in the sport. The tournaments—the Masters, the

U.S. Open, the British Open, and the PGA—are considered to be challenging and pressure-

                   2. be called
filled. No player can ~~called~~ great unless he has won a Major.

In 1953, three of the four tournaments—the Masters, the U.S. Open, and the British

                                 3. became
Open—were won by the same man, Ben Hogan. That year, Hogan ~~was become~~ the only golfer

to have won these three tournaments in the same year. Hogan didn't enter the PGA, partly because it was held too soon after the British Open and partly because Hogan hadn't really

4. recovered

~~been recovered~~ from a near-fatal accident in 1949. Perhaps, too, Hogan didn't enter the PGA

5. given

because it hasn't ever been ~~giving~~ the same respect as the other tournaments. Yet, golf great

Arnold Palmer, who has won the other Majors, regrets not having won this tournament.

A "magic" number in the sport of golf is 18, the number that represents the most Major

6. won by a

tournaments that have been ~~won a~~ single individual: Jack Nicklaus. This record, which

7. been approached

hasn't ~~approached~~ by any other competitor, may never get broken. Nicklaus made it clear that

these four tournaments were the ones he was training to win. Because Nicklaus was the best

golfer of his era, he was copied by other professional golfers, and the Majors truly became the

tournaments to win.

After the PGA tournament, the last of the Majors, gets finished in August, other tourna-

8. are still played

ments on the professional tour ~~still play.~~ Competition isn't stopped, but for another year, the

9. crushed

winners of the Majors have been decided, and the losers have had their hopes ~~crush.~~ The best

of the pros may already have gotten started looking ahead to next year.

Guided Writing

Answers will vary.

TOEFL TIME

Questions 1–10

1. C   2. A   3. C   4. B   5. D   6. B   7. C   8. B   9. C
10. A

Questions 11–20

11. A (disappeared)   12. D (by their instructors)
13. A (*omit*)   14. B (introduced)   15. D (will be)
16. C (to be OR *omit*)   17. D (improved)   18. A (*omit*)
19. B (*omit*)   20. D OR being (appear)

Unit Nine

Chapter 18: Conditionals

GRAMMAR PRACTICE 1:
Overview of Conditionals; Factual Conditionals; Future Conditionals

1 Factual Conditionals

1. c. Cooler, nutrient-rich water is pushed deeper if   1. d. If El Niño conditions exist, then   2. a. if they built new cities, then   2. b. If they built on the coast, then   3. a. Scientists can get a wide range of accurate information on the Pacific if   3. b. If scientists understand El Niño better, then

2 Future Conditionals—Form and Function

2. If it is an El Niño year, Peru and parts of the United States and Europe will suffer from damaging floods.   3. Indonesia, Australia, and India will experience drought if El Niño happens.   4. Many countries will have flash floods if more rain falls as a result of El Niño.   5. If El Niño occurs, the next year will be a La Niña year.   6. If countries have drought during El Niño, they will have too much rain during La Niña.

3 Guided Writing

Answers will vary.

GRAMMAR PRACTICE 2:
Present Unreal Conditionals

4 Present Unreal Conditionals—Form

2. weren't, wouldn't get   3. would answer, asked   4. were, would be   5. wanted, wouldn't forget

5 Present Unreal Conditionals—Function

2. a. F   2. b. T   3. a. T   3. b. T   4. a. F   4. b. F

6 Factual versus Unreal Conditions

2. didn't hurt, would still have   3. lived, would respect   4. would not hit, were   5. go, are

7 Guided Writing

Answers will vary.

GRAMMAR PRACTICE 3:
Past Unreal Conditionals

8 Past Unreal Conditionals—Form

2. would have caused, had erupted   3. might/could have taken, hadn't been   4. had seen, could have told   5. had happened, would have died

9 Past Unreal Conditionals—Function

2. a. T   2. b. F   3. a. T   3. b. T   4. a. F   4. b. T   5. a. F   5. b. F

10 Past Unreal Conditionals

2. If the chamber had been above sea level, ocean water wouldn't have rushed into it.   3. The volcano would have remained standing if it hadn't collapsed in the explosion.   4. If the explosion hadn't been so loud, people in Australia couldn't have heard it.   5. The wind from the explosion would have circled the earth more times if the force of the explosion hadn't dissipated.

11 Guided Writing

Answers will vary.

Chapter 19: More About Conditionals

GRAMMAR PRACTICE 1:
Other Forms in Conditionals

1 Conditionals with Conditions and Results in Different Times

1. b. If a louder noise than the explosion of Krakatau occurred, we have no record of it.   1. c. People pay attention to hurricane warnings if they lived through a strong hurricane when they were young.   2. b. The oceans wouldn't be as deep as they are now if many glaciers hadn't melted since the last Ice Age.   2. c. If erosion from the Colorado River had stopped, the Grand Canyon wouldn't exist.   3. b. If the weather could be controlled, the 1999 drought would have been avoided.   3. c. If people didn't adapt to their environments, Eskimos wouldn't have adjusted to very cold places.

2 *Should (Happen To)* and *Were To*

2. If a tsunami should happen to threaten a populated area, many people would be evacuated.   3. If a wildfire were to start in an isolated area, it would probably be allowed to burn.   4. If a volcano should happen to send a huge amount of ash into the atmosphere, global temperatures drop.   5. If another Ice Age were to occur, the climate would change dramatically.

3 Inverted Conditionals

2. Should you live on a fault line, you might also live close to a volcano.   3. You would have heard quite an explosion had you been near Krakatau in 1883.   4. You would see lava glowing were you to fly over the island of Hawaii at night.

4 *If So* and *If Not*

Do you know what to do in a tornado? ~~If you don't know what to do in a tornado,~~ **If not,**

this is a good time to learn. First, know whether your community has a warning system.

If so,
~~If your community has a warning system~~ make sure that you know what the warning is.

If not,
~~If your community doesn't have a warning system~~ make sure that you have a radio so that you

can find out what is happening. Then look at your home. If you have a basement, that is the

If not,
best place to be in a tornado. ~~If you don't have a basement~~ the next best place is an interior

room with no windows.

5 Guided Writing

Answers will vary.

GRAMMAR PRACTICE 2:
Sentences with *Wish* or *Hope*

6 *Wish* and *Hope* About the Present and Future

2. started   3. won't start   4. were   5. will cooperate
6. will burn OR burns   7. could   8. can also save   9. could
10. will work OR can work OR work

7 *Wish* and *Hope* About the Past

2. were   3. had started   4. had known   5. hadn't waited
6. had rained   7. hadn't had to   8. learned   9. had been
able to

8 Guided Writing

Answers will vary.

GRAMMAR PRACTICE 3:
Alternatives to *If*; Implied Conditions

9 Alternatives to *If*—Form and Meaning

2. b. Even if we have sophisticated technology, we can't
control snow.   3. a. Only if we prepare for snowstorms

Unit Wrap-up

Error Correction

1. without
It's hard to talk about natural disasters ~~or else~~ talking about economics. If that weren't

2. wouldn't have moved
true, the Weather Bureau, which often predicts weather-related disasters, ~~didn't move~~ from the

Department of Agriculture to the Department of Commerce in the 1940s.

Most Americans don't know that two people died in the Great Plains blizzard of 1886. If

they know anything about that blizzard, they usually remember that 90% of the cattle on the

can we lessen their damage.   3. b. Unless we prepare for snowstorms, we can't lessen their damage.   4. Unless you've seen "white" out conditions, it's hard to believe that visibility could be so poor.   5. a. Even if people in a blizzard know an area well, they can still get lost.   5. b. Whether or not people in a blizzard know an area well, they can still get lost.
6. a. As long as you are warm and have food and water, you should survive a blizzard.   6. b. Providing you are warm and have food and water, you should survive a blizzard.

10 Implied Conditions

A. 2. If there isn't heavy, dense snow, avalanches are less
likely to occur. OR If there weren't heavy, dense snow,
avalanches would be less likely to occur.   3. If the conditions are right, an avalanche can travel two miles.   4. If
vegetation doesn't hold the snow, an avalanche can more
easily start. OR If vegetation didn't hold the snow, an
avalanche could more easily start.   5. If backcountry
skiers aren't aware of avalanche conditions, they may find
themselves in a dangerous predicament.

B. 2. Dry snow avalanches go around trees. Otherwise,
avalanches push trees out of their way.   3. Without avalanche crews to compact snow with machines above
avalanche zones, there might be more avalanches.
4. With explosives, crews can start a small avalanche to
avoid a bigger one.   5. Avalanche crews must train carefully, or else they may endanger themselves.

ranges of the Great Plains died. Ranchers wouldn't have lost so many cattle if the weather

   3. hadn't
~~wouldn't have~~ been so severe.

In the 1988 Yellowstone Park fires, one principle concern was for the businesses around

the park. In the event that fires threaten private property or Old Faithful, the Park Service

  4. always tries OR will always try
~~would always try~~ to put them out, but that year there was another concern. Business people

                          5. wouldn't come
were concerned that if too much of the Park burned, tourists ~~didn't come~~ to the area.

In fact, people came to Yellowstone after the fires just to see the damage. They wished that

the fires hadn't happened, but they were curious to see what had changed. Otherwise, they

6. wouldn't have
~~wouldn't~~ come.

Despite the risks, people continue to build on lands that are susceptible to natural disas-

                              7. will
ters. Unless we make good judgments about using sensitive areas, we ~~would~~ continue to pay

for mistakes in natural resources, property, and lives.

Guided Writing

Answers will vary.

TOEFL TIME

Questions 1–10

1. D   2. A   3. B   4. B   5. B   6. A   7. C   8. A   9. A
10. D

Questions 11–20

11. A (would have)   12. B (wouldn't have been)   13. B
(were)   14. B (enjoy)   15. A (Only if)   16. D (influenced)
17. B (hadn't moved)   18. C (*omit*)   19. D (*move* can *after
views*)   20. B (otherwise)

Unit Ten

Chapter 20: Noun Clauses

GRAMMAR PRACTICE I:
Noun Clauses

1 Noun Clauses

2. wondered (why) had looked

3. believed (that) would reveal

4. realized (that) had

5. were horrified (that) had locked

6. wondered (if) would appear

GRAMMAR PRACTICE 2:
Types of Noun Clauses

2 Forming Sentences with *That* Clauses

2. That emotional risk and conflict are basic to the romance
genre is well known. OR It is well known that emotional risk
and conflict are basic to the romance genre.   3. Romance
writers insist on the fact that their readers are intelligent.
4. Romance writers don't pretend that their books are fine
literature.   5. They believe in the fact that they write
extremely well-crafted, balanced entertainment.

3 Guided Writing

Answers will vary.

4 Responding with *So* or *Not*

2. don't think so OR think not   3. suppose so   4. seems so
5. am OR 'm afraid not   6. hope so

5 Noun Clauses with *Wh*-Words

2. why your fingerprints aren't on it   3. why you wiped it off
4. what time it was when you found it   5. where you were
at the time of the murder   6. when you usually go to bed
7. why you went to bed early that night   8. why you have
lied to me

6 Noun Clauses with *Wh*-Words; Expressing
Uncertainty

2. how tall it was   3. who else has seen the creature
4. where we first spotted it   5. when we saw it   6. what the
creature did when it saw us   7. how we escaped   8. who
will go to show you the place we saw the monster

7 Noun Clauses with *if/whether*

A. & B. 2. Whether or not he is looking for me   3. if he saw
me following him to her house yesterday or not   4. if I
have done the right thing or not   5. whether or not he
loves me   6. whether or not I will ever find another love
like him

8 Guided Writing

Answers will vary.

Chapter 21: Noun Clauses in Reported Speech; Quoted Speech

GRAMMAR PRACTICE 1:
Overview of Quoted Speech and Reported Speech

1 Punctuating Quoted Speech and Identifying Reported Speech

A. & B. "Hello, Doctor," a woman's voice said. "My name is Margo."

"Hello, Margo," I replied. "I can't see you. The video must not be on."

"Oh, I know. I'd like to use audio only for a while if that's OK," Margo said.

"Fine. So what's the problem?" I asked.

"It's my son," she said. "He says that he's in love with a hologram."

I thought to myself, "Oh, great. Another one. The third this week."

"He told me he's found his life partner, but I want him to spend more time with biological

beings," she continued.

"Do you know why he doesn't have more biological friends?" I asked.

"Well, we're a little isolated," she said. "He doesn't have much exposure to biological

beings, and he says he doesn't like them. My husband and I try to spend time with him, but

we're very busy."

2 Quoted Speech; Verbs Used to Introduce Speech

2. "Hugo, that's my son, used to introduce me to his holograms," Margo replied. "He told me that he understood them
better than biological beings. His father and I are, well, intellectuals, so it's no surprise that he is, too."   3. "Well, I think
you and your husband should encourage Hugo to develop
his physical side, not just his intellect. Swim. Go for a walk.
Do things together," I suggested.   4. "Doctor, I think I'd better turn on the video now," Margo answered me. "There's
something you should know."   5. "Oh, great," I told myself.
"I wonder what this means."   6. "You see, Doctor, we are
computers," Margo explained. "We took some of my programming and some of my husband's and put them together
to form Hugo. We had to have technicians put together the
physical components, but Hugo is our son."   7. "Well, this
is a surprise!" I exclaimed. "So why did you contact me?"
8. She replied, "I picked your name out of a database of psychologists. I thought that if I could get a human's perspective,
I could figure out what to do about Hugo."   9. "Then you
know nothing about me?" I asked her. "Because I'm not
human, either. I'm an experimental program in an artificial
intelligence institute at a major research university."

3 Guided Writing

Answers will vary.

GRAMMAR PRACTICE 2:
Reported Speech

4 Changes in Verb Tense in Reported Speech

2. he had been gone   he had planned
3. her   had planned
4. had been   their   had wanted   them
5. she   I   had seen her
6. I was   I hadn't seen him   I had seen him   I would have told her
7. she was going   her
8. was

5 Changes in Modals in Reported Speech

2. he had to leave   he couldn't
3. he was going to be   he shouldn't be
4. he   might   it   he might not be able to cross
5. he should have written   his   he could have had me   it
6. I would tell his

6 Changes in Time and Place Words in Reported Speech

2. that morning   then   3. here   4. two days before
5. here today

7 Changes That Occur in Reported Speech

2. Mrs. Donovan said (that) she must have screamed after the man had grabbed her.   3. Mrs. Donovan said (that) he had made her horse run so that she couldn't jump off.
4. Mrs. Donovan said (that) if he hadn't tried to cross the river his horse might not have thrown him off.
5. Mrs. Donovan said (that) he couldn't swim and (that) she couldn't help him.   6. Mrs. Donovan said (that) she was happy to be here in my office, but (that) she was very tired.
7. Mrs. Donovan said (that) she had to get some sleep then, but (that) she would talk to you later.

8 Guided Writing

Answers will vary.

GRAMMAR PRACTICE 3:
Questions, Commands, and Requests in Reported Speech; Noun Clauses after Verbs or Adjectives of Urgency

9 Questions, Commands, and Requests in Reported Speech

2. where the Westerns were   3. what time the library closed
4. what she should do to get a library card   5. to put her name on the list to reserve the next Tony Hillerman novel
6. to keep some books for him for a few minutes   7. if anyone had turned in his wallet   8. not to worry

10 Noun Clauses after Verbs or Adjectives of Urgency

3. attracts / will attract   4. tell   5. have   6. are   7. not be used   8. not embarrass

Unit Wrap-up

Error Correction

                1. that
No one would disagree ~~if~~ reading is important for teenagers. Diana Tixier Herald, author

                    2. are
of *Teen Genreflecting*, believes that good readers ~~be~~ avid readers and often these avid readers

are readers of genre fiction. She knows that genre fiction doesn't always get much respect.

Nevertheless, Herald contends that escapist reading of genre fiction is an ideal outlet for

teens, who have different needs from people of other age groups. That the teen years are a

                3. that
time of self discovery is clear. She argues ~~if~~ genre fiction fits the needs of teen readers. She asks

    4. if OR whether
herself ~~that~~ teens can divide the world into more manageable parts by selecting and reading a

type of genre fiction that appeals to them.

5. teens
For her book, Herald wanted to know how ~~do teens~~ select genre fiction. As a librarian, she

6. if teens . . . more OR if teens . . . more or not OR whether or not teens . . . more
wondered ~~if or not teens would read more~~ if a library organized the books in a different way.

She had noticed that teens pay attention to the labels on the books they read. She believes

that they are the only readers who ask for books, not by author and title, but by the imprint

7. offer
(specific publisher). She recommends that a library ~~offers~~ genre collections, clearly identified

as such, to make books more accessible to teens.

8. whether
Herald also thought ~~about if~~ the books should be displayed differently. She feels that it is

9. be
important that teens ~~are~~ given the opportunity to see the covers, too. She says that making the

books more accessible to teens will encourage them to become avid, and thus good, readers.

Guided Writing

Answers will vary.

TOEFL TIME

Questions 1–10

1. B   2. D   3. B   4. A   5. C   6. C   7. D   8. C   9. A
10. B

Questions 11–20

11. A (That)   12. C (whether)   13. A (*Omit*)   14. B (not to ask)   15. B (not have)   16. C (take)   17. C (is)   18. B (whether)   19. A (that)   20. C (has)

Unit Eleven

Chapter 22: Adverb Clauses and Phrases

GRAMMAR PRACTICE 1:
Adverb Clauses

1 Identifying Adverb Clauses

Successful business owners need to know the reasons behind people's purchases

why   when
(so that) they can meet the needs of their clients or customers. (While) they are thinking about

starting a new business, owners need to budget time and money for market research. They

when
need to know the likelihood of the success of their business (before) they invest a lot of time

and money. Starting a business ~~where~~ *where* it won't do well can be frustrating and expensive, so

they try to find out as much as possible about their potential customers. In the end, they

hope that they have the right information to make good decisions, and they proceed

how
~~as if~~ they are going to succeed.

GRAMMAR PRACTICE 2:
Types of Adverb Clauses

2 Adverb Clauses of Time and Reason

2. Until   3. since   4. Whenever   5. As soon as   6. before
7. because   8. As long as

3 Adverb Clauses of Time and Reason

2. since we started watching this program. T

3. Just as the program was getting more exciting T

4. as I can't stand commercials R

5. Once this happens T

6. Since the program isn't on R

7. as it can make you get fat. R

4 Adverb Clauses of Result

3. I paid such attention to the beautiful model that I didn't notice the name of the product.   4. It's such an expensive car that I can't afford to buy it.   5. I've seen so many commercials recently that I can't remember any of them.   6. I have so few opportunities to watch television that I haven't seen those commercials.

5 Direct Contrast or Opposition

2. While OR Whereas teens in the past were not the main shoppers in the family, teens today make many of the shopping decisions. OR While OR Whereas teens today make many of the shopping decisions, teens in the past were not the main shoppers in the family. OR Teens in the past were not the main shoppers in the family, while OR whereas teens today make many of the shopping decisions. OR Teens today make many of the shopping decisions, while OR whereas teens in the past were not the main shoppers in the family.   3. While OR Whereas adults often buy a product for practical reasons, teens usually choose a product because it's cool. OR While OR Whereas teens usually choose a product because it's cool, adults often buy a product for practical reasons. OR Adults often buy a product for practical reasons, while OR whereas teens usually choose a product because it's cool. OR Teens usually choose a product because it's cool, while OR whereas adults often buy a product for practical reasons.   4. While OR Whereas teens in the past didn't have much money to spend, teens today spend an average of $99.00 per week. OR While OR Whereas teens today spend an average of $99.00 per week, teens in the past didn't have much money to spend. OR Teens in the past didn't have much money to spend, while OR whereas teens today spend an average of $99.00 per week. OR Teens today spend an average of $99.00 per week, while OR whereas teens in the past didn't have much money to spend.

6 Reason versus Weaker Contrast and Opposition

2. Although   3. Since   4. Despite the fact   5. As OR Because   6. In spite of the fact   7. Though   8. As OR Because

7 Adverb Clauses of Purpose

2. The firms seek out influencer teens in order that they can get their opinions on the latest trends in fashion and other areas.   3. They survey influencer teens so that they can find out what's hip in the minds of a teen.   4. Teen responses are analyzed in order that the firm can make recommendations to companies like Nike and Pepsi.   5. Companies pay for market research so that their products will be successful with teens.

8 Adverb Clauses of Manner

2. as if OR as though he is (a professional athlete)   3. as if OR as though I were (starving)   4. as if OR as though she is (a famous actress)   5. as if OR as though they did OR needed more clothes

9 Guided Writing

Answers will vary.

GRAMMAR PRACTICE 3:
Adverb Phrases

10 Identifying Adverb Clauses and Adverb Phrases

Paco Underhill, managing director of Envirosell, has been called a retail anthropologist

    R

because he has been recording and analyzing what customers do in stores for the last 20 years.

    R

Having spent hours studying video tapes of shoppers, he is an expert on shopper behavior. He

            C

knows that although the merchandise in a store is important, the layout of the physical space

                         T

of a store can make or break that store. When he enters a store, he quickly evaluates where

                                  R

and how the merchandise is displayed. Observing the movement of shoppers, Paco Underhill

is able to advise his clients on how to set up their stores for success.

11 Adverb Phrases of Time and Reason

3. When preparing display windows, retailers should angle them to the left.   4. Walking along, shoppers will be able to see the merchandise in the display windows.   5. Entering a store, shoppers are walking at a fast pace.   6. Walking fast, they need time to slow down.   7. Moving too fast, a shopper will miss anything in the first fifteen to twenty feet of the store.   8. NR   9. Having studied thousands of hours of videotape of customers entering stores, Paco Underhill also believes in the invariant right.   10. This means that (after) entering the store, shoppers invariably turn to the right. 11. NR

12 Adverb Phrases of Contrast and Opposition

2. NR   3. Though both needing to be enticed to buy accessories, men and women buy them at different times and places.   4. NR   5. While (being) able to make choices in style and size, men prefer help in matching colors.

Chapter 23: Connecting Ideas

GRAMMAR PRACTICE 1:
Connectors

1 Coordinating Conjunctions—Punctuating Sentences; Parallel Structures

2. NC   3. They tried to show that they had both a good product and good service. OR They tried to show both that they had a good product and that they had good service 4. The PC companies "sold" their computers, their knowledge, and their help with problems. OR The PC companies "sold" their computers, knowledge, and help with problems. 5. Customers could either buy a prepackaged system or put together their own systems. OR Either customers could buy a prepackaged system or they could put together their own

systems.   6. They could ask for help or (they could) use their own judgment.   7. The customers were supported while buying the computers and after completing the sale. 8. Selling after-the-sale service seemed to be effective and successful, for many PC customers appreciated the extra help. OR Selling after-the-sale service seemed to be effective and successful for many PC customers that OR who appreciated the extra help.

2 Omitting Words

2. The company that made Macintosh computers had a different and unique approach.   3. Macintosh advertised that it was fun, for individuals, and easy to use.   4. Macintosh computers came out in different colors and were sold to many young people.   5. Macintosh computers and PC's have supporters and detractors.

3 Punctuating Sentences Connected by Transitions

In the late 1990s, one of the most popular investments was in companies associated with the Internet; however, (OR .However,) since many of these companies weren't making a profit, their values were hard to assess. Many investors saw the Internet as a new way of doing business; they, therefore, (OR business. They,) didn't want to be left out of any important future developments. In addition, buying Internet stocks became trendy, despite the lack of dividends. Other investors recognized the potential of an accelerating trade in Internet stocks; consequently, (OR stocks. Consequently,) they were able to buy low and sell high. One company more than tripled its initial opening price on the first day that it was traded, for example.

GRAMMAR PRACTICE 2:
Relationships Expressed with Connectors—
Addition and Time

4 Addition with Paired Coordinating Conjunctions
and Transitions

A. 2. Our shoes both support your feet and make your legs
look elegant.   3. You'll either be satisfied or get your
money back. OR Either you'll be satisfied or you'll get
your money back.   4. Neither you nor your friends are
going to be disappointed in our shoes.

B. 2. HealthyDog dog food tastes great; furthermore, (OR .
Furthermore,) HealthyDog dog food is good for your dog's
health.   3. Your dog's coat will be shiny; your dog, (OR .
Your dog,) in addition, will be more active.   4.
HealthyDog will change the way your dog feels. It'll(; it'll)
make you happy, also.

5 Time Connectors

2. The products we buy are designed to wear out.
Meanwhile, models and parts change. In the end, we have to
buy something new because we can't repair our "old" stuff.
3. Often, before we buy something, advertisers have tried to
convince us that we not only want but need their products.
Then, we ourselves begin to believe that we need the products. Finally, we buy what we want, not necessarily what we
need.

6 Guided Writing

Answers will vary.

Unit Wrap-up

Error Correction

    1. As
    Though fiber-optic, digital, and satellite technologies advance in the next ten years,

they will give advertisers new tools to use television and the Internet interactively.

 2. Because of that OR Therefore,
Such that, advertisers will be able to target very specific markets. For instance, custom-made

ads will target such specific markets as a particular age group or a specific zip code. Whereas

                                                    3. they'll
advertisers' messages were delivered to large general audiences before, so they'll be delivered

to the narrow audiences most interested in the product or service. For example, advertisers

can target sports fans or dog lovers. Thus, micro-marketing will replace mass marketing.

Furthermore, the technology will give consumers the power to order products

4. and OR in addition to
in addition information instantly. Whenever they want a product, consumers will have only to

click a button to get it.

GRAMMAR PRACTICE 3:
Other Relationships Expressed with
Connectors

7 Reason and Result Connectors

2. therefore   3. so   4. As a result   5. On account of
6. for   7. so   8. Because of   9. consequently

8 Contrast and Opposition Connectors

1. b. People remember the jingle, but they don't remember
the product.   1. c. People remember the jingle; however,
(OR . However,) they don't remember the product.
2. a. Although famous people are often used in ads, they
sometimes have a negative effect on the product.
2. b. Famous people are often used in ads, yet they sometimes have a negative effect on the product.   2. c. Famous
people are often used in ads; nevertheless, (OR . Nevertheless,)
they sometimes have a negative effect on the product.
3. a. Despite the fact that the slogan is recognizable, the
company may stop using it.   3. b. The slogan is recognizable; nonetheless, (OR . Nonetheless,) the company may
stop using it.   3. c. The slogan is recognizable, yet the company may stop using it.   4. a. Whereas this company's logo
is good, its slogan is poor. OR This company's logo is good,
whereas its slogan is poor.   4. b. This company's logo is
good; in contrast, (OR . In contrast,) its slogan is poor.
4. c. This company's logo is good; on the other hand, (OR .
On the other hand,) its slogan is poor.

9 Guided Writing—Exemplification

Answers will vary.

Several companies are working on ways to blend Internet and television advertising. A

                                                                    5. but
viewer will be able to not only view the product on a television ad, <u>and</u> also split his TV screen

                                                6. it is coming OR coming
and click on the web site for more information. Although <u>is coming</u>, the evolution of

interactive television and Internet advertising will be a slow process.

7. In addition OR Additionally OR Moreover OR Furthermore
<u>Consequently</u>, there is also technology which will allow consumers to block advertising and

control what advertising they watch. Interactive advertising will give both advertisers and

consumers more choice, convenience, and control. But, privacy issues must be addressed.

                                                        8. (who) uses
Advertisers must control who gets access to information and and <u>using it</u>. Either the advertising

                                            9. or
industry will regulate itself to protect consumer privacy <u>nor</u> it will lose the trust of the consumer.

Guided Writing

Answers will vary.

TOEFL TIME

Questions 1–10

1. C 2. D 3. D 4. A 5. B 6. C 7. B 8. A 9. D
10. B

Questions 11–20

11. B (is chlorophyll no longer) 12. C (as if) 13. B (fear)
14. D (have self-confidence) 15. B (is) 16. C (*omit*)
17. B (but) 18. A (Because they had) 19. C (smooth OR
to smooth) 20. B (nor)